Books by Dan Wooding

Guerrilla for Christ
(co-authored with Salu Daka Ndebele)

Supernatural Superpowers
(partly based on *Exit the Devil*,
which was co-authored with Trevor Dearing)

Train of Terror
(co-authored with Mini Loman)

DAN WOODING and RAY BARNETT

ZONDERVAN
PUBLISHING HOUSE
OF THE ZONDERVAN CORPORATION
GRAND RAPIDS, MICHIGAN 49506

UGANDA HOLOCAUST
© 1980 by Dan Wooding and Ray Barnett

Published simultaneously in Great Britain by
PICKERING & INGLIS LTD. of London and Glasgow.

Library of Congress Cataloging in Publication Data

Wooding, Dan.
  Uganda holocaust.

  1. Persecution—Uganda.   2. Amin, Idi, 1925-
3. Uganda—Church history.   I. Barnett, Ray, joint
author.   II. Title.
BR1608.U45W66   272'.9'096761   80-434
ISBN 0-310-41800-3

Printed in the United States of America

We dedicate this book to the courageous
believers of Uganda.

Contents

Part V—Final Days

Photo section after page 128

Foreword

IT IS A CHALLENGE and a privilege to write a foreword to such a book as this. The best introductory statement on this overwhelming subject is that which is found in the Letters to the Hebrew believers, in which the writer says:

> Should I go on? There isn't enough time
> to tell the whole story of those who stood—

and this stand cost them everything.

But the most descriptive remarks as to the real nature of these heroes are to be found in verse 34, chapter 11 of Hebrews. Their superhuman exploits—against their natural weakness—

> They were *weak*—but were made *strong*.

We have a tendency to idealize such men and women as superhuman and extraordinary. But the truth is that in each of them we observe a repetition of the "burning bush" that is never consumed!

We stand amazed as we watch the spectacle. And in the silent, humble, suffering witness of the truth, we see in shining reality the radiant character of God. As we watch a Janani Luwum, we see God, not as essentially "all-powerful"—which He is—but as essentially "all-loving," even to the point of sacrificing Himself for those He loves.

Yes, "they were weak," but in their weakness God demonstrated His timeless quality: "suffering, victorious love."

True revolutionaries are these witnesses of Christ. They usher into the arena of human history a *new way* of resisting evil, they resist to the point of shedding their own life blood. They refuse to use the cheap, old method of resisting the oppressor by violently taking away his life. Instead they offer their own lives in resisting evil. This is their Master's way. It is the new way—the living way!

These modern martyrs, like lights, shine out in a darkened, hostile—though superficially permissive—world. As they stand, in bloody sweat, utterly alone, humbly and silently protesting, they declare judgment on a guilty world.

But they stand as encouraging beacons to all who believe in Christ, and they shed hope on the way of suffering. We are taught great lessons, not of mere human heroism, but of true human values, of the preciousness of human life. The intrinsic rights of every man and woman, and above all, the power of suffering love.

These Christians demonstrate to us in no uncertain terms the fact that resistance is not, first of all, destructive violence. They have shown us a new way of resisting oppression. Instead of destroying the oppressor, they have resisted him constructively, giving him a chance to change. "Father, forgive them" is the great utterance from the greatest Sufferer of all time—Jesus, the Crucified.

May the stories of these men and women shed light on our darkened world. May they inspire the Christian community to resist all evil actively in love, and so bring hope to this despair-filled world.

—*Festo Kivengere*
Bishop of Kigezi, Church of Uganda

Preface

It is difficult to believe that a man so much like Hitler could rise to power and carry out a holocaust while the entire world stood by watching. Yet it happened, and among those who were victimized were thousands of Christians who, like the Makerere believers, had only one charge against them—their faith in God. Because of this, the Uganda holocaust is more than an incident to be reported in world history books. It is an important chapter in the history of the Christian church from which we have much to learn—about faith, about the sovereign love of God, about the world in which we live, and about the value of life itself. It is for this reason that we write this book.

—Dan Wooding and Ray Barnett

Acknowledgments

The authors would like to thank Mike Watson and Suzanne Nelson for their invaluable help in the preparation of this book.

They also wish to thank BBC; Richard Bewes; Wallace Boulton; Joan Hall; Barbara Harmon; Bev Hubble; Louis Jarvis and Janyce Chalifour of Copytron, Fraser Valley, Canada; Lydia Mukashaza; Michael Page; Chris Rees; Scripture Union; Susan Scroggs; Leo Slingerland of E.O. Television; Jean Wilson; David Wood; Andrew Wooding; and World Vision International.

Photographs were supplied by Dan Brewster, Camerapix-Keystone, Mary Hayward, Bev Hubble, Paul Latham, Uganda Ministry of Information and Broadcasting, *Munno,* Religious News Service, Dan Wooding, and World Vision International.

Maps

Northeastern Africa and the Near East

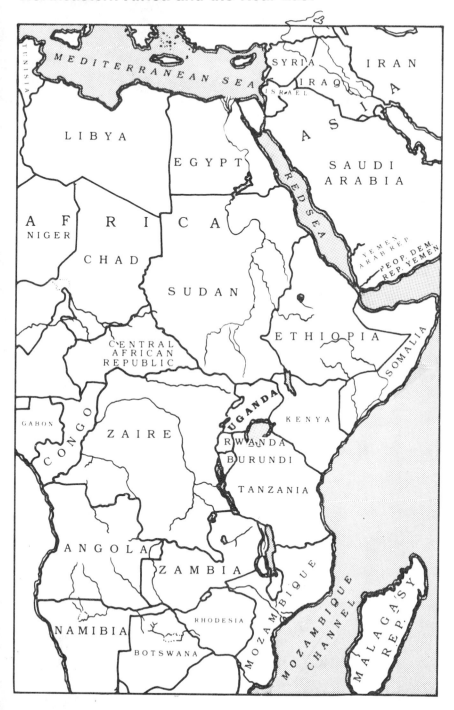

Chronology

1875	Explorer Henry M. Stanley in Uganda
1877–1879	First missionaries arrive and are welcomed
1884	Kabaka (king) Mutesa dies; is succeeded by his son Mwanga
1886–1887	Christian martyrs burned alive
1929	Beginning of Christian revival
1941	Festo Kivengere converted
1948	Janani Luwum converted
Late 1950s	Idi Amin involved in brutal episode against the Turkana, a nomadic Kenyan tribe (Ugandan government ignores incident)
March, 1962	Internal self-government established in Uganda; Benedicto Kiwanuka is first prime minister
April, 1962	Elections place A. Milton Obote in power as leader of the Uganda People's Congress party
October, 1962	Uganda becomes an independent country within the British Commonwealth; Sir Edward Mutesa is president
1964	Canonization of Ugandan Christian martyrs
1966	Prime Minister A. Milton Obote suspends the constitution and is given full authority as president
1966	Erica Sabiti is elected first African archbishop
1969	In Libya, Gadhafi overthrows King Idris
Jan. 25, 1971	Idi Amin overthrows Obote in a coup, while Obote is in Singapore attending a Commonwealth Conference

1971	First meeting of Amin and Gadhafi, both Moslems
Early 1972	Amin's troops given command to do anything necessary "to maintain public order and security"
March, 1972	All Israelis expelled from Uganda
Throughout 1972	All Asians expelled
Sept. 21, 1972	Judge Benedicto Kiwanuka arrested
End of 1972	58 Christian missionaries expelled
Jan. 13, 1973	Kiggundu murdered (editor of *Munno* newspaper)
Feb. 10, 1973	Public executions throughout Uganda
June, 1974	Janani Luwum enthroned as archbishop
1974	Amin's initial ban on certain sects and church denominations
1975	Alleged sacrifice of Amin's son Moses
June, 1976	Raid on Entebbe Airport by Israeli troops
Feb. 10, 1977	Bishops sign open letter to Amin, protesting his persecution of the Ugandan people
Feb. 17, 1977	Uganda radio announces the death of Archbishop Luwum
September, 1977	Amin's second ban, this time banning 27 sects and denominations; permitting only Islam, Roman Catholic, Uganda (Greek) Orthodox, and Church of Uganda (Anglican)
1977–1978	Memorial to honor Ugandan Christian martyrs
April 12, 1978	Arrest of 200 Makerere Church people
Oct. 30, 1978	Uganda invades Tanzania
Early 1979	Beginning of Tanzanian invasion of Uganda
April 5, 1979	Kampala taken by Tanzanian invaders; Amin begins flight northward
April 6, 1979	Entebbe taken
April 13, 1979	Yosef Lule becomes president
April 18, 1979	Fort Portal taken
May 20, 1979	Gulu taken
June 20, 1979	Godfrey L. Binaisa becomes president, replacing Yosef Lule
July, 1979	Christians conduct a worship crusade

Part I

Persecution

1

Sentenced to Be
Burned Alive

THE BELIEVERS SAT HUDDLED in a circle with guns pressed against their necks waiting to be burned alive. As they waited for the execution orders to arrive from General Mustafa Adrisi, Idi Amin's second-in-command, sadistic guards taunted them about how they would die in the flames.

Just as Adrisi was responsible for their execution orders, he was also responsible for their arrest. Earlier he passed by the Makerere Gospel Mission to Uganda during one of their services and heard them singing. He immediately ordered that the Christians be arrested the next time they met.

On April 12, 1978, Adrisi's plot became a reality. Soldiers invaded the church and began firing indiscriminately at the six-hundred-strong congregation. With crazed eyes, Idi Amin's soldiers sprayed bullets at the platform. As the gunfire zoomed skyward it riddled holes in the asbestos roof. The assistant pastor, Jotham Mutcbi, who was on the platform, sank to his knees in prayer.

Amid the mayhem, hundreds more quickly dropped to their knees between the pews. With upraised arms they began to praise God. The sturdy red brick church was filled with a cacophony of incredible sound—a combination of prayer, praise, and bullets.

Suddenly another sound was heard. A musician from the church orchestra, Joseph Nyakairu, raised his trumpet and blew it with all his might.

"The soldiers immediately ceased fire and retreated in terror," says Nyakairu with a wry smile, showing us the very trumpet he played on that fateful day. "Obviously they thought we had our own

23

private army and I was signaling for them to come to the rescue. But, after a short time they regained courage, crept back, and began shooting again. My trumpet was 'executed' and now it is damaged beyond repair.''

In the ensuing confusion, nearly four hundred people managed to slip away from the church. But at least two hundred remained on their knees and continued to worship the Lord, knowing that death could be imminent. The congregation was under arrest!

The soldiers ordered the worshipers out into the church's neatly kept grounds and made them lie flat on their faces. As the members lay there in their Sunday-best clothes, the army men committed acts of appalling violence.

"Some soldiers were jumping on the head and chest of a young man with their heavy boots," says Obed Rubaiza, one of those arrested. "His 'crime' was that he tried to run away. They beat him with sticks and rifle butts. We didn't think he would live, but God spared his life."

The sadistic soldiers forced many of the people to lie on top of each other in heaps ten-high. The people at the bottom were badly crushed and in agony, almost unable to breathe.

Relief from this position did not come until trucks arrived to take them away. As the two hundred church members were pushed into them, many were clubbed by soldiers and climbed aboard the trucks with gaping wounds in their heads.

Thinking back to the event, Assistant Pastor Mutebi shares, "As the lorries proceeded to the State Research Bureau, a house of death for nearly all who enter, the spirit of the Lord was with us and we were singing a hymn called 'God Is Good.'

"I don't think we even considered anything worse would happen to us than perhaps being kept in prison for a time. We knew we hadn't committed any crime."

When they arrived at the dreadful headquarters of Amin's "gestapo," the group was ordered to surrender all valuables, including their Bibles. Assistant Pastor Mutebi forgot to take off his tie, and consequently he was smashed in the face by a guard belonging to Amin's tribe, the Kakwas.

After all valuables had been handed over to the guards, the group was led outside and ordered to sit on the ground in a circle. Trumpeter Joseph was dragged away from the group, thrown face down into a gutter and beaten savagely with sticks until his back was almost broken. The other believers were confronted by the commander of the killer squad who demanded to know who their leader was. When he discovered that the senior pastor, Joshua Musoke, was not with them, he was incensed.

"Pastor Joshua is at another of our churches," Jotham Mutebi tried to explain. A guard grabbed him by the neck and pushed him into a car filled with armed guards.

"Take us to find your missing pastor," they ordered the young Christian leader.

They drove at high speeds toward Pastor Musoke's home in a little compound near Namirembe Hill.

During the ride the guards in the car asked Pastor Mutebi why the church had been holding a service. Mutebi tried to explain that their church was registered under the Companies Act as Glad Tidings of Uganda. As he proceeded to explain that they were unlimited in the religious services they could hold, the guards cut in and accused him of being a conspirator. Deeming this crime as worthy of a beating, they began crashing a pistol butt down on his head and slapping him across the face.

Mutebi was relieved when the painful blows ended and the group arrived at Pastor Musoke's house. The guards quickly discovered that he had not returned from his trip, and they decided to go back to the church. Mutebi says, "They removed electric fans, the undamaged musical instruments, amplifiers, and speakers, and put them in the car. Stopping at one of their homes, they unloaded their loot, and the driver pulled out a sword. He held it close to my neck as if he was going to slit my throat. After attempting to frighten me, he put the sword away and they began driving back to the State Research Bureau."

At the office Mutebi was shoved into a stinking basement corridor where 115 of his brethren from the church sat gasping for breath. The women were in a separate part of the murder factory. The heat was intense and the stench of blood and urine was sickening. Mutebi moved along the stifling tunnel, which was sealed off near the end. Amin had hoped to pass through this tunnel from his lodge to watch the killings or even personally take part in them, but was forced to use another route. Apollo Lawoko, a senior civil servant, says that he witnessed Amin killing prisoners. Once he saw Amin hammer a police official to death. Another time, the self-styled Field Marshal, wearing a gas mask and two pistols, helped beat to death a group of soldiers. Inside this corridor the young pastor found a group of the believers taking turns cradling the head of the youth who had tried to escape and had been beaten outside the church. Because of the intense heat, most of the group had removed their shirts and some were using them as a pillow for him.

As Mutebi listened to their conversation, he learned the disturbing story of what had happened to his "brothers and sisters" while he was away.

The State Research men threatened to surround the groups with cans of gasoline. One of the believers, George Kasozi, was recognized by a former classmate who had joined the Bureau. This man from State Research gleefully announced that the Christians were all to be burned alive.

"Now George, you pray before we set you all on fire," he said with a sneer. "And George, don't forget to pray for us that live only for today and could be dead tomorrow."

George stood to his feet and courageously began praying for his friends and the guards. As he did so, they hurled stones at him and began beating him with sticks.

"Even a murderer would not have been treated like that," Obed Rubaiza told us. "Then they began slapping and cursing the women of our group."

The two hundred sat in silent prayer as the State Research men, most of them wearing their "uniform" of dark glasses, platform heel shoes, and bell-bottomed trousers, mocked them.

Many of these believers recalled how the first Christian martyrs in Uganda had also died by fire. In 1875 explorer Henry M. Stanley (famous for the greeting, "Dr. Livingstone, I presume") arrived in Uganda and described one of its kingdoms, Buganda, as a center of civilization in the heart of Africa. Two years later the first missionaries were received warmly by Kabaka (meaning king) Mutesa. Although he remained a Moslem, he listened carefully to the Christian teachings. Many of the page boys at his court heard the preaching and reading of the Scriptures and were greatly influenced. In 1882 and 1883 the first baptisms took place. Then Kabaka Mutesa died and his young Moslem son, Mwanga, became the new kabaka, or king.

A difficult time followed for the Christians. In 1885 five servant boys and two Christian women were arrested. Four of those arrested were released, but three of the young servant boys, aged eleven to fifteen, were condemned to death in an effort to stamp out Christianity. At their execution the boys had their arms cut off and were thrown into the fire. Eleven-year-old Yusufu, the youngest, pleaded: "Please don't cut off my arms. I will not struggle in the fire that takes me to Jesus." At their execution the boys sent a message to the king, "Tell His Majesty that he has put our bodies in the fire, but we won't be in the fire for long. Soon we will be with Jesus, which is much better. But ask him to repent and change his mind, or he will land in a place of eternal fire and desolation." That day it is reported that forty adults became Christians.

The persecution and martyrdom led to a remarkable growth of the Christian church, as the message of the gospel spread to all sections of Uganda.

Now, about a hundred years later, Christians were once again facing persecution by fire because of their faith.

"As soon as Adrisi signs the document you will all be burned alive," taunted one Nubian as he toyed with the metal chain around his neck bearing a picture of Idi Amin.

But some miles away from where they were imprisoned, on that very day, Adrisi and some of his aides were recklessly playing a dangerous game of overtaking each other on the main Jinja-Kampala road. Eye witness George Muwanga-Kamya, editor of *Munno,* the influential Roman Catholic daily newspaper in Kampala, remembers what happened.

"I was in a taxi with my fiancee fifteen miles from Kampala, when two Mercedes Benz cars shot past us at great speed. One was white, the other was green.

"I suspected someone important was in one of them. The two cars took turns overtaking each other at great speed when suddenly the green car, carrying Vice-President Adrisi, hit a Fiat 128 head-on.

"Adrisi's car careened into a ditch full of water. We were ordered at gunpoint to stop. I got out of the taxi, rushed over and dragged the vice-president out of the car. He was deep in the water and as I helped him he cried for his mother. I noticed he had six pistols around his waist. He had terrible cuts on his face and obviously was in a lot of pain. I understand both his legs were badly fractured.

"My fiancee, a nurse, tried to administer first-aid, but the panic-stricken guards began shooting to disperse us and the other people who had stopped. One of them walked over to the driver of the Fiat, who was unconscious and lying slumped over the wheel, and shot him through the head.

"They bundled the moaning Adrisi into the undamaged white Mercedes and rushed him to the hospital in Kampala. Later, he was flown to Cairo for treatment.

"He ended up a cripple in a wheelchair, and finally Amin turned against him." It was this event that saved the courageous believers. When the signed order from Adrisi did not appear, the guards led the prisoners back to their prison cells.

At one o'clock the next morning, as the men were struggling for breath in the six-foot-high, five-foot-wide tunnel, they heard ominous footsteps in the corridor.

Paul Kinaatama, a teen-age prisoner who had been a believer for only two years, remembers what happened. "The guards wanted first of all to kill some of us, but instead they dragged off two other prisoners from a nearby cell, not to kill them but to force them to wash away the blood of recently executed prisoners. As they returned, a drunken guard aimed his rifle at one of the prisoners. The bullet just missed him. This made the guard so angry that he lunged at him with his bayonet and pierced his left arm."

The State Research men, whose badge of office was to grow their little fingernails into long, curved talons, were regularly coming for men and taking them away, reports Obed Rubaiza.

"Many prisoners were probably either taken to Namanve Forest on the Kampala-Jinja road, where thousands of people were shot, or they were released into the streets during darkness and told to run. In the latter event they would have been shot in the back as if they had tried to escape."

Next day, most of the prisoners were taken to the Central Police Station. As the church members were taken out, they were struck with clubs and one man had his arm badly burned with the stub of a lighted cigarette.

There was more brutality to come when they arrived at the police station. Paul Kinaatama says, "As we entered, we passed by a line-up of men who beat us on the head and back with sticks. I was praying all the time and I didn't really feel it."

Timothy Okalany, a young carpenter who had been attending the Makerere Church for the first time, describes the ordeal of one of the young women at the police station. "A guard came for one of the sisters. He wanted to take her to his office and rape her. But she stood there bravely and told him, 'If you want to kill me, you kill me here. I'm not going with you.' Fortunately, the other guards intervened and the man left shamefaced."

Okalany goes on: "At the police station we were divided into groups and one group at a time was taken to Luzira Prison. This was difficult because we knew we could be killed there.

"As we arrived at the prison, each person was given three whacks on the buttocks with a stick and then we were put in cells—the women in one part of the prison, and the men in another.

"We were about fifty to a cell. For several days it was difficult to sleep on the bare floor. But after five nights we were given some blankets, which made it somewhat easier.

"The other prisoners were confused when they heard that we had all been arrested for only praying.

"It was a great time of learning for us all and we realized we had to accept suffering as part of the Christian life. Many of our group were sick because of the awful food, but through it we learned to give ourselves to prayer. Those who were sick in the cell were prayed for and healed.

"Even though we were starving, we declared days of prayer and fasting. We realized that man does not live by bread alone. For three days each week we fasted from 7:00 A.M. to 6:00 P.M. Sometimes we hoarded food that was brought for us, eating it after the fast ended.

"We found great blessing in this. None of us were depressed. The men were divided in seven cells but we found a corridor outside the cells where we met twice a day for testimony, praise, and prayer. We were not stopped by the authorities, and other prisoners would join us. Many were converted during this time. I remember that one mentally-disturbed prisoner regained his sanity after he accepted the Lord."

The imprisoned group became a source of great inspiration to the believers who came to visit them.

One young Christian, Levy Odida, wrote to English missionary Cynthia Mackay, who was on furlough, and described a visit. In her letter she says, "It was all the Lord's doing. I could not imagine it.

Elvis Muhaabwa encouraged us so much in the faith. In fact the prisoners were spiritually rich and full of indescribable joy and peace. Surely nothing can separate us from the love of God. God is so wonderful. We came back changed.''

Meanwhile Pastor Mutebi and his five friends were still at Nakasero. They were accused of being the ringleaders, of being members of the CIA, and of dealing with the Israelis. They experienced a period of starvation and sadistic tortures. Mutebi, whose serene nature made him the brunt of the guard's cruelty, particularly suffered.

"One day a guard ordered me to smoke a cigarette," says the diminutive clergyman. "I replied that I was a Christian and I didn't smoke. He became very angry and ordered me to walk just within range of his rifle. I stood there. Then he took aim.

"Other prisoners who were not believers were so frightened they shouted, 'Smoke, smoke.' They were sure this was the only way my life would be spared. They were also afraid that if the bullet went through my body it might hit one of them.

"When he realized that this wouldn't work, the guard instructed me to pass my hand through the cell bars and began levering it against a bar, trying to break it. But God protected me and despite the terrible pain it did not snap.

"Then he began trying to burn me on the face with his cigarette. Miraculously it didn't sear my skin. Next he beckoned me to come closer. He started hitting me with the rifle, but still he was unable to break any of my bones.

"Finally he gave up and we began a time of prayer for him, that God might change his heart. The following day the torture and abuse ceased. With an apparent new respect, he referred to us as the 'born again' Christians.

"We were his responsibility for four days. During this time he allowed us to do some light duties, such as picking up rubbish outside. He warned the others to treat us well because we were Christians. Previously, no prisoners were allowed outside in the fresh air. Undoubtedly, God had done a work in his heart.''

Eventually, after two harassing weeks, the six "ringleaders" were transferred to the Central Police Station. There they found to their delight a born-again woman officer. "She was like our mother," says Pastor Mutebi. "Every morning she came to visit. When someone brought food for us and was not allowed in, she would bring it.

"She bravely prayed with us in the cell. If discovered, she would have suffered grave consequences. She also smuggled a Bible to us, which was wonderful. We found Psalm 23 and Isaiah 43 a tremendous encouragement."

At times other prisoners were roughly shoved into their cell. Mutebi and his friends did all they could spiritually to help these other non-Christian prisoners by sharing their testimony and praying with them.

"Many committed their lives to Christ during this time. Since liberation, fifteen ex-prisoners have joined our church," says Assistant Pastor Mutebi.

But between the times of spiritual refreshment, they had to endure the pain of constant beatings.

"We would be lined up and made to squat. Then a policeman would come down the line and beat each of us with a stick," says Mutebi.

"One day, an officer split open my head with an iron bar as I squatted there. Most of the time he had to be careful because of the senior officers who were watching. When they weren't looking, he would really beat us. But again God preserved us, and we weren't as badly treated as some of the others."

Other prisoners were living evidence of what was happening in that chamber of horrors.

"We would see men with burns all over their bodies," says Rubaiza. "They would tell us of the nightmare they had had to endure. Many suffered electric shock torture when wires were put on their ears or fingertips.

"One night we pleaded with a young man to stop describing how they had cut a piece off his arm and ear. He was killed the same day we left.

"Another young man had a knife thrust into him and a fellow prisoner had to pull it out of his body."

Church members who had not been arrested risked their freedom to visit Mutebi and the others at the police station.

"When asked if they, too, were Christians, they would reply, 'Yes.' Some officers would say to them, 'Perhaps we should also keep you inside.' But the believers didn't let that frighten them," says Mutebi.

"We were allowed to talk to our visitors across a table. Despite the guards, we joyously laughed and encouraged each other. It was really wonderful.''

Then, unexpectedly, the six men were released. The date was May 28, 1978. It appeared that the Moslem Supreme Council needed cells for some of their prisoners, and so the little group was freed. Also, it was discovered that Amin had not signed the detention order; Adrisi was the only one who had signed it.

The six men went to a house where church members were praying for them. Naturally there was much rejoicing as they walked in. Tears of joy flowed freely and the news of their release spread like wildfire. Soon great numbers of people arrived from all over the area, bringing gifts of food and money.

Although these six prisoners were allegedly the ringleaders, it was to be another month before the rest of the imprisoned church was freed. On June 30, 1978, they too walked to freedom. Miraculously, not one of their number had died.

Part II

The Deeds of a Dictator

2

Amin—
A Very Mixed-up Man

IDI AMIN'S PRIVATE HELICOPTER droned over the Kenyan town of Kisumu, located on the shore of beautiful, crystal-clear Lake Victoria, the world's second largest fresh-water lake, and the source of the river Nile.

The year was 1973. Amin, just two years into his reign, was flying in for a courtesy visit with the district commissioner of this lakeside town. Kisumu, despite the beauty of its surroundings, was once a pesthouse; vulnerable to malaria, dysentery, blackwater fever, and many other tropical scourges.

"Look, Your Excellency, your reception committee," said a helpful aide as the massive president peered below. Directly beneath them a large gathering of people stood in neat lines.

Amin, a man with an ego as big as his enormous frame, beamed with delight. He ordered the "chopper" pilot to land so he could address the huge crowd. The flyer radioed the back-up helicopter containing more of the dictator's entourage, and relayed the president's instructions.

Amin's transport touched down at the side of the crowd. A puzzled American woman and Silas Owiti, a Kenyan pastor, hurried over to greet the Ugandan president. "What is President Amin doing at a seminar for Christian preachers?" they thought curiously.

The woman was Mrs. Daisy Osborn, wife of American evangelist T. L. Osborn. Rev. Osborn had been teaching five thousand African pastors and preachers how to present the gospel more effectively. He had then lined them up in tidy rows for a photograph to be taken.

Meanwhile, a tiny reception committee was waiting for the president at Kisumu Airport, his real destination. They shuffled impatiently, wondering what had happened to their VIP. President Amin still had not discovered he was at the wrong place. The evangelist stood bemused, as Amin strode toward the platform to join him.

Little did Amin know that Rev. Osborn had been praying for many months to meet him personally, to present him with the claims of Jesus Christ on his life. Soon it was explained to Amin that he was attending a Bible teaching seminar. Continuing the meeting, T. L. Osborn prayed. The president remarked emotionally, "I feel like Moses standing on holy ground." He then addressed the crowd in his faltering English.

"President Amin said he felt the Ugandan people needed the same message of Jesus we were giving to these people in Kenya," recalls Mrs. Osborn.

Following his speech, Amin was enthusiastically cheered by the large audience, which was amazed at his presence in the evangelical meeting. The "Life President" shook hands with Rev. Osborn and his wife, then departed as abruptly as he had arrived.

The American evangelist concluded the seminar, still puzzled by the strange incident. Almost immediately a messenger arrived with an invitation for the couple to dine with Amin at the New Kisumu Hotel.

Daisy Osborn remembers well her astonishment at this second meeting with the unpredictable Ugandan president.

"First he invited us to come to Uganda to conduct a seminar similar to the one we led in Kenya," she says. "President Amin assured us we would be very welcome and asked when we could come. To see if he was really sincere about this, we encouraged him to send us an official invitation. He promised to do so.

"Later we learned Amin had announced on radio and television that we were coming for a crusade. During the broadcast he made an edict that everyone in Kampala would have to attend the meetings." (The Osborns waited in vain for an official invitation.)

After the meal, Rev. Osborn, never a man to pull punches, spiritually challenged the former Uganda heavyweight boxing champion.

"For forty-five minutes Amin listened as my husband shared with him the message of the gospel," says Mrs. Osborn. "He stood by the side of the table at attention like a soldier the whole time. The message was very direct. It all centered around the supernatural ability of Jesus to transform a life."

Tears began to roll down the dictator's deep black face as he listened to the evangelist and his wife. When they were finished he walked unsteadily to where American missionary May Dodwitz was sitting with her twin sister.

"Everyone stood up as he left the Osborns. For some reason he just stepped over and shook our hands," says Mrs. Dodwitz, a missionary from Florida. "There was a real charisma about the man. His eyes were tear-stained and he was obviously very moved by what he had heard. We had great hopes he would be saved."

The Osborns felt this meeting was a crossroad for Amin. "At the time, we felt he could go one of two ways," says Mrs. Osborn. "He could have accepted Christ and become another Saul of Tarsus. We are sorry at how things turned out—not unhappy he was removed, but for all that happened in those eight years."

Like Saul, he became a persecutor of the church. He ruled over Uganda with unprecedented brutality.

This was not the only time Amin was confronted with the message of Christ's love. Ugandan and European believers attempted to present the way of salvation to him.

Bishop Festo Kivengere explains, "I knew President Amin quite well. He had heard the gospel, and in many ways appreciated it. The president told the bishops he had been taught all about Jesus Christ when he was young. He said some of his closest relatives were 'born again.' The meaning of these terms were not unfamiliar to him." The bishop, who had to flee the country for his life, became the world-wide spokesman on behalf of the suffering church.

Miss Joan Hall conversed with the president when he opened a school where she was headmistress at Bweranyangi, in West Ankole. She is presently home secretary of the Ruanda Mission Church Missionary Society (CMS) in London, England.

Miss Hall says, "I walked around the school with the president and over lunch related to him the tremendous effect Ugandan Christians had on me. I told him this had changed my life and really given a new dimension to me spiritually.

"'Here at the school we begin with morning prayers,' I said. 'The prayers in the evening are led by the students.'

"'Good,' said Amin as he turned to me. 'I want you to continue with that.'

"He seemed to keep up a dual role by saying one thing and doing another. It was hard to believe I was speaking to the same man I knew was committing such atrocities.''

Besides T. L. Osborn, another American to witness to Idi Amin was Dr. Ralph Wilkerson, pastor of the large Melodyland Church, close to Disneyland in California.

As time was fast running out for the president in 1978, Dr. Wilkerson, who believes he has been called to minister to world leaders, paid a desperate visit to Uganda in an attempt to win him for Christ.

He spent many hours talking to Amin in private and was even invited by the dictator to appear on Uganda television to ''pray for the nation.'' This he did, but Dr. Wilkerson declined to go into details of the meetings they had, saying they had been confidential between him and the president.

One of Amin's severest critics, Dr. George Kanyeihamba, leader of the Uganda Human Rights organization based in London, does believe that Amin had a change of heart near the end of his reign. The change, says Dr. Kanyeihamba, who during Yosef Lule's short term as president was Attorney-General, came about as Arab aid began to dry up.

''Amin had seen the church not so much as a threat to his person, but to his policies,'' he says.

''When Arab countries, especially Saudi Arabia, either reduced or abandoned aid, he more or less said, 'If you can't beat them you might as well join them,' and he started giving gifts to the church.''

Dr. Kanyeihamba cited a gift from Amin toward a proposed twelve-story Church of Uganda House in Kampala as a centenary memorial and means of income.

''I'm told that Amin gave a considerable contribution to the building of the place. He also gave gifts to the archbishop of the Roman Catholic Church for their centenary celebrations in 1979. So he was a very mixed-up man.''

Although the president gave a sympathetic ear to his American visitor and gave conscience-easing gifts, the merciless killing machine continued.

Amin's rise to power did not come through one event; rather, Idi Amin began climbing the ladder of political ranks nearly two decades before he took over Uganda.

Early in his political career, in the late 1950s when he was one of only two African officers in the army, he was charged with brutal actions against the Turkana, a nomadic Kenyan tribe. These charges were conveniently forgotten when Uganda gained independence from Britain in March of 1962.

Under the new Ugandan government, Milton Obote was elected Prime Minister in April. Six months later Sir Edward Mutesa of Buganda was selected by Parliament to be Head of State and President of the country. These presiding officials selected Idi Amin to be Uganda's representative when the Congo Rebellion broke out in 1965. In 1966, shortly after the rebellion ended, Amin and Prime Minister Obote were both charged with receiving a share of the thousands of dollars looted from the Congo.

Infuriated with the charge made by a Buganda supporter, Obote suspended the constitution, ousted Sir Edward Mutesa from the presidency, and wrote a new constitution which undermined the regional power possessed by Buganda. He also wrote the *Common Man's Charter,* which envisaged an end to capitalism, foreign economic control, and labor inequities. In its place, Obote planned a new order based on collectives and state control of industry and trade.

The country did well under Obote. After independence from Britain, medical services tripled, primary and secondary education reached out over most of the country, and Makerere University had twice as many students. The gross national product increased by more than ten percent over the 1962 figures. But, after Obote nationalized eighty-five companies, foreign capital began to be withdrawn, and other problems surfaced. Violent robbery reached an unprecedented pitch, and unemployment was increasing while earnings fell.

So when Major General Amin staged his coup on January 25, 1971, while Obote was in Singapore at the British Commonwealth Prime Ministers' Conference, he was hailed as a hero by Ugandans and by most of the world.

On swearing-in day Britain recognized Amin's government, a lead soon to be followed around the world. The ceremony, at Kololo airstrip, took place to the sound of a twenty-one-gun salute, traditional drums, horns, and ecstatic applause. Amin stood in an open car without the usual escort of motorcycles and police cars. Holding a Bible in his right hand, Amin swore he would "truly exercise all functions of the Head of Government and do right to all manner of people without fear, favor, or ill will."

Idi Amin Dada appointed himself head of state, minister of defense, and commander-in-chief of the armed forces. He had become dictator over Uganda, a country of ninety-one thousand square miles, or twice the size of Pennsylvania, but with half as many people, a population of about twelve million.

Journalists Joseph Kamau and Andrew Cameron wrote in their book, *Lust to Kill* (Corgi), "Three weeks after the take-over, seventy army officers and more than two thousand men had died. Within three months ten thousand civilians had been slaughtered. Crocodiles basked beneath the Karuma Falls Bridge, the Bridge of Blood, spanning the river Nile. They grew both fat and lazy. Idi Amin Dada cancelled elections and filled his prisons.

"The honeymoon was over. Uganda turned to the horror of Amin's *lust to kill.*"

THE COURAGE of many of the Christian preachers was at times tremendous. Mrs. Mary Davies, who worked with her husband at 150-bed Ngora Hospital in Teso District, tells of Archbishop Erica Sabiti. In 1966 he was elected as first African archbishop, with his province stretching across one thousand miles to Rwanda, Burundi, and Boga-Zaire. He preached in Ngora church at the fiftieth anniversary celebration of the founding of this Church of Uganda hospital which was started by the Church Missionary Society.

Recalls Mrs. Davies: "The church was packed to the doors, and except for about six of us expatriates, it was a completely Ugandàn congregation. In his sermon the archbishop talked about African culture. 'What is our culture?' he asked. 'It was fear, superstition, and darkness. The missionaries made us what we are now. They came to us at great sacrifice to themselves, to bring us the light of our Lord Jesus.'

"We thought that was a very brave statement to make to such a large congregation of Ugandans, because even then, Amin's spies were everywhere."

Mr. and Mrs. Davies, from Huddersfield, England, eventually left their hospital work for home. In January, 1978, they returned to give short-term help at the hospital.

"Things had deteriorated in every material sense, but the people were flocking to the churches," says Mrs. Davies. "In Teso, a poor district at best, giving had increased tenfold."

God did not allow the Ugandan Christians to suffer under Amin's satanic regime without the spiritual weapons to defend themselves.

A revival movement, which began forty years before and revolutionized the lives of many barren Christians, had swept the country. It was called the East African Revival and followed a time of spiritual dryness in the Ugandan Church.

The movement began in 1929 when an English missionary doctor, Joe Church, sat physically and spiritually exhausted with an African friend, Simeoni Nsibambi, a government official. A terrible famine had swept Rwanda and thousands had died. They, together with many others, lamented the tragedy of a lukewarm, nominal Christian church that seemed as powerless to energize its own members as it was to evangelize the untouched tribes beyond Lake Muhasi.

But something stirred in the doctor's heart as they sat under a tree on Namirembe Hill while on holiday in Kampala. They spent three days reading the Bible together.

Patricia St. John tells the story in *Breath of Life* (Norfolk Press), ''He prayed passionately for the scattering of the mists of superstition and sin, and the shining forth of the light of the Gospel, and the site of the beautiful spreading acacia tree seemed like holy ground to be claimed for God.''

Soon others realized that their lives had changed. Their fervor spread; the hills and valleys echoed to gospel hymns.

Whole communities were told the New Testament message by small groups of believers. Many people saw visions and came crying to the churches. Converts returned stolen property and forgot old feuds.

One of those whose lives were changed was Festo Kivengere. The revival reached him in 1941.

An element that stamped the East African Revival as a genuine New Testament experience was its ethical aspect. In every great move of the Spirit there has been a deep understanding of the nature of sin. Mistakes and excesses there may have been, but ethical standards have leaped upwards and restitution been freely made. Willing admissions, too, have been made for wrongs that were committed.

Said James Katarikawe (a Ugandan who studied Theology, Anthropology, and History at Oak Hill Theological College, London) in a thesis on the *Rise and Progress of the East African Revival Movement:* ''As the Holy Spirit began to work in many people's hearts, there was deep conviction of sin. Many spent sleepless nights as they began to realize for the first time their spiritual destitution; many hidden sins were repented of, and hypocrisies revealed. Nothing could escape the searching light of the Holy Spirit.''

He mentioned one big lesson that has come out of the revival. ''We have come to learn from all this that where Jesus is, there is no room for tribalism, or denominationalism: all colors look beautiful and racialism has no room either. They are all one in Christ Jesus.''

Many thousands were deeply affected by this great move of the Spirit in East Africa. This was part of God's preparation for Idi Amin's persecution that was yet to come.

3

Justice—The Amin Way

BENEDICTO KIWANUKA, the Chief Justice and former Prime Minister of Uganda, was sitting quietly in his office, working on legal papers, when three of Amin's special police burst in. They were each wielding two pistols.

"You're under arrest, big man," said one of the State Research men, brutally slapping a pair of handcuffs on the law chief's wrists.

"Grab his shoes," the man in the dark glasses shouted to one of his accomplices, who roughly pulled them from Mr. Kiwanuka's feet.

The date was September 21, 1972, and the time was about 3:00 P.M. The raid took place at the Kampala High Court in the middle of a session of the East African Court of Appeal, attended by judges from all over that region.

What made the arrest even more surprising was that the Chief Justice was chairman of the important legal conference, and had apparently taken time out to deal with papers requiring urgent attention. This was yet another example of Amin's contempt for the might of the law.

The legal head was forcibly carried downstairs in full view of the other judges, thrown into a Peugeot 504, and driven off at high speed toward the Kampala International Hotel.

"People were alarmed when they saw what was happening," says young Steve Kiwanuka, the Chief Justice's student son, in his home, surrounded by pictures of his father with world figures.

"My father was slapped twice and everyone was afraid to do anything because the men were armed. Police stood idly by without intervening."

But why should the police intervene? They, too, were part of the Amin terror machine. If the dictator had decided the Chief Justice's time was up, it was none of their business.

Mr. Kiwanuka was then apparently bound at the wrists and ankles, and taken to Entebbe, where it is said he was presented like a chicken ready for the oven to the gloating "Life President." Amin is believed to have told him exactly what he thought of him.

One independent witness said he saw Mr. Kiwanuka in the military jeep heading for Entebbe.

Some days later, the Chief Justice was seen unshaven, barefoot, and exhausted at Kampala's notorious Makindye Military Prison, wearing tattered and stained denims.

A prisoner later recounted how Kiwanuka was quickly recognized, despite his disheveled appearance, as he moved slowly in a communal cell. Inmates rushed over to talk to him, but he was so badly beaten that he could hardly utter a word.

So how did Kiwanuka die? "We heard that my father was hammered to death by an Army sergeant while a group of senior officers watched," says Steve, without a trace of bitterness.

The Chief Justice's abduction took place four days after a force of about a thousand Obote guerrillas staged an abortive invasion of Uganda from Northern Tanzania. Some think Amin suspected that Kiwanuka was involved in the plot. But that theory couldn't have been more ludicrous, because Kiwanuka, who on March 1, 1962, was sworn in as the first Prime Minister of Uganda, had later been interned by Milton Obote. It was Amin who, in January, 1971, released him as one of several Obote detainees.

"When Amin came to power he appointed my father as Chief Justice, but almost immediately began reducing the importance of the job," says Steve. "Because he feared my father's popularity, Amin stopped him from going to official ceremonies."

The pair clashed strongly over a habeas corpus case on September 8, 1972, when Chief Justice Kiwanuka issued a judgment in favor of British businessman Donald Stewart, detained in Makindye Military Prison. The Chief Justice, ordering the detaining authorities to attend a further hearing, said there was a prima facie case of wrongful detention to be answered. He pointed out that Stewart had been held by the military which, at the time, did not have the full powers of arrest.

Amin was furious over the judgment, and Kiwanuka confided in friends that it was only a matter of time before he would be arrested, especially since he had already given a number of stern warnings to the authorities for exceeding legal powers.

Amin later criticized in public "a prominent Ugandan from Masaka,"—Kiwanuka's home. He also stepped up his propaganda campaign against Kiwanuka, in whom the government, he said, had "lost confidence."

Maxensia, the Chief Justice's widow, recalls: "Amin wanted my husband to invent evidence, but he would not do that. He told the president, 'You cannot interfere in court matters.' Later that day Amin phoned and said to him, 'So you say that I don't have power. All right, we'll see!'

"Amin feared my husband because he had the support of the people. He thought he was a threat, which was really foolish.

"My husband was from the Buganda tribe and a Roman Catholic, and Amin particularly hated Catholics. He wanted to make Uganda into an Islamic state. Every day my husband would go to the Catholic cathedral at Rubaga at 6:30 A.M. to pray. He would say to me, 'We have all got to pray earnestly for our country.' It was better for him to die than to compromise with Amin."

The two men also disagreed over Amin's decision to order fifty thousand Asians in Uganda to leave the country within ninety days. The instruction, said Amin as he spoke at the barracks at Tororo, near the Kenyan border, had come from God in a dream. As Asians almost totally controlled Uganda's trade, factories, plantations, and industries, they were an ideal target.

As a committed Christian, Kiwanuka did not feel that Amin should use God as an excuse for his inhuman decision to deport these people, whose only home was Uganda, and who formed an affluent middle class.

Steve says, "People began advising my father to run, but he didn't fear death. He boldly declared, 'No, why should I run? I have promised to serve my people, and that is what I will do.'

"One of his closest friends was Father Clement Kiggundu, editor of *Munno* [Your Friend], the Luganda language Catholic newspaper. They constantly would discuss the situation. [Kiggundu, too, suspected his life was in danger.]

"My father told Father Clement as they had lunch here one day:

'We cannot leave the country just because we are threatened. If we are to die, let us die like martyrs.'"

After her husband's disappearance, Mrs. Kiwanuka tried in vain to make contact with Amin to find out what had happened. "But he wouldn't see me," she tells us.

"We thank God, however, that he didn't take our house. We have been surviving somehow. I don't have any feeling toward Idi Amin. All I know is that God will punish him.

"My faith has helped me a lot during this time. Like my late husband, I am a devoted Christian."

On the wall of her home is a large picture of Jesus Christ. Beside it are two other photographs—one of her late husband, and the other of Father Clement, who was one of the next on Amin's Roman Catholic hit list.

Underneath the picture is the handwritten inscription by Mrs. Kiwanuka: "I leave you peace. Love one another as I loved you."

GEORGE MUWANGA-KAMYA, then a trainee reporter on *Munno* and now its editor, talks for the first time about that terrible day.

"Father Kiggundu had arranged a business trip to Masaka and had told his driver to wait for him at the office so they could set off on the eighty-mile drive to the south," says Mr. Muwanga-Kamya, a soft-spoken man in his early thirties.

"When the editor didn't arrive, the driver was very concerned, so one of the staff phoned his home at Kisubi, fourteen miles along the Kampala-Entebbe road. He was told by a fellow priest that Clement was not home and had not been there all night.

"Alarmed, we began phoning all the places he could possibly be, including the archbishop's residence at Rubaga, but we could not trace him.

"Around three o'clock, we had an anonymous phone call at the paper. The caller said that a red Peugeot car, similar to the one belonging to our editor, had been spotted in the Namanve Forest." This was ten miles toward Jinja on the main road from Kampala.

"So all the staff members, including myself, went to the scene and found that it was his car. It was completely burned out," says Muwanga-Kamya.

"About ten yards from the vehicle, which had all its tires punctured, was the charred body of Father Kiggundu. It was a terrible sight. In tears, we went to the police and they came back with us to the spot. We collected the remains of his body and took it to Mulago Hospital.

There, Dr. Joseph Kafero, the chief pathologist (who later examined the bullet-scarred body of Archbishop Luwum, and is now dead), conducted a post mortem in which he concluded that Father Kiggundu had been shot and later burned.

"So we then took the mortal remains to Rubaga Cathedral and put them on public display in an open coffin. It was a horrible sight. His head and feet were badly burned and his body shriveled. All that was left was a pile of bones and burned flesh.

"From the Saturday evening until the following Monday, people filed past him. Many were crying. I know I cried."

Christians from all over Kampala were stirred beyond words at this latest illustration of Amin's terrorism against the church.

Among those who paid silent tribute to the late editor was young Steve Kiwanuka. "I went to the cathedral and viewed his body. It smelled like roasted meat. It was so nightmarish that I couldn't sleep for three nights."

The burial took place at the cathedral on Monday, January 15, and was conducted by Bishop Albert Baharagate. Even the leader of the Moslem religion in Uganda was there.

"There was no official representation from the government, not even a message of condolence from Amin or anyone else in his office," says the present editor.

"Nothing was said of the killing on radio, television, or in the official newspaper, the *Voice of Uganda*. This was not surprising."

So why was the *Munno* editor so savagely murdered? One reason may be that he was quietly piecing together the story of the murder of the Chief Justice, and Amin feared he was getting a little too near to solving the riddle for comfort.

Another possibility, up to now never suggested, was his link with Christians in the United States.

Says George Muwanga-Kamya: "He had returned two years earlier from the States, where he had taken a degree in journalism. His friends over there began sending him money to help the Ugandan Catholics."

The president did not permit the churches to receive money from abroad, so the checks were sent to Kiggundu personally. He used the gifts to pay the fees of many of the students, and also purchased a motorbike for a member of the paper's staff.

Perhaps Amin found out about the American money and thought it was being given to overthrow him.

THE CONFLICT BETWEEN AMIN and the Roman Catholic church took a turn for the worse when, at the end of 1972, he decided to expel more than fifty European missionaries, because they were found without residence permits. He said that the missionaries were mercenaries and spies.

The London Times on December 4, 1972, carried the story, datelined Kampala. The correspondent said Amin had accused the Roman Catholic archbishop, the Most Rev. Emmanuel Nsubuga, of connections with Israelis and of South African plots against the Ugandan regime.

"Monsignor Nsubuga called on General Amin with two other Roman Catholic bishops to ask him to reconsider his decision to expel fifty-five European missionaries here," said the *Times*.

"Before this subject was discussed, however, the president gave a warning against people who tried to bring confusion in the country, and produced copies of two letters. He said one had been addressed to the archbishop by a Ugandan lawyer living in Nairobi and the other purportedly was written to a Dutch-born Roman Catholic bishop here by a representative of El Al, the Israel airline.

"General Amin said the first letter 'urged the archbishop and his group' to ferment tribal and religious divisions in the Ugandan Army and to work to frustrate the government's objectives. It also referred to 'military comrades' and the support from South Africa and NATO.

"The second letter, whose full text was released to the press, referred at one point to the British Securicor Company. Part of it read: 'We have decided with my comrades here that on the operation day we shall have to use the Securicor wireless communications to all our seven groups to achieve the success with our comrades up-country. Mr. Ezer has been in contact with the "S" chief. All the arrangements have been made.' The identities of 'Mr. Ezer' and the 'seven groups' were not elaborated.

"General Amin told the archbishop the letters were very dangerous and could have caused bloodshed in the country."

The archbishop and the Dutch-born Bishop of Jinja, the Rt. Rev.

Joseph Willigers, immediately issued a statement about the stormy meeting. Part of it read: "The Catholic bishops categorically denied having brought into the country spies or mercenaries disguised as missionaries. While the persons falling under the government's order are technically in an irregular situation, all of them entered the country legally. Their present situation, which is no doubt technically illegal, was simply due to the fact that the applications for permission to remain in Uganda have not yet been processed by the Immigration Office." They pointed out that all the foreign religious personnel employed by the Catholic Church had their passports stamped at the arriving points into Uganda. They said that, when asked by the government officials, they have always submitted the aliens' quarterly returns. They assured their Catholic community that they have never brought any mercenaries into the country."

Then Pope Paul came onto the scene. He wrote to Amin shortly after the president had announced plans to "Africanize all religions in Uganda." His letter was in reply to one from the president about recent events in the country. Pope Paul assured President Amin that the Roman Catholic Church in Uganda was firmly committed to the spiritual and material well-being of Uganda's people.

Referring to Roman Catholic priests in Uganda, Pope Paul said in his letter he was certain President Amin would facilitate their activities, which were directed to the common good.

He wrote: "We would greatly appreciate it, Mr. President, should there arise problems which concern the Catholic Church and the Republic of Uganda, if the same method of friendly contacts were followed, in order to arrive at just and balanced solutions for the benefit of both sides.

"We are happy to reassure you, Mr. President, that the Catholic Church is firmly disposed to contribute in every possible way to the spiritual and material well-being of the people of Uganda.

"To this end the priests, brothers, and sisters, both Ugandans and of other nationalities, are totally dedicated. We warmly recommend them to your benevolence, certain that you will, as in the past, appreciate and facilitate their activities, which are directed to the common good."

He also referred in the letter, delivered by the Papal Pronuncio, Archbishop Luigi Bellotti, to Uganda's expulsion of non-citizen Asians.

Pope Paul said he was confident General Amin would be sensible to the "moral and human aspects" and that he would "know how to harmonize the interests of the nation with the rights and interests of each individual person, acting always with justice and humanity."

When the nine Italian missionaries of the fifty-five missionaries who were expelled from Uganda arrived home, they praised the "courageous and firm conduct" of the Ugandan Roman Catholic bishops. In interviews broadcast by the Vatican radio, the missionaries said that the bishops "have not neglected a single step" to justify their presence in Uganda.

Someone who watched the dangerous situation with deep concern was Amin's Foreign Minister and then brother-in-law, Wanume Kibedi. He tells us: "The archbishop was a very courageous man. One of the most courageous men in Uganda. There's no doubt that when he was made cardinal he fully deserved it because I know he went through hell. How he survived Amin, only God knows."

Mr. Kibedi, who is not a Catholic, says he believes Rome honored the archbishop because he was operating in a "lions' den" in Amin's Uganda.

But nothing would placate the mad dictator. President Amin then warned religious leaders in Uganda that they would be tried by military tribunal and executed if they misused their influence and created discord and confusion.

He said: "Those spreading this propaganda want to create confusion and misunderstanding so that the people of Uganda fight among themselves. The members of the Defense Council will not allow this to happen. Any religious leader who brings confusion will be dealt with by the military tribunal."

And those close to Amin knew that this was no idle threat.

Possibly one of Idi Amin's greatest mistakes during those eight years of misrule was to allow the shrine of the martyrs at Namugongo, just outside Kampala, to remain standing. Three times in 1977, and again in 1978, thousands of Christians assembled at the simple forest memorial to honor the twenty-two Christians who were burned alive for their faith in 1886 and 1887.

"We remembered, on those occasions and others, that all those martyrs refused to deny Christ," says the shrine caretaker and director of the adjacent Uganda martyrs' seminary, the Rev. Godfrey Charles Baira of the Church of Uganda.

Just as the never-ending killings, mutilations, and tortures of Christians run like a bloody thread through Uganda's stormy history, so does the astonishing growth of Christianity. The Roman Catholic Church has now become the largest single Christian group in the country, with about 5,640,000 members. There are 3,120,000 Protestants; 2,520,000 African Traditionalists, including those who worship gods of wood and stone; and—despite Amin's Islamic crusade—only 720,000 Muslims, who make up a minimal six percent of the total population.

The Roman Catholic Church celebrated its centenary in Uganda in February, 1979, as Amin's terror reign was coming to an end.

It all began when on February 17, 1879, a dilapidated canoe was beached at Entebbe on the shores of Lake Victoria, and it has been faithfully recorded by a friendly, pipe-smoking French-Canadian member of the White Friars, Yves Tourigny, at his office close to Rubaga Cathedral.

He wrote that in the canoe were Father Simeon Lourdel and Brother Amans Delmas, two white Fathers. The king, Kabaka Mutesa I, let them stay in Buganda. They set up a mission, were joined by colleagues, and started baptisms.

The early years were difficult. Some tribal chiefs were openly hostile, and once the missionaries even had to leave the country. But during those three years their converts proved their faith, and the young church grew. When they returned in 1885 there were twice as many Catholics!

Continually, new groups of missionaries joined the pioneers, and in 1893 a seminary opened. Now there are nearly five hundred Ugandan priests and over one thousand six hundred African Sisters.

Even during the years of growth the Catholic Church suffered, particularly during the world war, when priests died in military service, or were interned.

But there have been exciting moments, too—Pope Paul VI's visit in 1969, the canonization of the twenty-two martyrs of Uganda by that same Pope in 1964, and the appointment as Cardinal of Archbishop Emmanuel Nsubuga in 1976.

Indeed, as Yves Tourigny says, it has been a hundred years of trials and blessings.

4

Amin Tries to Rewrite the Bible

AFTER EXPELLING THE ISRAELIS from Uganda on the instructions of Colonel Muammar Gadhafi of Libya, Idi Amin began to really hate Israel. It became so overwhelming that he decided to re-write part of the Bible and take out all references to Israel.

Uganda's former foreign minister, Wanume Kibedi, now a lawyer in London, England, tells what happened. Amin, he says, had discovered that daily Bible readings, put out by organizations like Scripture Union, contained references to Israel and the children of Israel. He became very angry about this.

Kibedi, whose sister Malyamu was Amin's first wife, recalls: "Amin was very upset about this because he felt it was 'political propaganda' by the church."

What made matters worse for the Moslem tyrant was that these daily Bible readings were being broadcast over the government-controlled radio.

"He decreed that this had to stop immediately, because it was 'all political,'" says Kibedi.

Amin summoned the then Archbishop of Uganda, the Rt. Rev. Erica Sabiti, to a cabinet meeting on this matter. The archbishop told Amin and the cabinet that if they tried to ban all references to Israel in the Scriptures, the results could lead to bloodshed.

The church leader said: "We are not doing this for political reasons, but because we are merely following the Bible, and if you are prepared to see more martyrs, so be it, but we are not going to change our religious beliefs."

So, in spite of Amin, "Israel" stayed in the Bible.

Even Gadhafi was enough of a historian to realize that Israel could not be so easily ignored.

The contrast between no two men could be greater than that between General Idi Amin and Colonel Muammar Gadhafi of Libya. When they first met, Amin had grown fat from the good life, with a grin that was deceptively jovial. Gadhafi was self-disciplined and chillingly thin from his diet of sour milk and dates.

Yet these two unlikely allies forged a partnership that gave a new dimension to the African crisis—an alliance that, for the first time, crossed the traditional boundaries between the warring Arab world and strife-torn Africa.

Even in their approach to their common Moslem religion, the differences were striking. Gadhafi was austere and deeply devoted to the Koran. Alcohol and all forms of permissiveness were forbidden in Libya. He had one wife and a small son. Idi Amin, by contrast, enjoyed extravagant tastes. He had five wives, and enjoyed quantities of alcohol.

This strange pair first came together in 1971, when the Ugandan leader visited Libya. At the time, President Amin's regime was being heavily subsidized, armed, and trained by the Israelis. And Amin actually flew in an Israeli jet to Libya to see the extremist Arab dictator.

It was love at first sight. The intellectual Gadhafi fascinated the illiterate soldier from Africa. He also wooed Amin with promises of massive financial and military aid, obviously relishing the opportunity to have Israel thrown out of an African country.

Journalist Daniel McGeachie says, "So great was the Arab's personal influence, as well as his offers of money, that Amin went home and threw out all the Israelis.

"Overnight he began to worship Gadhafi. He developed a hatred for the Jews that, outside the Arab world, has been equaled only by Hitler."

By the end of March, 1972, the Israelis had cleared out. But Israel waited patiently for her chance to teach Amin a lesson. It came in late June, 1976, when an Air France plane, hijacked by the Popular Front for the Liberation of Palestine, arrived at Entebbe Airport. The incredible raid on the airport by Israeli troops is now history. But it did more than humiliate Amin; it also lifted the whole nation, weighed down under his reign of terror.

"On the morning of the Entebbe Raid, practically the entire nation had been secretly tuning into overseas broadcasts and had gotten the incredible news of the freeing of the hostages," a missionary tells us.

"Everywhere I went I noticed a restrained look of triumph on the faces of the people. No one actually mentioned the Israeli raid, but one could sense that deep down they were thrilled that at long last someone had taught Big Daddy a lesson he would never forget."

Amin's mentor Gadhafi was born in a Bedouin goatskin tent and, in 1969, at the age of 28, he overthrew King Idris in a bloodless coup. Unlike Amin, who was once a sergeant, Gadhafi never promoted himself from the rank of colonel, which he held before the takeover. Nor has Gadhafi assumed the title of president, preferring to remain chairman of Libya's Revolutionary Council.

"Under Gadhafi's rule, Libya's staggering oil wealth has snowballed through skilled negotiations with the British and American oil men," says Daniel McGeachie.

At the time the strange alliance was being formed between the two leaders, the Lord Privy Seal in the British Government, Lord Jellicoe, said, "The Libyan involvement has grave implications." He was right.

Next Amin turned his attentions to oil-rich Saudi Arabia, probably the strictest of all the Moslem lands. He arrived in Riyadh aboard a special plane, and was received by King Faisal. (Amin previously visited Mecca after representing Obote's government at the funeral of Nasser in Cairo.)

This successful visit was returned by the king—"The pope of the Moslem religion," as Amin described him—with Faisal being royally received in Uganda. King Faisal was the country's second state visitor since the military coup nearly two years before. (The first was the crazed Emperor Bokassa 1 of the Central African Empire. His extravagant military dress first inspired Amin to start awarding himself medals. However Amin never went quite as far as the now ousted Bokassa, who spent a quarter of the impoverished country's annual income on his coronation.)

The president's fever for the Moslem faith reached its height during the visit of the Arab king. Faisal brought with him royal gifts, including an enormous platter of gold and a golden sword. He told the impressed Amin: "With this sword, Moslemize your country."

Faisal's visit, however, did cause Big Daddy a few headaches.

When the Saudi king was a guest of Amin at Nile Mansions, Kampala, the country was suffering from a food shortage. The king was a lover of fruit, and Amin, afraid that a sparse table might affect the huge loan he was after, quickly imported some melons—one of Faisal's favorite fruits. Consequently, Amin got his money and the Arab leader enjoyed his food.

The melons? They came from Israel.

By the end of the year Arab aid was flooding in. The first big check, for about $5.2 million (US) was handed to Amin on behalf of King Faisal, who also promised to buy Ugandan coffee, tea, timber, and ginger. He pledged he would energetically support the Uganda Moslem Supreme Council.

Amin was actually hoodwinking many of the Arab leaders into believing that Uganda was already a Moslem nation. And this is why they were so generous. But his Arab visitors were perturbed when confronted with Christian churches, hospitals, colleges, and schools. And when they were in Kampala City, they could not avoid the sight of the towering Namirembe and Rubaga Cathedrals.

To counter this, Amin started a Moslem hospital in one of the former Aga Khan buildings in the capital.

"All medicines intended for other hospitals were diverted to this hospital, so others had no medicines," says Fred Jagwe, an Episcopalian from Kampala.

"And because of the greediness of the Moslems, they would charge exorbitant amounts for treatment."

He cited the case of one non-Moslem who had brought his child in for treatment, and then threatened to leave the youngster there for good, unless they reduced the sky-high fee.

When the Asians were expelled, almost all the businesses that they owned were handed over to Moslems. Also those of this faith could easily get permission for allocation of foreign exchange for imports.

"The ticket for everything was to have a Moslem hat on your head," says this Ugandan Christian.

Mr. Jagwe claims that many of these privileged people in Amin's Uganda were illiterate. He says, "It is interesting to note that learning goes hand in hand with Christianity, while when the Arabs came to Uganda, they didn't go to school but just traded. And if they went to school at all, it was to learn to read the Koran. The first Christian missionaries to Uganda brought education here."

In his attempt to Moslemize the country, Amin ordered for a time that only Moslem music could be played over the air, at Easter and Christmas time.

"Amin even abolished Boxing Day [the day after Christmas Day], but when he saw that all other nations were celebrating that day, he had to reinstate it," says Jagwe.

"He then declared Friday a public holiday. One Moslem told me that many people were going to be converted to Islam because of this. But I saw no one converted because of it. Our worry was that sooner or later he would ban Sunday."

The believers began to feel that if he could, the dictator would then try to abolish Christianity altogether in Uganda.

"The clergy and the laymen said that if the president does abolish it here, we will pray in our houses rather than become Moslems," says Jagwe.

A Kampala-based Roman Catholic believes that the friction between Catholics and Moslems in the country dates back to when twenty-two Ugandan saints were murdered in 1886 and 1887 by Islamic King Mwanga.

"During the years that followed, the church tried to close the gap which existed between the two religions," says Deogratias Lwanga.

"But the coming of Amin to power in January, 1971, and his long ambition to turn Uganda into an Islamic republic, revived the past quarrels and misunderstandings of the two religions. Amin made himself head of the Islamic religion and their chief spokesman.

"When he appeared on the scene, he saw how powerful the churches were. This made him jealous of them. He saw no reason why the Islamic religion should be inferior to the other two churches.

The first step he took was to remove the differences that existed among the Islamic community. He united them under the umbrella of the Uganda Moslem Supreme Council. After uniting them and having won their support, he wanted to use them to campaign for an Islamic republic.

"He did not consider the many years and hardship the church had passed through to concrete her foundation. He wanted his revolution to take place immediately—a thing which was impossible to happen in Uganda."

Both Libya and Saudi Arabia fell for Amin's lies and gave generous donations to the Jihad (holy war) Fund to be used, in the words of a visiting Libyan diplomat, "to eliminate the few remaining Christians and turn Uganda into a Moslem state."

Obviously taken up with his importance as a Moslem evangelist and intent on converting Uganda, Amin announced to the inaugural board meeting of the Uganda Development Bank: "Every hundred years God appoints one person to be very powerful in the world to follow what the Prophet directed. When I dream, then things are put into practice."

One day in December, 1974, he "dreamed" that he should dismiss all three hundred members of the Moslem Supreme Council. He accused some of them of preferring girlfriends and expensive cars to religion. However, he eventually decided to keep them on.

It seems that Idi Amin was not in any position to criticize other Moslems for their behavior. For instance he was a heavy drinker, despite the fact that his religion forbade alcohol.

"He drank most of the time. It was nothing for him to consume a bottle of whisky or brandy a day," says his former brother-in-law, Wanume Kibedi.

"He would sit down and keep pouring it into a glass which eventually, I think, gave him gout. Then he cut down seriously. In fact, he abstained for a time, but then he went back to it."

Kibedi said that Amin "treated the people of Uganda as if they were just animals." He added: "I can't believe that anybody who would call himself a devout Moslem could behave like that."

Amin was also into drugs and pornography. When he fled north as the Tanzanians took Entebbe and then Kampala, journalists went into State Lodge, a huge whitewashed villa overlooking Lake Victoria, and found a large stack of pornographic magazines.

Depravity, drugs, and death were his stock in trade at parties. Amin insisted that guests at his parties take amphetamines and barbiturates by the handful. Evidence from secret files found after Idi Amin fled Kampala shows that he would raid hospitals for drugs to be used at the parties.

The latest sex movies from London would be screened and the unfortunate girls, some only fifteen or sixteen, who had been ordered to attend, would be gang raped, often to death.

The president even incurred the wrath of Uganda's Moslems in September, 1977, when he staged public executions during the holy month of Ramadan. A group of Moslems in East Africa sent telegrams to Egypt's President Sadat and Saudi Arabia's king appealing for them to intervene.

Fifteen Ugandans were executed by firing squad in Kampala before a crowd of up to fifty thousand people, many of whom were ordered to watch at gunpoint.

The fifteen—twelve of whom were convicted, by a special military tribunal, of plotting to overthrow President Amin—were shot in front of the Queen Elizabeth Tower, a clock tower built in 1954 to commemorate the queen's visit to Uganda.

The firing squad consisted of thirteen soldiers dressed in camouflage uniforms. Each condemned man was lashed to two sand-filled oil drums and executed individually.

One, however, did not die immediately, and he was killed with a second volley.

Schools were closed, and even young children were forced to watch the killing. A hospital was also closed, and patients and staff were forced at gunpoint to go to the execution site.

Afterwards the bodies of the fifteen men were taken to Cape Town View, the president's lakeside home at Entebbe, so that he could see for himself that they were dead.

As the pleas for mercy for the condemned men had been made from African leaders, religious groups, and others, Amin's aids suddenly answered that the president was in a coma after an operation on his neck. But this was an elaborate hoax used to persuade Moslem countries that Amin was unable to grant reprieves.

Amin decided he was a great man and did not need to heed anyone. He bestowed upon himself eight top medals in an effort to out-do Bokassa, and then vowed to erect a memorial to Queen Victoria and a statue of Hitler in Kampala—after expressing surprise that he had seen no such statues in West Germany.

Regularly the dictator took over the microphone at the government-controlled Uganda radio. He caused confusion among his top officials with his random announcements over the air.

"The ministers took to carrying notebooks, and, as soon as he started to talk, began scribbling down what they were meant to do," recalls Henry Kyemba, in his book, *State of Blood* (Paddington Press, USA, and Corgi, UK). "I was supposed to coordinate the instructions to various ministries. This was fine to start with, because it followed, more or less, the procedures laid down by the colonial civil service, but soon it became impossible to keep track of all the orders."

To be informed of the decisions Amin had made, it was necessary to read the newspapers and listen to Uganda radio. Government officials used the radio as their guide.

Colleagues often explained their actions to Kyemba by saying, "The president told me to do it—didn't you hear it on the radio?"

Sometimes Amin would go on the air as "Big Daddy" or "Dada" (grandfather) as he liked to call himself, but often he would try to disguise himself as "a government spokesman" and would ramble on about anything that came into his head.

During March, 1976, while again posing on the air as an official, he launched into an attack on the Roman Catholic Archbishop of Kampala, Cardinal Emmanuel Nsubuga, who had just arrived back at Entebbe from an unusual trip to Zanzibar in Tanzania. He had gone to collect the remains of Father Leon Barbot and Brother Delmas Amans, two of the first Catholic missionaries to settle in Uganda.

"The remains had been exhumed and the archbishop was bringing them back to Kampala," recalls George Muwanga-Kamya, editor of the Catholic daily paper, *Munno*. (This paper was founded in 1911 by a French priest, Father Julien Gorju, and now sells ten thousand copies a day.)

"The archbishop and his aide brought them back in two small boxes. They were photographed with the boxes at Entebbe. Amin, claiming to be the 'government spokesman,' went on the air and said how shameful it was for the archbishop to be carrying a woman's handbag. The president added that 'he looked like an importer of women's handbags.' "

President Amin then said: "Anyway, how can human bodies fit into such small boxes?"

"To defend himself, the archbishop called a press conference. He told the assembled journalists that after one hundred years a body was nothing more than dust, and could now easily fit into a small box.

"No other papers, radio, or television carried his explanation and we were ordered by Amin not to publish it," says Muwanga-Kamya. "But in spite of this, we carried the whole text of the press conference. A week later, Amin, again as 'the government spokesman,' suddenly went on the air saying he had 'received a proposal from the people that *Munno* should be banned.' "

And when Idi Amin "received" such proposals, he meant them to be carried out. On August 1, 1976, as the editorial staff were settling down to another busy day meeting deadlines, the office was raided by members of the police Special Branch.

"As they dashed in they found a reporter, James Luyima, reading an anti-Amin leaflet he had picked up on his way into work that morning," says Muwanga-Kamya, who was then working as a subeditor on the paper.

"They immediately declared that *Munno* had printed the leaflet and arrested the editor, John Serwaniko, and the two reporters. They were taken to the Central Police Station and the office was closed down. Then Amin made a public statement, saying that our editor was dealing with South Africans, Israelis, and Rhodesians, as well as being agents of the 'malicious propaganda spread by the BBC against Uganda.'"

Reports around the world said the trio had been killed by Amin's gangsters. We discovered this was not true and spoke to James Luyima.

He recalls that day: "I was reading a leaflet called *Blood, Blood, Blood,* which was thought to have been written by some people at Makerere University. The message of the pamphlet was to unite and overthrow the government. I had just picked it up in the street on the way in.

"After a short stay at the Central Police Station, we were transferred to Luzira Prison. We were called 'The President's Prisoners.' Often we were beaten with sticks or kicked with their boots. During one beating my shoulder was badly damaged."

Then suddenly, without warning, a guard brought the office keys to the imprisoned editor and told him he and the reporters were free men and could reopen the office.

That was January 1, 1977. After a few weeks the editor left, and George Muwanga-Kamya took over.

From then until the downfall of the Amin regime, Muwanga-Kamya was under constant pressure, and needed tremendous courage and insight to avoid being arrested.

"One day I was summoned to see the Permanent Secretary, Mr. Abdullah Amin, who told me he had discovered we were getting features from Catholic agencies in Rome and in the United States. [The censors opened all the paper's overseas mail.]

"He said the government didn't want me to use this material anymore and that I must write a 'strong letter' to both of them telling them to stop sending it. He ordered me to send him a copy of my letters. So I sat down and drafted two strong letters. I then sent the carbon copies to Mr. Amin, and 'forgot' to send the originals. The material kept coming."

Muwanga-Kamya says the intimidation was often more subtle. "We needed foreign exchange to import newsprint for our newspaper, and the Bank of Uganda kept us waiting for long periods. This was their method of applying pressure."

The editor finally found a way around the foreign exchange problem. "In 1979, during our centenary celebrations, gifts of newsprint came in from Holland to the Uganda Catholic Secretariat," he says. "The Secretariat would then give us the paper. It was a way of getting it in by the back door."

He adds: "Although we had problems getting foreign exchange, Amin's friends had no trouble at all. All the cash necessary was available when they wanted to buy their Mercedes-Benz cars."

After the killing of Chief Justice Kiwanuka and Father Kiggundu, *Munno* reported a Women's Council resolution calling for probes into "disappearances."

Exiled Education Minister Edward Rugumayo claims Amin "went on to liquidate many of the important Catholics in the civil service and the business world—many Catholic prison officers, administrative secretaries, and others. President Amin further attacked the nuns and priests in the press for allegedly acting as spies. He also turned against Protestants."

One leading Protestant killed was Michael Kagwa, president of the Industrial Court. Kagwa, who was extremely wealthy (he even possessed a Mercedes sports car with its own television), had a pretty girlfriend, Helen Ogwang, in whom Amin was interested. He was seized by the president's bodyguards at the Kampala International Hotel swimming pool. His shot and burned body, together with his car, was found on the outskirts of the city, near Namirembe Cathedral.

In a bid to cover up the killing, the government offered a fifty-thousand shilling (nearly five thousand dollars US) reward for information about the situation. But, of course, no one dared claim it. Helen Ogwang was later assigned to the Uganda Embassy in Paris, from where she defected.

Rugumayo said a death list was drawn up, containing more than two thousand names. At least ten "assassination squads" roamed the country with impunity, seeking their victims.

Speaking during Amin's reign, he said, "The pattern is a familiar one: They enter an office, call their victim out, put him in the boot [trunk] of the car or just inside the car. And that is his end. On some occasions, they ambush their victim along a motorway, or along the road leading to his home. Previously, most of the victims were men, but now women have fallen victims of his [Amin's] deadly plans."

The former minister added: "He [Amin] considers himself first and foremost as a Nubian Kakwa, secondly as a Moslem, thirdly as a West Niler, and fourthly as a Ugandan." Consequently, he said, his closest associates come from one or all of these categories.

Rugumayo's account of Amin's evil deeds were both explicit and frightening.

"The methods of killing during the first months of the coup included straight-forward shooting or beating. With the disposal of dead bodies becoming a problem, the soldiers resorted to throwing bodies of their victims either in rivers, swamps, or even water reservoirs. This was found to be unsatisfactory, as human bodies tend to float and to attract vultures. Later on, they were simply thrown into the bush and left there to rot or to be eaten by wild beasts, or were burned in petrol [gasoline] fires."

The Nazi torturers would probably have learned a few harrowing methods from Amin's principal killers.

"The victims would line up, and the first one would be ordered to lie down while the prisoner next to him would be ordered to smash his head with a huge hammer. Then the third person would be ordered to demolish the second prisoner's brains, and so on until the last man, who would either be shot by Toweli [head of the Public Safety unit] or be killed in the same brutal manner by a police officer.

"The victims' heads would be smashed beyond recognition by one of the appointed executioners.

"Slow killing is a common practice. Toweli would shoot into a man's arm, leg, or chest, and let him bleed to death.

"Another method is to cut off any of the man's organs, such as an arm, leg, genitals, and let him die in agony. Sometimes these organs would be stuck into the victim's mouth.

"There is a technique of cutting a victim's flesh, and forcing him to feed on it raw, until he would bleed to death while living on his own flesh. The other despicable method is to cut a man's flesh, have it roasted and let him feed on it until he dies.

"There are in Makindye Prison very deep and dark holes in which certain prisoners are kept. These holes are filled with ice-cold water in which prisoners are kept and are fed once a day on some form of diet, and are at the same time tortured until they die.

"There are other horrible methods of torture which are too terrible to describe, such as sticking bayonets through prisoners' anuses or genitals; or women being raped and afterwards having their reproductive organs set on fire while they are alive.

"The instruments of murder, torture, and human degradation have been perfected by Amin. Most of the bodies of important people are put in incinerators and those who cannot be burned for one reason or another are buried, while wrapped in a cloth, by prisoners who would not live to tell the tale. In some towns the army, after their killing sprees, carry the dead bodies into the nearest town or hospital mortuary. Nobody can venture to ask any questions. The following day the town or city cemetery workers are told to bury the dead without asking any questions."

The vile ingenuity of these beasts seemed to know no end. For instance, electric shocks were used in torture cells at Naguru Police College. Power terminals were attached to the genitals, nipples, neck, or face. Eyes were gouged out of victims and left hanging from their sockets.

Iron bars, car axles, hammers, and wooden mallets were used to smash limbs and joints. Prisoners were beaten for long periods with vicious rhinoceros whips. The wheel torture was also used, where a victim's head was forced into the center of the metal wheel rim of a truck. A boot was pressed against his neck, and guards held his legs. Then his back was whipped, and the torturers struck the rim of the wheel with iron bars until the man collapsed from the unbearable pain tingling through his head.

Women's breasts were hacked off with bayonets; hands and feet were chopped off; victims' stomachs were slashed open and their intestines pulled out. Some prisoners were forced to walk over up-turned nails and were then subjected to physical exertion until they collapsed or were beaten down.

Some groups of people, called burial squads, were fed only on human flesh. Others were forced to dig their own mass graves, trenches along which they were lined up and then shot. Bodies that did not fall neatly into the trench were pushed in by the next group of victims lining up to die.

In a damning report from the International Commission of Jurists, based in Geneva, President Amin was accused of being responsible for up to ninety thousand deaths during the first two years of his regime.

The United Nations did nothing about these endless atrocities. And the African states made no attempt to restrain the black Hitler in their midst.

An ignorant world continued to laugh at the antics of Crown Prince Idi. Television comedians made a good living by impersonating him, and others became hits with their friends by imitating a speech of Idi's in his own brand of pidgin English.

One person who thinks Amin was definitely not a clown is Dr. Ted Williams, probably Uganda's most experienced medical missionary doctor. The Nairobi-born medic, who works with the Africa Inland Mission, helped found the seventy-five bed Kuluva Hospital in Amin's West Nile region. He worked with Dr. Dennis Burkitt on research into the growth, now universally known as Burkitt's lymphoma, which was killing hundreds of African children. The important research eventually established that the cancerous growths could be successfully treated with drugs.

"We were told that he was a buffoon and all that, but he was not. He was very intelligent," says the doctor, who is now in his sixties.

"Christians in Uganda regarded him as devil-possessed. And if you want to check that, just think of the times that he did outrageous things—like chucking the Asians out. Also, look at the many times he escaped assassination attempts.

"No, despite his lack of education, he was a very clever and cunning man, devilishly cunning."

5

Did Idi Amin
Sacrifice His Son?

"TAKE AIM . . ."

The firing squad lifted their rifles to their shoulders and waited for the order to squeeze the trigger. It came almost immediately.

". . . fire."

A volley of bullets cut down the three men standing bravely together. But even as the hail of fire ripped into them, their faces were radiant. In a split second they had gone to be with Jesus. The venue for this terrible spectacle was a stadium in the southern Uganda town of Kabale. The date was February 10, 1973.

This was just one of many public executions the president had announced over the radio. He said that several men had been arrested "for subversive activities." The country's military tribunal had decided, as a warning to others, that each would have to be shot in his home area.

Most people in the country were horrified by the barbarity of the announced plan, and Festo Kivengere, the Bishop of Kigezi, was one of them. He happened to be in the Ugandan capital, Kampala, when the order was announced. Immediately Bishop Kivengere called the president on his private line and requested an interview.

Surprisingly, Amin invited the Church of Uganda bishop to "come straight over." He had previously announced that any citizen with a complaint could personally talk it over with him, but he never honored that pledge.

After they had exchanged a few formalities, Kivengere came straight to the point. "Your Excellency, I am troubled about the announcement to publicly execute these men who have been arrested.

We appreciate very much that you have never introduced martial law, but have allowed the courts of Uganda to function as usual.

"You have often said you fear God. God created human life in His own image, and therefore, I plead that these men be given a chance to defend themselves. You graciously gave to one of your army officers, who shot a Kenyan soldier, a chance to plead his case in court. Now that he has been proven guilty no one can complain."

Then pointing to one of Amin's children, who happened to be in the room, he said, "See this little boy of yours, sir? God will allow him the time he needs to grow into a man. So when you think of taking a life away, first consider it carefully before acting."

The bishop waited for the giant president to erupt into a wild rage, but amazingly, he didn't. After thoughtfully weighing Kivengere's words, he made no firm commitment to commute the death sentences, but left some hope.

For a few days nothing happened. Kivengere and his flock prayed for a stay in the execution. But finally the Defense Council had its way and the public killings were scheduled.

Bishop Kivengere asked for permission from the authorities at least to speak to the local Kabale men before they died, and this was granted. Two of his fellow ministers went with him.

"The men were brought in a truck and unloaded," said Bishop Kivengere, in his book *I Love Idi Amin* (New Life Ventures). "They were handcuffed and their feet were chained. The firing squad stood to attention. As we walked to the center of the stadium, I was wondering what to say to these men in the few minutes we had before their death. How do you give the gospel to doomed men who are probably seething with rage?"

"We approached them from behind, and as they turned around to look at us, what a sight! Their faces were all alight with an unmistakable glow and radiance. Before we could say anything, one of them burst out: 'Bishop, thank you for coming! I wanted to tell you. The day I was arrested, in my prison cell, I asked the Lord Jesus to come into my heart. He came in and forgave me all my sins! Heaven is now open, and there is nothing between me and my God! Please tell my wife and children that I am going to be with Jesus. Ask them to accept Him into their lives as I did.'

"The second man told us a similar story, excitedly raising his hands, which rattled his handcuffs.

"Then the youngest said: 'I once knew the Lord, but I went away from Him and got into political confusions. After I was arrested, I came back to the Lord. He has forgiven me and filled me with his peace. Please tell my parents (they are evangelists in the diocese) and warn my younger brother never to go away from the Lord Jesus.'"

Kivengere felt as if he should be talking to the soldiers, and not to the condemned men.

"So I translated what the men had said into a language the soldiers understood. The military men were standing there with their guns cocked, and bewilderment on their faces. Those in the stadium who were near enough could hear it, too. The rest could see the radiance on the faces of the condemned, which showed they were forgiven souls. The soldiers were so dumbfounded at the faces and words of the men they were about to execute that they even forgot to put the hoods over the prisoner's faces!"

British missionary Lillian Clarke takes up the story: "Festo was so moved with their testimonies that he was in tears. As the men, who were handcuffed and chained together, began walking to the other end of the stadium where they were to be shot, they jumped up and down for joy and said it was all right because they were going to be with the Lord." They were quickly and violently executed.

All over Uganda at 2:00 P.M. East African time a total of twelve men—all but one of them alleged Obote guerrillas—were publicly executed by firing squads.

The story did not end there. The next Sunday, Kivengere preached to a large crowd in the hometown of one of the executed men. Despite the feeling of death which hung over the congregation, the bishop told them the inspiring testimony of the brother from their area, and how he died praising Jesus. Suddenly the whole congregation erupted into a great song of praise to the Lord. Many turned their lives over to God at that service. It had the same effect in many other churches around the region.

Kivengere was later told that the soldiers who formed the firing squad were deeply affected by the sight of those three men standing with the glory of God shining on their faces.

But the executioners had to do their job. After the Kabale execution, Lt. Col. Ali, the officer presiding there, said: "Anyone disturbing the stability of Uganda will be crushed."

In West Acholi, more than ten thousand crowded onto Gulu Golf

Course to watch John Labeja and Amos Obwona die. Golf tournaments in the town had never drawn such a crowd.

A twenty-four-year-old mathematics teacher at Kyambogo College, James Karuhanga, was shot near the district commissioner's office at Mbarara. As Karuhanga was blindfolded, the crowd began chanting, "Kill him. Kill him. We don't want guerrillas."

The twelfth man to die that day was Badru Semakula, who had been sentenced to death for robbery. Before he faced a twelve-man firing squad in Kampala, three priests—a Catholic, a Protestant, and a Muslim—were allowed to approach the hogtied prisoner and conduct prayers.

The killings spotlighted a link with Uganda's pagan past. The last public executions in the country had taken place during the British Colonial Administration, half a century before. Three men were then publicly hanged at Malongwe village near Kampala after being found guilty of murdering a young girl and dismembering her body for witchcraft rites.

These superstitious practices had not died out and witchcraft was something that Idi Amin knew all about. Exiled Education Minister Edward Rugumayo revealed the shocking truth behind Amin's pagan practices in a memorandum after his resignation. He was addressing African heads of state and government.

After describing Amin as a "racist and a fascist; a murderer and a blasphemer; a tribalist and a dictator," he spoke about Amin's deep-rooted superstition. "He is surrounded by witch doctors, fortune tellers, soothsayers, and all manner of bogus persons. He relies more on these men than on the actual facts as they exist. Hence his reliance on 'dreams,' apparitions, and other occult practices, and his inability to realize the importance of pertinent information relating to his government."

Amin's main seer for a time was "Dr." Ngombe Francis, a Zambian bush "prophet" who early in January, 1971, had predicted Milton Obote's overthrow. So Amin could not resist inviting the tiny seer to Kampala. Then before television cameras, Francis performed various alleged psychic feats.

The Zambian, who frequently boasted, "I can predict anything," grew rich after Big Daddy admitted him to his close entourage. Boosted by Amin's generosity, he opened consulting rooms in Nairobi, and soon became a reported dollar millionaire, with a luxury mansion in Zambia, two houses in Kenya, a villa on the Cote D'Azur, three Mercedes-Benz cars, a British sports model, and part ownership of a four-seater helicopter. However, he had one weakness that even he couldn't predict. That was his gambling. On one occasion "Dr." Francis admitted his losses exceeded $50,000 (US).

Amin's obsession with witchcraft was also confirmed by Henry Kyemba, Amin's former Health Minister, who fled the country in 1977. He claims that on one occasion in September, 1976, when they were talking at the President's Lodge at Nakasero, Amin told him: "I have eaten human meat. It is very salty, even more salty than leopard meat."

"Amin is certainly superstitious enough to engage in blood rituals," wrote Kyemba in his disturbing book *State of Blood* (Paddington Press, USA, and Corgi, UK) published while Amin was still in power.

"He regularly visits witch doctors both in Jinja, where friends of mine have seen him entering the witch doctor's house, and in Kampala. Witch doctors are consulted in Uganda, particularly by Moslems, as astrologers and psychiatrists are consulted in the West.

"Amin usually goes to them because he needs advice on some problem or other—he may wish to have an 'enemy' name, for instance, or he may want to know what action to take to avoid assassination. No doubt his sessions follow the same pattern as other, similar consultations. The client comes bearing a chicken, goat, or some other offering. The witch doctor tells the client to sit in a darkened room, then asks a number of questions to elicit the information that will later form the basis of his advice. He then mumbles a few incantations, before telling the client what he should do. He may also provide the person with some beads to be worn as amulets, or he may give him a magic chant to be used on particular occasions. The consultation is then at an end."

He added: "Amin also frequently consults the head of the Moslem religion in the army, Colonel Khamis Saafi, who is himself a firm believer in witchcraft. The colonel once came to me with a request to transfer a Mulago nurse, because, as he put it, she was bewitching a former lover to make him impotent. He said that if she was sent to a remote area the spell would be broken. I did not oblige him."

Idi Amin even took to keeping severed heads and human organs in a refrigerator of one of his homes. This gruesome claim was made by a house servant who fled to Kenya. The servant, Moses Aloga, who worked in one of Amin's residences, the "Old Command Post at Kampala," says that Amin's fifth wife, Sarah, discovered the head of her former lover in the refrigerator.

Sarah made her bizarre discovery, says the former servant, when she visited the "Old Command Post" and persuaded the servant to take her into what was called the Botanical Room. This was where the president entertained close friends, and it was always kept locked. Aloga, whose job was to clean the room, kept the keys to the room and to the two refrigerators that stood there.

When he was asked by Mrs. Amin what was kept in one of the refrigerators, he told her that he thought it was for drinks for the president's important visitors. But she was not content with his answer, and asked again about the refrigerator, which she said she had not seen open since she had married Amin.

"I'll give you a large sum of money if you will open the fridge for me," she told him.

He told her that both he and another servant, Abud Khalim, were responsible for the key to the refrigerator. "If I open it for you, my life will be in danger," he said.

Obviously not going to be put off so easily, Sarah promised him she would not tell anybody.

"Look, if you will open it, it will be a secret between us and I will give you a job at my own house with a bigger salary."

So after this he opened the padlock which joined the refrigerators by a chain. She opened one which contained beer and other drinks. Then she opened the left-hand one.

She gasped, transfixed in horror when she saw that in it were two heads. One was the head of Jesse Gitta, her former lover. She looked at it for a few moments, then tried to take it out. Her body was trembling and full of fear. She began crying hysterically and then collapsed in a faint.

The other head was that of a woman called Ruth Kobusingye, a beautiful girl who had been coming to Amin and whom he suspected was running around with other men.

The servant first tried to lift the unconscious Sarah, but couldn't, so he picked up the refrigerator key and ran out, forgetting to lock the door. Amin arrived shortly afterwards with his bodyguard. Also with him were Colonel Juma Oris and Lieutenant Colonel Mondo, as well as Major Farouk Minawa, commanding officer of the State Research Bureau at Nakasero.

Amin found Sarah, who had by now come out of her faint, lying on the floor crying. When he noticed the open refrigerator door he started to beat her and she began screaming. He grabbed his terrified wife and dragged her into the main room. He had a pistol in his other hand and kept shouting, "I will kill you for this." Colonel Juma Oris pleaded with Amin not to harm her, but he pointed his weapon at the colonel and said to leave him alone.

Sarah was savagely beaten by her husband and then dispatched to Tripoli in Libya, where her face and body healed after the attack.

Human organs were often brought to Amin and kept in the refrigerator. It is said he kept the heads and human organs, such as hearts and livers, to bring him good fortune and ward off the "evil eye."

Another former employee of the dictator claims that he had the ears of executed whites delivered to him on a platter. And Abraham Missuule-Minge, who was a secret police officer, says it happened at least fifty times.

He claims that Amin often ordered couples facing execution to have sexual intercourse in front of him, promising them freedom if they pleased him.

"Amin would lounge about sipping Russian wine and roar with laughter as the couples had sex on the floor," he says.

Probably the most spine-chilling story of Amin's adherence to black magic is the shocking claim that he sacrificed one of his sons, Moses. Supposedly Moses was ritually slaughtered in front of his father. It was said to be a blood sacrifice to appease the gods, and to save Amin's own skin.

In public, Amin posed as a devoted family man. He adored being photographed with his principal sons among the legion of thirty-six children he has fathered. Often he dressed them as exact replicas of himself.

In particular, his favorite, Moses, went everywhere with him. But the persistent rumor is that the present Moses is an imposter.

This incredible claim, which appeared in the *London Daily Mirror,* was told by Dr. Ally Kawuma, a personal physician to General Idi Amin for three years, until he suddenly found himself out of favor. After gaining safe refuge in Scotland, he gave an appalling account of how he believed the president was led to sacrifice his own son.

It happened in 1975 when Amin feared he would be overthrown, Dr. Kawuma says. With his strong belief in black magic, it was decided only one thing could prevent this—the death of one of his own family.

Dr. Kawuma continues, "The details of the savage blood rite were disclosed to me by the man who wielded the ceremonial dagger to slit the boy's throat—a Rwandese witch doctor called Mohammoud.

"It took place near a small, seven-room statehouse kept for Amin at Entebbe. The building is unusually shaped—round, and with two side doors, instead of a main entrance.

"A driveway circles the metal-roofed house, which is only lightly-guarded and has only two powerful security lights illuminating its small, but attractive grounds.

"It was from there, between June and October, 1975, that Amin left to participate in that terrible deed, in that lonely countryside nearby."

It happened, claims the doctor, at a time when communists were infiltrating the country—and Amin feared that he would be overthrown in a Marxist-backed coup.

"There were rumors of this story, but all the details were given to me by the man who slaughtered the boy, Mohammoud himself, a man I was to meet often in the close coterie of trusted confidants Amin surrounded himself with.

"Stealthily, and in the middle of the night, Amin had the little boy brought, in a drugged stupor, to the secret clearing.

"There he was met by Mohammoud, the witch doctor. Only five feet, four inches tall, the witch doctor was a small, very ordinary looking man of forty-five, who wore the flowing white robes often adopted by Moslems.

"The little boy Moses, aged only seven, was laid on the ground, while Mohammoud began his incantations to the gods.

"Watching with Amin were at least two trusted relatives—known as 'elders,' and as steeped in the beliefs of witchcraft as Amin himself. There may also have been intelligence officers from the army present.

"The incantations ceased. Mohammoud bared his knife—and with one terrible, deep incision severed the throat of the human sacrifice.

"He placed a gourd to the gaping wound to collect the flowing blood. And when it was full, he handed that ghastly container to Amin."

Amin, he says, then knelt holding the gourd of his son's still-warm blood in front of him. Clasping it in both hands, he told the gods what he wanted—an end to the troubles that threatened him in his land; the ridding of the Communist menace; the destruction of his enemies; and his continued life presidency of Uganda.

"He handed the blood-filled gourd back to Mohammoud, who later took it to another secret spot, where it was left for the gods to drink," says Dr. Kawuma.

"The body of the child was taken away and disposed of—I never heard the details of how it was done. I imagine it was buried in an unmarked grave."

Dr. Kawuma believes that Moses was the son of Amin's now-divorced first wife, Malyamu, a headmaster's daughter and sister of the former Foreign Minister, Wanume Kibedi.

When Dr. Kawuma tackled Mohammoud about the dark secret, he says Mohammoud told him: "It was necessary." The witch doctor also revealed that Amin was given the choice of victims for the sacrifice—either a wife, son, or daughter. He chose Moses.

Dr. Kawuma claims the present "Moses" is not the original son of that name—he is six months to a year older than the child Amin sacrificed. Now the former dictator treats the replacement Moses as the reincarnation of the innocent boy who gave up his life to prolong the existence of his mad father.

In his London law office, Mr. Kibedi, in an exclusive interview, says he could neither prove nor disprove the shocking story. "The point is that I have denounced Amin from beginning to end. There's no doubt about that, and if I had complete information about this, certainly I would talk about it. I've heard of that incident, but I cannot say that this is true or not."

Kibedi says his sister, Malyama, Moses' mother, could not verify the story either. "I know that if it happened, we would have heard information. Obviously, although we haven't been in Uganda for years, we weren't cut off after we left his regime. We were in touch with the people in a secret sort of way."

Mr. Kibedi says there was "no end to the list of crimes committed by Amin against people in Uganda." He adds: "Take into consideration the fact that two of his wives died in the most abominable circumstances after they'd left him and my own sister barely escaped death. In the course of one day, she was involved in two put-up accidents. There is no doubt whatsoever that he is capable of anything. As to whether he did this thing or not I cannot testify that I knew personally."

So is the story true or not? "Well, I don't know," he says.

Part III

The Death of
Archbishop Janani Luwum

6

Prisoners at Nakasero

As JAMES KAHIGIRIZA lay helpless in the airless, stinking cell at Nakasero, he could hear the voice of the sadistic State Research boss, Major Farouk Minawa, barking out a list of names.

In nearby Cell One were about fifty Ugandan soldiers. And as Minawa took the roll call from outside the cell, they answered by numbers.

Suddenly he seized a machine gun and pointed it through the tiny opening at the top of the cell door. Kahigiriza heard the deadly chatter of the weapon as Minawa fired indiscriminately into the crowd of screaming men. When the bullets were exhausted, the SRB man started calling out the names again. This time there was no answer.

"Then he got some tear gas, and wearing a gas mask, started pumping it into the cell. Since the gas could not go through the other end, it had to come back underneath the door of our cell, which had a metal door with open bars," says Kahigiriza, who had been a Prime Minister in the Acholi Kingdom government during the time when Uganda was still a British protectorate.

"We all started coughing and sneezing, and holding our clothes to our mouths and noses, rising up to get fresh air from the small ventilator at the top of the basement; but all in vain.

"We, in fact, thought they were intending to kill us with guns, after shooting the soldiers. Finally the air cleared, but it was considerable time after the tear gas had been pumped in.

"A few days afterwards, Minawa came and apologized to us. He said, 'The gas was not intended for you, but to drive out any soldiers who might still have been alive.'

"This gas did affect one of our friends that night, a Mr. Nyagahima, who became mentally disturbed, and told us that in the morning he would tell the Nubian guards how bad they were. We desperately tried to persuade him not to say anything, as it would endanger his life, but he refused.

"Next morning, when a guard named Kabugo came in, a Moslem of the Buganda tribe and very aggressive, Mr. Nyagahima asked him why they had 'wanted to kill us with gas.' This question angered Kabugo, who picked up a sweeping brush and started beating him. But Mr. Nyagahima overpowered him, took the brush, and hit him over the head. We could not separate them, as all our hands were tied. Kabugo managed to escape from the beating, and ran outside. But he was quickly back with a contingent of soldiers.

"They caught Mr. Nyagahima and started beating him on the head with iron bars. Then he was dragged up to Minawa's office for 'questioning' and he never came back. He was murdered."

Kahigiriza describes the "mopping-up" operation in the massacre cell. "Washing the pools of blood, after removing all the bodies, took the guard almost seven hours. The cell was hosed down from a large hosepipe brought down from a tap upstairs.

"Sometimes the guards would let us drink from the pipe, but that was awful because it had been dropped in the blood of the dead soldiers."

The nightmare began for James Kahigiriza, a distinguished-looking man in his fifties with graying hair, when he strolled into his office at the Uganda Land Commission, Kampala, on February 15, 1977. He had glanced briefly at the usual gathering of people waiting to see him about land applications and other matters dealt with by his busy department.

But before admitting them, one by one, he decided to dictate a few urgent letters to his personal secretary. He had just completed that task when three men opened the door of his office and rushed in. Their strange clothes made him suspect that they were not among his usual callers.

"One was wearing carpet slippers and the other two were in high-heeled shoes and bell-bottom trousers," recalls Mr. Kahigiriza, a committed Christian and a member of All Saints Church, just four hundred yards from the notorious State Research building.

"One introduced himself to me as John and then mentioned the names of the others, which I now believe were fictitious. I could see that they were Nubians, and therefore Moslems.

"After they had finished their introduction, the leader told me that I was wanted to 'make a statement' and they had come to take me to write it. I asked where I was being taken, but they refused to tell me."

One of them then opened his small briefcase, pointed inside it, and said to Kahigiriza, "If you want to know what my identity is, here it is." The top civil servant saw to his dismay two pistols lying snugly there. "I thought that I could well be shot there and then," he recalls, as we sat talking in the cool of the evening at the Namirembe Guest House, Kampala.

He told us how, almost instinctively, he made a grab for the telephone to call his boss, Lt. Col. Erunayo Oryema, the Minister of Land and Water Resources. But he was too slow. One of the young men seized a pair of handcuffs from his briefcase and, while another roughly held his arms, snapped them on him.

While Kahigiriza was struggling with the men, Joseph Mubiru, his Secretary to the Commission, entered the room.

"Mr. Mubiru appeared and was extremely disturbed to find me in this state. I said to him, 'You can see that I am being arrested.' The Commission Secretary was then ordered to sit down. Before being led at gunpoint from my second-floor office, I removed my wristwatch and handed it to Mr. Mubiru, and told him to take it to my family and tell them what had happened.

"Our ministry is always a busy place and there were normally a lot of people moving up and down the corridors; but this time I did not see a single person; there was no one around until I got outside.

"One of my captors went quickly ahead, opened the rear door of a waiting car, then sat himself in the driver's seat. When I arrived at the car, I saw a number of machine guns on the floor. I immediately made up my mind to resist getting in. I told them I did not see any reason why I should. 'Since you have guns, why don't you kill me now?' I said.

"They tried to push me into the car, and I started to shout. I knew nobody would actually come to my rescue, but I would, at least, alert people to the fact that I had been arrested. My shouts were successful and people peered anxiously through the windows to observe what was happening."

By now his captors were getting angry, and they grabbed him

roughly. One held his legs, another his head, as they bodily forced him into the car. In the melee, Kahigiriza lost one of his shoes, which was left lying in the gutter as the car screeched off toward the Speke Hotel.

As he sat stunned in the back of the car, one of the Nubians turned to him and said, "We know you people had planned to kill us, so we have decided to kill you first."

Puzzled by the comment, Kahigiriza, a peace-loving man, questioned what he meant by "you people." But the trio did not reply; they sat with sullen stares, looking ahead.

Suddenly the car came to a halt at Nakasero, and, as the gate to the house of torture swung open, Kahigiriza glanced quickly back at his home church across the beautiful green. He knew this could well be the last time he would ever see the building where he worshiped so regularly.

He was manhandled down to a basement, where he was told to sit on the floor and wait. A few minutes later a guard came in and ordered him to remove his remaining shoe, belt, and other belongings. The guard also confiscated three thousand shillings, the equivalent of nearly $400 (US).

"The Moslem guard then opened the door to a dark tunnel and pushed me in. I found about ten other people inside, most of them Langi, and badly beaten," he says.

"The tunnel was very narrow and I was given a gunny sack to sit on. The place was so narrow that I could not stretch my legs properly. When I tried to, they would touch the opposite wall. For us to be able to stretch at all, the person facing me had to cross his legs over mine.

"There was one fluorescent light inside, but that was not switched on unless they were bringing in a prisoner or taking one out. Another striking thing about this cell, which was known as Cell One, was that the only ventilation was a small opening on top of the door, used by the guards to speak to the prisoners.

"At first I was left near the door. My only opportunity to gulp in fresh air, if you could call it that, was when new prisoners were brought in.

"The stench was almost unbearable, mainly caused by a big trash can kept in the cell and used as a toilet." Handuffed and helpless, Kahigiriza sat cramped on the floor of this hell-hole with only the Lord to comfort him. He soon discovered one of the reasons for his sudden arrest. A young Nubian who came to see him that evening said: "You are one of those big politicians wanting to overthrow the government." Kahigiriza naturally denied the ludicrous charge, but was told ominously: "You will have to answer for this."

"In the evening, I called my friends in the cell to have a word of prayer," says Kahigiriza. "I led the prayer, and then everybody joined in. I did this for the next three weeks, every morning and evening. But if footsteps were heard in the middle of a prayer, we kept quiet for a while until they receded. Being caught praying in the cell would have brought dire consequences for all of us."

For the first twenty-four hours, no one in the putrid tunnel was given anything to eat or drink.

"Of course we could not sleep, as there was no space to lie down. That whole terrible first night was spent watching them bring in more prisoners, and then beating and torturing them," says Kahigiriza. Later he and most of the prisoners were moved out of Cell One to a nearby cell.

As the hours passed, new prisoners were dragged in, many of whom he knew personally, and most of whom were about to be murdered. Kahigiriza tried to give spiritual comfort to as many as possible, knowing he, too, could soon be brutally murdered by the sadistic Nubian State Research officers.

He watched some of the cream of Ugandan society arrive. "Byron Kawadwa, director of the Uganda National Theater, was brought in badly beaten. He died in terrible agony. He desperately needed water to drink, but there was no one who could assist him. There was, of course no water in the cell. His body was taken away in the morning.

"Also brought to the cell opposite ours was a young man called Dr. Kadama, who was in private practice in Bugerere. He was arrested, being found with an album of photographs of Milton Obote and Grace Ibingira [once Amin's Ambassador to the United Nations, who fled from the dictator's service], when they visited the UN soon after Uganda's independence in 1962.

"For this 'crime' he was killed."

Not everyone died, however. The former Prime Minister recalled one young man, a self-employed electrician from Jinja, who was accused of "abusing the government when the Israelis came to rescue their hostages from Entebbe." He bribed his way out of Nakasero by paying the guards 15,000 shillings ($2,000 US).

"I learned after my release that he paid the money, and then ran away to Kenya," says Kahigiriza.

He witnessed another ghastly sight one night shortly after the massacre of the soldiers in Cell One. He describes it: "Farouk Minawa had arrested a young officer, a captain from the South Nile District, and he brought him in our cell and then shot him dead before us, with his pistol. He told us that this officer was planning to kill him, but he got him first."

Kahigiriza and the rest of the surviving prisoners had no option than to get used to these appalling conditions. "We all had to use one mug, which was dipped in a bucket of water that had been used to clean our hands," says Kahigiriza. "We were not allowed to wash our faces or clean our teeth. I would usually dry my hands on part of my already filthy clothes. My clothes were never removed from my body until the day I was released. I would rub my teeth with part of my dirty coat."

Old, young, fit, sick, all were murdered indiscriminately at that house of death. "During my stay of three weeks at Nakasero, I witnessed the murder of not less than one hundred people," says Kahigiriza. Every night there were murders. Each evening a guard would select those to be killed from either of the two underground cells where we were, and then take them away.

"After midnight, a guard would return with one or two other soldiers and read the names of more people he wanted to die that night. Then he would open the door, and as each prisoner came out, one guard would open his handcuffs, then turn his hands at the back and tie them.

"Then, at gunpoint, they would all be led outside. If you did not hear your name, you knew your life had been spared for that night. Then from our underground cells we heard the noise of banging and screaming, and we knew that Amin's men were carrying out their executions.

"After they wiped everyone out, the sound of vehicles carrying away the dead bodies could be heard; this was about 2:00 or 3:00 in the morning. Normally they would return about 5:00 A.M. By the time I left the prison, I knew the awful sound of these particular trucks so well that at my house on Nakasero Hill, I would still hear them. I would wake my wife and ask her, 'Do you hear that vehicle? They are taking the bodies away.'"

Kahigiriza was not even told why he had been arrested until a week had passed. "Interrogation used to take place after midnight, and those taken faced threats and beatings," he says.

"My turn came one night when a guard arrived, stood at the door of my cell, and called my name. I got up, and he opened the door and then ordered me out at gunpoint.

"He told me to go ahead of him. As we reached the reception area, I did not know where he was taking me. Then he directed me to a room on the first floor. When I entered the room, I saw a jet-black Nubian stretched out on a sofa. He was wearing dark glasses and had a pistol beside him. I was told to sit on a chair at the table. Behind me was another angry Nubian with a machine-gun, and on my left was another man with a rope, which could have been used to strangle me. On my right was yet another Nubian with a cane, known as a Kiboko, for beating.

"The young man who brought me from the cell, by the name of Lieutenant Nasur, gave me paper and pen. He told me that I was required to write a statement and that I should 'tell the truth,' because they already had all the facts. 'What sort of statement do you require me to write?' I asked. He then claimed they knew that I belonged to a group calling itself the 'Intelligentia Group' and that I knew where it was based. 'Now tell us where you were going to get the money and weapons to come and kill us and then take over the government,' he snapped. 'We also know you have been going to Nairobi from time to time. Tell us why.'

"I was terribly shocked, because apart from knowing the meaning of the word 'intelligentia' from the dictionary, I had no idea about the existence of this group. For about five minutes I was motionless, not knowing what to write. All the time I was being threatened by these men, who said that if I did not write out this statement, my life was in danger. I knew they were not joking.

"I wrote a short statement and told them that I knew nothing of these allegations. I also told them the last time I was in Kenya was December, 1973, and I had never been back, nor had I ever telephoned any friend in Nairobi. I concluded by writing that this was all I had to say.

"I handed over the papers to Lieutenant Nasur who, after reading them, angrily tore them up and threw the pieces in my face. He informed me that this was 'nonsense,' and that I should write another statement. I replied that if it was time for me to die, I was prepared. 'I would rather die than tell lies,' I said. I then began writing again and wrote down an identical statement as before.

"Reading through it, Lieutenant Nasur turned to me and said that I would be returned to my cell, but soon I would have to face the consequences of my actions."

Back in his cell, Kahigiriza waited for death to come quickly, with prayer as his only comfort. He occupied his time by trying to help and encourage other prisoners in worse condition than he was in. Many had been beaten so badly on the buttocks that they could not stand or sit, and would have to kneel for hours with their rear ends exposed so they could heal.

Being handcuffed twenty-four hours a day was another terrible experience. "Even if you wanted to go to the toilet, they would not release your hands. I visited the toilet three times in the whole of three weeks I spent in this place."

Lice were also a constant aggravation for Kahigiriza and his fellow prisoners. "Since there was no washing of either our bodies or clothes, the lice were on us all the time. These small insects covered my body and I would spend most of the night trying to kill them, which was most difficult with both my hands tied.

"I remember one night, I discovered a piece of broken razor blade on the floor and I asked a friend to cut open my undershirt, which was very dirty. When he did, it revealed that my body was crawling with these lice. He kindly removed them one by one. However, removing them didn't really help, because they were inside my trousers. There was virtually no respite or sleep for those three weeks.

"With all these things happening, I praise God that I did not go mad. I believe the reason for this was the wonderful times of prayer I had privately, and with the other prisoners.

"If I would sometimes forget, one of the others would say, 'Mzee [old man], it is time for prayers. Please lead us.' After this time of refreshing, we all felt our spirits uplifted. Sometimes we would even be able to joke with each other."

Suddenly, on the evening of March 6, 1977, at about 7:30 P.M., they came for Kahigiriza. "Lieutenant Nasur came to the door and called me to come out. Thinking it was my turn to die, I waved my friends good-by, and mentally prepared myself for death as he led me upstairs to the reception area.

"At a distance, I heard someone saying, 'Remove the handcuffs.' I could not believe they were being removed from my hands, which by now were badly swollen.

"I was then told to get into a Mercedes-Benz car which was parked near the door, and Lieutenant Nasur warned me: 'What you have seen here, leave here. Don't tell anyone else.'

"As we drove back to my house, which wasn't far away, I still couldn't believe that I was being released. When we stopped at my gate at about 8:00 P.M., two of my daughters, Jennifer and Solome, came running towards me. I was fearful for them and beckoned them to go back into the house and ask any visitors there to leave, so I could be alone with my family. I was in such an appalling condition that I didn't want them to see me.

"The driver drove me back a way and waited on the road to allow any visitors to leave.

"When I entered my home, my wife and children all stood by the door and, as I got out of the car, instead of the family feeling happy that I was free at last, they all seemed really sad. In fact we all burst into tears.

"What a great reunion it was, with all of us sitting on chairs with tears dropping like a waterfall. I found it impossible to speak because I still couldn't believe that I was out.

"As we all recovered our composure, I began to discover the impact of my arrest on my family. I heard that one day my eight-year-old son Joseph had stood on the balcony of our home and said, 'You know, mommy, if my daddy doesn't come back, I shall drop off this balcony and fall down and die. If I don't die there and then, I shall run into the road and be crushed by a passing car.'"

We asked this impressive, dignified man why he did not run away after his release.

"By doing that, I felt I would have been despising the power of God who had saved me from the monster, Amin," he says most emphatically.

"There are not enough words in the dictionary to describe Amin, except to say that I think he is the most criminal person in the world since the tyrant reign of Attila the Hun.

"In my opinion, Amin even excelled Attila, the man he so loved. At one time Amin wanted to name a hotel here after him. Attila once said, 'Where I have passed, the grass will not grow again.' Indeed, the same applies to Amin. Where he passed, the grass will never grow again.''

How could Kahigiriza survive such an ordeal? "It was by God's mercy," he says. "I believe God saved my life for a purpose."

The reason, he believes, is so that he can tell the truth about the murder of a great Christian leader, the Archbishop Janani Luwum.

7

The Empty Grave

THE LID OF THE COFFIN creaked slowly open in the half-light. A group of believers watched breathlessly as one of their number pried open the rough wooden casket. Gradually the rusty nails holding down the lid gave way and, as he drew it back, the group gasped. By the flickering gleam of a hurricane lamp, they saw the body of a purple-clad man.

"It really is the archbishop," said a middle-aged woman, peering at the familiar figure. Tears welled up in her eyes and ran down her ebony face.

"And look," said another woman, leaning over her shoulder, "there are bullet holes in his body."

A lookout nervously stood guard at the little iron-roofed church at Mucwini, a village near the Sudan border in the East Acholi District of northern Uganda. The small group, who knew they were risking their lives by their action, began carefully examining the body.

The noise of chirping crickets scythed in through the heavy tropical silence as they examined the corpse. There were two gun wounds, one in his neck where a bullet had apparently gone through his mouth and out again, the other in his groin. The man's purple robe was stained with blood, his arms were badly skinned, his rings had been stolen, and he was shoeless.

The woman who had first recognized her archbishop, Janani Luwum, lovingly ran her shaking hand over his stiff body and then whispered: "Thank you, Jesus, for the life and death of Janani. For through it, I know, many will come to know you."

They were all gazing quietly, reverently, at the body of a martyr, a man who was killed for daring to stand up to the black Hitler of Africa—His Excellency President for Life (sic), Marshall Al Hadji, Dr. Idi Amin Dada, proud bearer of a chest full of bogus decorations; the VC (Victorious Cross), DSO (Distinguished Service Order), MC (Military Cross), and CBE (Conqueror of the British Empire in Africa in General and Uganda in Particular). For the boastful dictator was conducting a *black holocaust,* a holy war, for Islam against the Christian church in a land that Winston Churchill once described as "the Pearl of Africa."

The man he killed, Janani Luwum, was born in 1922 in Mucwini. He was one of the Acholi, an energetic, hard-working people. As young Janani herded the family's cattle, goats, and sheep, he could never have dreamed that he would rise to such high office and then be asked to pay the supreme sacrifice.

The turning point in his life came during the great East African Revival. At half past noon on January 6, 1948, in his own home village at Mucwini, he came to know the Lord. His conversion came as a result of the preaching of Yusto Otunno and his wife Josephine, members of "balokole," a word which comes from the Luganda word meaning "saved ones." This movement swept through the church like a raging bush fire, and previously "dead" Christians moved out of the confines of their churches to tell others to repent and be saved by the cleansing blood of Jesus.

Margaret Ford, who was later Luwum's secretary, says in her book *Janani* (Lakeland): "On their arrival, Janani's father, Eliya Okello, and other Christians welcomed them in the name of Jesus Christ. During the preaching Janani felt convicted; twice he broke out in heavy sweat. When this happened a third time, he confessed Jesus Christ as his Lord and in tears repented of his sins, crying aloud before God and men, so that the villagers came running to see what was happening.

"Janani asked Otunno and his wife to pray for him, that the Lord would lead him, and protect him from backsliding. At the end of the meeting Janani gave his testimony. He told the people: 'Today I have become a leader in Christ's army. I am prepared to die in the army of Jesus. As Jesus shed His blood for the people, if it is God's will, I will do the same.'"

And he did!

Luwum was enthroned as archbishop in June, 1974. He was only the second African to head the province, which also covers Rwanda, Burundi, and Boga-Zaire.

Almost immediately he became a real thorn in Amin's flesh by standing up for his beliefs. The trouble began when, in 1975, Luwum refused to give Church of Uganda funds to Amin to help build a Moslem mosque in Kampala. Amin had squandered $14M (US) in foreign exchange donated by the Arabians to build the Kampala mosque. (It now stands, a half-completed "folly" in the city, an item for ridicule, as its prayer tower minaret is crooked.)

Less than two years later Amin told Luwum he wanted some of the British money from the church's centenary fund to finish the mosque. Luwum refused, so the president sent Lieutenant Colonel Erinayo Oryema, Minister for Land and Water Resources, to persuade him to reconsider. He failed, so Amin then dispatched Mr. Charles Oboth-Ofumbi, his Internal Affairs Minister, to try again. This, too, was rejected, and so Amin hatched a crude plot to incriminate the arch-bishop, claiming he was trying to overthrow him.

The campaign of hatred against the archbishop began in earnest when his home near Namirembe was searched for weapons. After the incident, he sent Amin a written report as part of a formal protest.

Luwum described how he had been awakened by the barking of his dog about 1:30 A.M. on Saturday, February 5, 1977. "The fence had been broken down and I knew some people had come into the compound. I walked downstairs very quietly, without switching any lights on. As usual, I stopped at the door."

The archbishop saw there an Acholi named Ben Ongom, whom he knew. "Why Ben, you look in a bad way," he said. "What's the matter?" As he studied Ben's bruised and cut face, he had no idea that this man had been forced to become a latter-day Judas Iscariot in return for a mere few hours of life.

Before he could say any more, a group of soldiers rushed in, pointed guns, and screamed, "Show us the arms!" Luwum kept calm and replied: "What arms?" "There are arms in this house," they shouted. The archbishop repeated that there were no arms.

The men pushed into the building. Their leader, a Nubian speaking in Arabic, jabbed his rifle into the archbishop's stomach while he was frisked for arms.

"The leader," said the archbishop in his report, "pushed me with the rifle, shouting: 'Walk, run, show us the arms, take us to your bedroom.' So we went up to our bedroom where Mary, my wife, was asleep. We woke her up and they began crawling underneath the bed. They opened the wardrobe, climbing right up into the upper deck of the cupboard. They searched the bedroom thoroughly, looking in suitcases, boxes, etc., but found nothing. They proceeded to search the children's bedrooms, repeating the same exercise thoroughly everywhere.''

As the frantic soldiers tore the house apart, the tragic Ongom, now handcuffed, told the archbishop in desperation that he had been found with ammunition. ''You see, sometime back we bought some and divided it up with Mr. Olobo who works in the Ministry of Labour in Kampala. I kept some and Mr. Olobo kept some. Now mine has been found and I am certainly going to die for involving myself in politics,'' Ongom said with a clawing fear in his voice.

It seems that he had led a search party to Olobo's home and then to the home of a fellow Acholi, Dr. Lalobo, the medical superintendent at Mengo Hospital. Despite nothing being found, both were arrested.

Ongom told the archbishop, ''I suggested to the security men that Dr. Lalobo might have transferred the ammunition to the archbishop's house. This is why we have come to you.

''Please help us. If the arms are not here, tell us the location of any Acholi or Langi [the tribes Amin hated most] homes at Namirembe so they may be searched.''

Said Luwum, ''We pray for the president. We pray for the security forces—whatever they do. We preach the gospel and pray for others. That is our work, not keeping arms.''

As they talked, the search continued. ''They demanded we open the study,'' Luwum wrote later. ''They searched there. We opened the chapel. They searched there, even looking underneath the Holy Table. They searched the food stores, putting their hands into sacks of sim-sim, millet, and groundnuts, trying to feel for hidden objects. We went to the guest wing. They searched through the toilets, bathrooms, etc. They searched the cars parked in the compound.

''My neighbors, Bishop Kauma and the Provincial Secretary, had phoned Old Kampala Police Station when they saw there were men with arms in our compound, thinking they were robbers. When the police came these men sent them away before they entered the compound. At about 3:00 A.M. these men left. They requested we open the gate for them to go out. But my wife suggested they should go the way they came. I said we were Christians; we had clean hearts. We would open the gates for them. They left and entered their cars which they had parked down the road. The number plates were covered."

Luwum had in his phone book a special "hot line" telephone number—Kampala 2242—on which he had been told he could reach Amin at any time of day or night. He finally got through at 9:00 A.M. but the operator asked him to call back an hour later "because the president is busy with visitors." The second time the operator stalled by saying the president had gone out with his visitors and could not be contacted by phone.

The archbishop then phoned Vice-President Mustafa Adrisi, a power-hungry, illiterate Moslem. He was "out," too. "Later on I managed to get Colonel Malyamungu [Amin's vicious executioner]. I told him of the incident, including the doctor's arrest and other arrests. He let me speak to the vice-president. I spoke in Swahili. He comforted me and assured me that he would call the people concerned and follow the matter up."

But Luwum heard nothing more from Adrisi. That evening Amin's security men descended on the Bishop of Bukedi, the Rt. Rev. Yona Okoth. He had been sick and was already in bed, following evening prayers. The bishop said later: "At about 10:00 P.M. my aunt reported two cars full of people near my home. They seemed agitated and were carrying guns. I got up and welcomed them."

By now the unfortunate Ben Ongom, who was continuing his enforced Judas act, was bound in chains. The security men with him said they had come to search the bishop's house.

"Do you think I have arms?" asked the indignant Bishop Okoth. "Is that my work? Are you crazy? I don't know what you are talking about."

"How many men do you have here?"

"A watchman and my driver," said the bishop.

"How many arms do you have?" asked one of the soldiers.

"I have a rifle and a shotgun which I use for hunting animals and birds. I possess the necessary legal documents."

Bishop Okoth's house was ransacked. "At once they scattered over the house, searching everywhere but finding nothing. They went into the sitting room, the food store, the bedrooms. At one point they found a large package. My new water pump had arrived and was still unpacked. They tore it open but found nothing. They searched and searched—every corner of the house. Then they heard a noise. One of the men shouted: 'Are there many people here?' I said: 'Take a lamp, go and see.' They came back and reported they had found only cows.''

The leader tried to apologize and said: "We are sorry we have to do this, but we have been given a directive from our boss. We are sorry but we shall have to take you."

"I am not afraid," said the bishop. "If it is death for me, it is the gateway to the Lord. If life, I will continue preaching the gospel."

He was driven to his second house, at Tororo in Eastern Uganda on the Kenya border. There they searched everywhere, but still found nothing.

Eventually they freed the bishop, but they cautioned him not to spread the news. "Go on working normally," they said. He replied: "These are not normal times. If you suspect me, a man dealing in spiritual matters, what of others?"

Amin and his sadistic followers were said to have killed five hundred thousand people—that is one in every twenty-two Ugandans. These soldiers demonstrated a viciousness unknown even among the most depraved commandants of Nazi concentration camps. They killed on whim. No one, prelate or peasant, was safe from their murderous caprice. Amin was a tyrant indelibly stained with the blood of those he had killed.

The church leaders decided they must act. On the following Tuesday the House of Bishops of the Church of Uganda, Rwanda, Burundi, and Boga-Zaire convened at the church's pleasant guest house overlooking the troubled city of Kampala on Namirembe Hill. There they began to draft a courageous letter to Field Marshall Amin which was, in effect, to be a death warrant for the archbishop. It would herald a period of terror equaled only by the days of horror for the early church.

The historic letter, signed by Luwum and eighteen Anglican bishops, said: "We humbly beg to submit our most deeply felt concern for the church and the welfare of the people whom we serve under your care.

"In presenting this statement we are in no way questioning the right of the government in administering justice to search and arrest offenders. We believe that government has established structures and procedures for carrying out this kind of exercise. These structures and procedures give the police, the intelligence, and the security forces a framework within which to work. When these procedures are followed in carrying out their day-to-day duties, this gives the ordinary citizen a sense of security. It creates mutual friendship and trust between such officers and the general public irrespective of uniform. But when the police and security officers deviate . . . in carrying out their day-to-day duties, citizens become insecure, afraid, and disturbed. They begin to distrust these officers.

"Your Excellency, you have said publicly on many occasions that religious leaders have a special place in this country and that you treat them with respect for what they stand for and represent.

"The gun whose muzzle has been pressed against the archbishop's stomach, the gun which has been used to search the Bishop of Bukedi's houses is a gun which is being pointed at every Christian in the church, unless Your Excellency can give us something new to change this situation.

"The security of the ordinary Christian has been in jeopardy for quite a long time. It may be that what has happened to the archbishop and the Bishop of Bukedi is a climax of what is consistently happening to our Christians. We have buried many who have died as a result of being shot. There are many more whose bodies have not been found, yet their disappearance is connected with the activities of some members of the Security Forces. Your Excellency, if it is required we can give concrete evidence of what is happening because widows and orphans are members of our church."

To rub salt into the wound, the churchmen moved on to a very sensitive subject with the dictator—their concern that Ugandan Moslems in powerful positions were coercing Christians into adopting the Islamic faith; that the killing of educated Ugandans had forced many to flee and that subsequent fear had made the progress of the country and its stability virtually impossible; also that suspicion and hidden hatred had destroyed the last vestige of mutual trust between soldiers and civilians.

They also pointed to the growing gap between church and state. "We had been assured by you of your ready availability to religious leaders whenever they had serious matters to discuss with you. You had even gone to the extent of giving His Grace, the archbishop, the surest means of contacting you in this country wherever you may be. But a situation has developed now where you have become more and more inaccessible and even when he tried to write he has not received any reply.

"While you, Your Excellency, have stated on the national radio that your government is not under any foreign influence and that your decisions are guided by your Defense Council and Cabinet, the general trend of things in Uganda has created a feeling that the affairs of our nation are being directed by outsiders who do not have the welfare of the country and the value of the lives and properties of Ugandans at their heart. A situation like this breeds unnecessary misunderstanding. Indeed, we were shocked to hear, over the radio on Christmas Day, Your Excellency saying that some bishops had preached bloodshed. We waited anxiously to be called by Your Excellency to clarify such a situation, but all in vain."

The letter was typed and copied, and was ready for distribution on Thursday, February 10, 1977. After signing the letter with fellow-bishops, Luwum said, "I am signing my own death warrant."

Margaret Ford, Luwum's secretary for several years when he was Bishop of Northern Uganda, and for a short time while he was archbishop, then left quickly for Kenya with a copy of the controversial document to present to the Archbishop of Kenya.

"It was kind of an insurance policy," says the Rt. Rev. Dr. Yustasi Ruhindi, Bishop of Bunyoro-Kitara Diocese. "The feeling was that if the document was published in the outside world, nothing could then happen to us or the archbishop."

Miss Ford arrived safely and publication went ahead, but it proved to be no protection from the evil dictator.

The following day the bishops met again and, for the last time on this earth, Luwum sat with his fellows and shared with them a Bible passage he had read with Mary, his wife, that morning. It was the story of the disciples trying to cross the stormy Sea of Galilee alone while the Master was praying in the hills: "And after bidding them farewell, He departed to the mountain to pray. And when it was evening, the boat was in the midst of the sea, and He was alone on the land" (Mark 6:46-47). Luwum turned to his bishops and said: "The Lord has seen us in the past four days making headway painfully. But I see the way ahead very clearly. There are storms, waves, winds, and danger, but I see the road clearly."

By now the group had requested an appointment with the "Life President," but there was still no word from him. On Saturday about half the bishops returned to their dioceses for Sunday, while the remainder stayed on in Kampala.

Finally, on Monday, February 14, the president sent for the archbishop alone. His wife Mary desperately tried to dissuade him from going. But he turned and said: "I will go. Even if he kills me, my blood will save the nation." Mary went with him to the State House in Entebbe.

Over a cup of tea Amin accused Luwum of plotting with Milton Obote, the former president and the man whom Amin had overthrown in a coup in 1971. Amin claimed that eleven crates containing automatic weapons, ammunition, and grenades sent to Uganda by Obote-backed plotters had been found by children near his house. The president then arranged for the allegations to be repeated on Radio Uganda, on television that night, and in the corrupt official newspaper, *Voice of Uganda,* the following day. There was no mention in any of the media concerning the letter from the bishops, which, while Luwum was with the president, was being delivered personally to all the cabinet ministers, religious leaders, and the secretary of the Defense Council.

Luwum could now see that he was being framed. Amin told the shocked archbishop that as soon as all the investigations were over, a public rally would be held so that Ugandans could judge the evidence themselves. They would hear that the weapons had been intended for Southern Africa liberation movements but were diverted for use against Uganda.

"God did not want bloodshed, and saved us," said Amin. "You must forget all these selfish subversive activities and preach the Word of God. Pray for peace in the country. We will keep cool and calm, but should never be mistaken for sleeping."

Luwum, who at first had been left speechless, hit back by saying that it was quite clear that Ben Ongom knew that if he did not find arms that night he would die. And Amin's men had provided no proof that weapons had been found near his house. "For the sake of myself and the church that I lead, I would like more concrete evidence about these serious and far reaching allegations," he said.

The archbishop left State House, and shortly afterward the bishops met again, this time at the Kampala conference center. The memorandum they issued said: "Our church does not believe in, nor does it teach its members the use of, destructive weapons. We believe in the life-giving love of Christ; we proclaim that love to all without fear. We speak publicly and in private against all evil, all corruption, all misuse of power, all maltreatment of human beings. We rejoice in the truth, because truth builds up a nation, but we are determined to refute all falsehood, all false accusations which damage the lives of our people and spoil the image of our country.''

Next morning the bishops and the archbishop, along with other religious leaders, many ministers, and diplomats, were summoned to the Nile Hotel for the rigged trial. They were dressed in their cassocks and wearing their crosses. Luwum was in full regalia. Television cameras were in position, as were three thousand soldiers, brought from various units all over the country, sitting on the ground in a huge semicircle in the forecourt of the hotel. In the center of the semicircle were neat lines of weapons: rifles, submachine guns, and grenades.

Among the large crowd on that hot day was Henry Kyemba, a Cabinet Minister who fled the country shortly afterwards. In his book, *State of Blood,* he recalled the scene:

''They were all brand-new East European weapons—exactly like those used by many units of the Ugandan army, and in fact supplied to ministers for official protection. Clearly, they were intended for some ominous purpose.

''We took our positions, along the front of the hotel, facing the seated soldiers. I was sitting almost exactly behind the bank of microphones set up for the speaker. We waited tensely in the hot sun for the president to arrive. He did not come. I learned later that he was watching the proceedings from his office above, striding back and forth between the office balcony and the television inside. At about 11:00 A.M. the proceedings were opened by Colonel Isaac Malyamungu. He reminded us that time and again the government had spoken of subversion. 'Here now,' he said, 'is the proof of it.'

''There then followed a reading of statements, by self-confessed 'conspirators,' of a reported attempt to overthrow the Amin government. The first and longest statement was allegedly from Obote himself and his henchmen. It was read by the former chairman of the Public Service Commission, Mr. Abdulla Anyuru. This man, aged about sixty years old, had retired and was living a quiet life in his own village.''

The statement was very similar to the archbishop's memorandum, and described how unhappy the people were, how Amin had mismanaged the country, and how people were being harassed and killed. In fact it was very close to the truth of Uganda at the time. The statement, of course, was a forgery and was read directly from the standard blue State House paper used for official documents.

The last part of the long speech implicated the archbishop and said he had received weapons. Luwum shook his head in denial at what was being read.

There were two other statements; one read by a Lieutenant Ogwang, an intelligence officer, the other by Ben Ongom who had by now been forced to grow a beard, a fashion associated with Obote guerrillas. In their statements, the two men "admitted" being given instructions from Obote. They also "admitted" having received the arms displayed there in the semicircle of soldiers.

After the statements had been read, Amin's Vice-President Adrisi asked for a show of hands from those soldiers who wanted the "conspiritors" to die. All the soldiers raised their arms, shouting in Swahili, "Kinja yeye!" (Kill them! Kill them!). It was just like the day of Christ's crucifixion.

"Put up your hands, all you who want them shot in public!" he said. The result was the same.

"Put up your hands, all you who don't want them to be shot." Naturally, no one moved.

Luwum's successor, the Most Rev. Silvanus Wani, a gentle, softspoken man, told us in Luwum's former home of that shocking day.

"We were terribly mistreated by the soldiers as we stood there," he says. "They pushed us all over the place and made us stand still from 9:00 A.M. until 3:00 in the afternoon.

"We didn't know what was going to happen. There was even the possibility of a public shooting.

"We were eventually taken into one of the rooms at the International Conference Center and were guarded by State Research people. We were there for about another four hours. During the whole time we were not given anything to eat or drink, not even water.

"Suddenly we were told that we could go home, and as we began to walk out, the late archbishop was told that Amin wanted to see him at Nile Mansions.

"Bishop Festo Kivengere and I, as Dean of the Province, tried to follow him, but they pushed us back. Still we went to Nile Mansions and were left waiting outside for another hour. We told the soldiers there: 'We would like to see our archbishop. Where have you taken him?' One guard said: 'We shall let you in in a moment. You wait.' But we kept on asking to see him and one of the soldiers guarding the entrance said: 'You must go. We shall bring your archbishop back to your place.' I said: 'I would like to wait here to go together with him.' They then insisted that we must leave. A police friend came over and whispered to us: 'You had better go because if you stay here for a long time you will possibly get in trouble.'

"When we got back we saw Mary, Janani's wife, and told her the news. She was very sad and started crying. Then she asked us if she could be taken back to Nile Mansions to try to see her husband. We took her, but she was driven back by the soldiers and not allowed to go in."

Luwum and his wife had a family of four boys and four girls, who, after his death, were forced to run for their lives to Kenya.

And he was now close to the time of his death. One of the last people to see him alive was James Kahigiriza, chairman of the Uganda Land Commission, who was arrested on February 15, 1977, and taken to State Research at gunpoint with handcuffs biting into his wrists. We asked him the reasons for his arrest. One, he says, was his generosity toward Janani Luwum.

"I happened to know the late archbishop personally, and was a member of his congregation in his diocese at All Saints Church, about four hundred yards from the notorious Nakasero State Research building," says gray-haired Kahigiriza. We were sipping tea with him at Namirembe Guest House in Kampala, where the bishops had signed the document that was to seal Luwum's fate.

"I had presented the archbishop with uniforms for our cathedral choir and also donated a throne during the consecration and enthronement of the new Bishop of West Ankole Diocese, Bishop Yoramu Bamunoba.

"These gifts had been noted publicly by the archbishop, and I guess that on both occasions State Research people noted what was taking place. That seems to have been my crime."

So Kahigiriza was slung into a stinking basement cell in that terrible house of killing.

"For more than twenty-four hours we were not given anything to eat or drink," he says. "Of course not all of us could sleep, as there was no space to lie down. All night more prisoners were brought in after they had been cruelly beaten and tortured.

"On the following afternoon we heard people being pushed down the steps and as they reached the door of our cell, I heard the names of Lt. Col. Erinayo Oryema, Minister of Land and Water Resources, and Charles Oboth-Ofumbi, the Minister of Internal Affairs, being mentioned. Suddenly the cell door was opened and they were roughly pushed in. I noticed Oryema had his military insignia removed, and both were without belts and shoes. The furious soldier escorting them yelled, 'So we pay you all this money so that you can then turn and kill us with your plots.' Another soldier brought their briefcases and they emptied the contents on the floor at the door.

"Soon to follow the two ministers were their drivers and body-guards, who were killed a week after their masters.

"About an hour or so after their arrival, a guard came and ordered everybody out, except the two ministers. We got out holding the gunny bags we sat on. Our hands were still handcuffed. We were told to enter a cell just opposite in the tunnel.

"This cell was about eight feet by eight feet, which was much better. In there we were given our first meal. It was about 4:00 P.M. and as the guards began to serve food, a number of people were also brought and pushed into the cell.

"I turned around to see who they were, and to my amazement I saw one of them was my archbishop, Janani Luwum. I noted he was wearing dark gray trousers and a black shirt; he was shoeless and both of his hands were handcuffed. He was still standing there in a state of shock when a young man in plain clothes slapped him hard on the cheek.

"'Who are you?' the man asked harshly. 'I am the Archbishop of Uganda,' Janani replied. Immediately another guard, by the name of Kabuye, hit him again. Janani, whose jaw had been broken by the blow, said to these men, 'You are hitting me, but I am innocent and I have done nothing. You are hitting me because you have power, but you would not have this power if it had not been given to you from God.'

"Then they ordered him to sit down and brought a plate of food for him to eat, which he could not do because of his broken jaw. I felt so sick because of his treatment that I also could not eat. In fact most of those men in the cell sent back their food, even though they were starving.

"Then came a guard who, at gunpoint, ordered us back to the tiny cell where we had left the two ministers. Janani went with us. As I slid back into that hell hole I saw Colonel Oryema was sitting opposite me. 'Could you please zip up my trousers?' he asked as I was about to sit down. Naturally, I obliged.

"After a few minutes I asked Janani if he would offer a word of prayer. He prayed for all of us. It was very moving.

"After a few minutes, the archbishop was called to come out of the cell. He was then told to put on his shoes and I thought he was about to be released.

"He came back in his full robes as archbishop, and when I saw him like that my faith was really strengthened. I felt that if he was to die, he was not to die like any other person, but as a personal representative of Jesus Christ.

"After about an hour, a guard stood at the door and called the two ministers and Janani to come out, and then added that other 'government servants' should follow.

"They all trooped out, knowing only too well that for some of them these were to be their last few minutes on earth. They left some of us behind. We went to follow them, and the guard said: 'You lot, stay behind. We will be coming for you.'

"About two hours later, in the evening, a tall young soldier, drunk with a lust for blood came shouting that he wanted to shoot a particular prisoner.

"I put up my hands and told him not to shoot, but he turned the gun on me and said, 'May I then shoot you instead?' I told him he could.

"I held my breath and prepared to meet my Maker as he leveled the gun at my head. Then he dropped it, took a deep breath, and said: 'If you think you are proud, where are the three people that were taken from here—the archbishop, Minister Oryema, and Minister Oboth-Ofema? Go on, call their names and see if they answer.

"We then realized they had been murdered, and our turn would probably come soon."

Cell-mate Apollo Lawoko, who was imprisoned for 196 days in the basement of Amin's infamous Kampala death chamber, tells of what happened to the archbishop and the ministers after they left the cell.

"Six of us, including those three, were taken upstairs to the office of Farouk Minawa [the head of the Bureau] where Amin was waiting,'' he says. "We had all been seriously beaten and the archbishop had conducted last rites before we left our cell."

Lawoko says that Amin ordered only the archbishop and ministers into Farouk's office. "We could hear Amin accusing them, saying, 'I know you were planning to kill me, to overthrow my government,' and we could hear their denials. We heard beatings with what sounded like big whips. Then after five or ten minutes we heard some shots. We were hurriedly taken back downstairs and the guards warned us that if we ever spoke about what was happening upstairs we'd be skinned alive."

Shortly afterwards, Lawoko says, another guard came. "He told us the 'sheik' of the Church of Uganda and the two ministers were dead and our turn would come next day."

We have been able to piece together what happened that fateful day. Luwum sat on the sofa opposite the president, and the archbishop would not be cowed as they sat face to face.

"You have prayed for peace in Uganda," Amin screamed. "It shows something was going to take place. You knew there was going to be bloodshed in Uganda."

Said Luwum calmly: "I have always prayed for peace in Uganda."

"Admit you knew about this plot, then the matter will end here."

But the archbishop would not admit to something that was not true. "I have nothing to do with the arms and I say once again, I am not involved."

"We were led to your house. You preached that God should save the people of Uganda from bloodshed," said the president.

During his interrogation, the archbishop refused to sign a confession, and was ordered to lie on the floor. His cassock was pulled up and two soldiers in turn whipped him. After the beating, Luwum began praying quietly, his words barely a whisper. This was the final straw for Amin, who was so incensed that he shouted angrily and wildly, using obscene language, and he struck the archbishop. Then he bellowed at an Acholi soldier in the room—he came from the same tribe as the archbishop—to "kill him; kill him." The shaking soldier aimed his gun and shot the archbishop in the groin. With that, Amin drew his pistol and fired into Luwum's face. The shot hit the archbishop in the mouth as he was lowering his head and turning sideways. Then Amin's guards rushed into the room, training their rifles on Oryema and Oboth-Ofumbi. Amin, suddenly shocked by what he had done, went over to the telephone and told someone at the other end of the line, "I have lost my temper. I have shot the archbishop. Do something." Oryema and Oboth-Ofumbi were shot by soldiers. The three, still just alive but bleeding profusely, were then pushed into a car by State Research officers and driven to the barracks of the Malire Regiment at Lubiri. Meanwhile a "road accident" was being carefully staged, using two already damaged cars.

Thousands of Christians throughout Uganda were stunned on February 17, 1977, as the Uganda announcer read in faltering English the 10:00 A.M. news bulletin.

"A government spokesman has announced with regret the death of the Minister of Land and Water Resources, Lt. Col. Erinayo Oryema; the Minister of Internal Affairs, Mr. Charles Oboth-Ofumbi; and the Archbishop of Uganda, Rwanda, Burundi, and Boga-Zaire, the Most Reverend Janani Luwum; after being involved in a motor accident yesterday in Kampala. The three men were being driven away from the Kampala International Conference Center by Major Moses for interrogation of their involvement in a plan to cause chaos in the country. The spokesman said the accident occurred when the three men were trying to overcome Major Moses in order to escape. Major Moses was taken to a hospital where he is still unconscious."

A later bulletin filled in a few more "facts" about the "accident." It said that the Range-Rover in which the trio were being driven in for questioning hit a second car only a few hundred yards from the Conference Center, slid across the street, and overturned. When the archbishop and the two ministers were taken from the wreckage they were already dead. The post-mortem examination, it was claimed, showed that Luwum died from a ruptured liver and lung and the others from internal bleeding and brain damage.

Amin was quoted on the radio as saying: "The accident was a punishment of God, because God does not want the others to suffer."

In the early hours of the next morning Janani's body arrived at Mulago mortuary, and Bishops Wani and Kivengere made desperate but unsuccessful attempts to recover it. The Health Ministry promised the church leaders that the archbishop's corpse would be handed over for a traditional burial service at Namirembe Cathedral on the following Sunday.

But by Sunday the situation had changed again. Brian Herd, who had been appointed Bishop of Karamoja by Luwum, says, "I was among thousands who converged on Namirembe Cathedral in Kampala for morning prayer and communion. We had just been told that the official funeral service for Archbishop Luwum had been canceled, and his body had already been interred in his home district. This was a disappointment to us, but on Sunday thousands of Christians gradually assembled and crammed into the cathedral, spilling over outside. There was an air of tension, but the people came to worship and to take their stand as Christians.''

Cynthia Mackay, a missionary from Yorkshire, England, and religious education advisor in the Province of Kampala, remembers that emotional Sunday:

"The radio announced that a memorial service at the cathedral was forbidden. But still thousands of people went to the ordinary 10:00 A.M. service. It was decided to let it continue and continue as so many people went for communion.

"A soldier came up the aisle and pointed out that the clergy were disobeying the directive. 'This service is not supposed to go on.' But the vicar said: 'This is an ordinary service that is going on a long time.'

"Then someone in the congregation spontaneously began singing the Martyrs' Hymn. We joined in and sang it again and again. The people began slowly moving outside the cathedral and just went on singing."

Bishop Herd says, "It took an hour for them to file from the cathedral, so great were the numbers. Outside was the empty grave which had been prepared for the archbishop."

The people gathered around the open grave site. Retired Archbishop Erica Sabiti spoke to the grieving Christians. "When we see an empty grave, it reminds us of the time when the angels spoke to the women at the empty grave of Jesus on that first Easter,' 'He is not here. He is risen!' " Sabiti continued, this time speaking of Luwum, "He is not here, but we know that his spirit has gone to be with the Lord Jesus. He is risen! Praise God!"

Bishop Herd recalls, "Instead of being something that discouraged us, the empty grave spoke to us of the victory that we have over death; that whatever happens to a person's body, there is an everlasting life that is quite indestructible.

"A great sense of strength and serenity spread through the crowds. Someone said that even if all the leaders were to go, still the church would go on. Many people were saying that as the first century of the Uganda church began with martyrdom and the church survived, so if the second century continues in the same way it will certainly not bring the end of the church of Christ.''

Miss Mackay recalls, ''Gradually people began singing, 'Glory, glory to the Lamb!' and soon that hilltop was full of victorious voices. They were singing in an absolute assurance of the resurrection. We knew there was victory over death and sin and hatred.''

That night many Christians in Uganda felt a transformation of their spiritual lives. A new courage and faith was born, that not even Idi Amin's Uganda holocaust could shake.

The body of fifty-two-year-old Janini Luwum, who was a tall, jet black giant of a man, had been taken by Amin's henchmen to Mucwini, his home village, a cluster of grass-thatched mud huts, set in the middle of arid savannah plains dissected by river beds.

At his mother's homestead, his mother told the soldiers: ''My son is a Christian. He cannot be buried here, he must be buried in the graveyard of the local church.''

So the soldiers took the coffin to the picturesque tiny hilltop church for a hurried burial.

Veteran British missionary Mildred Brown was working in the region translating the Scriptures into Acholi for the Bible Society. ''The soldiers had begun to dig the grave, but hadn't been able to complete the job before dark because the earth was so hard,'' she explains. ''They left the coffin in the church overnight, so they could finish the grave the next day.''

Thus the hardness of the ground gave the group of courageous believers at Mucwini that chance of gazing for the last time on their archbishop. Many of them had watched him grow up into maturity as a Christian leader of outstanding quality.

Miss Brown continues with her account, ''While the casket was in the church, the group took off the lid, first to make sure it was their beloved archbishop, and also because they did not believe the story of the 'accident.'

''This is the first time I, or anyone else, has spoken publicly about this matter. Before, nobody dared mention it because of the danger. But now Amin is gone; we can speak freely.''

The funeral at the village, seventy miles from the northern center of Gulu, was the next day led by Archdeacon Kesoloni Oni of East

Acholi, assisted by three other local clergymen, the Rev. Nelson Onono Onweng, the Rev. Jekeri Obua, and the Rev. Leuben Okech. Despite the danger from Amin's troops, local believers turned up in droves.

"The church was full," recalls the Rt. Rev. Gideon Oboma, Assistant Bishop of Northern Uganda. "The people were not afraid of the danger and were even preaching to the soldiers. They had said to themselves, 'If this is to be the time of death, let us also die. But if this is to be the time to stay and live on, this will be a strong Christian witness.'

"And witness they did. For one whole month, a group of believers kept vigil at the unmarked grave, over which they put a grass cover.

"They sang and thanked God for Janani's life. They even slept in the open. Day and night they stayed at the grave, with local Christians bringing food and drink to sustain them."

And while these brave men and women were risking their lives in memory of their beloved archbishop, the government-controlled newspaper, *Voice of Uganda,* published a call for President Amin to be made emperor and then proclaimed Son of God.

8

The Cover-up

As THE WORLD CONDEMNED the brutal killing of the archbishop and the two ministers, Amin began an unconvincing campaign to cover up his hideous crime.

He had produced a strange document called *Obote's War Call to Langis and Acholis Against Other Ugandans,* which was published by the government's Ministry of Information and Broadcasting. It claimed, among other things, that "the church's involvement in politics has almost become a disease."

The booklet, a copy of which we managed to obtain in Kampala, painted an Orwellian picture with compelling simplicity. The chapter implicating the church in a plot against Amin used the example of sectarian violence in Ulster. "Uganda does not want another Northern Ireland in Uganda," it said.

An obscure reference to nineteenth-century missionaries stunting the development of an African state of Uganda was also included in an attempt to instill hatred of the church into the people.

The book included photographs of a Japanese automobile, with a caption which said, "This is the car in which the two ministers and the late archbishop, Janani Luwum, died while being driven from the Nile Mansions for interrogation." A picture of the other "accident car"—a Range-Rover—was carried with a caption that said, "The accident was fatal and the three unfortunately met their untimely death."

Believing the best form of defense to be attack, the writer of Amin's document said: "Some arms were captured near the home of Bishop Okoth of Tororo, who received them and transported them to

Archbishop Luwum, because he was at the border where the arms from Dar es Salaam through Nairobi could easily be channeled. After the search of Bishop Okoth's house, he was also left intact but the arms were transported to Kampala. Though the arms, ammunition, and grenades were of Chinese make they were originally given to liberation movements in southern Africa but were diverted for use against Uganda.''

Under the title *The Fatal Accident Car Driver, Major Moses Okello, Tells the Story of How It Happened,* the booklet carried what it purports to be Major Okello's account. With a little help from Amin's writers, it begins with the arrest of the two ministers and the archbishop.

"Soon after the three people had entered the car," the story begins, "he [Major Okello] drove away from the Nile Mansions towards the Officers' Mess, where all officers are interrogated before being taken to any other place. Major Okello stated that he was seated in the car with only three other people. Next to him in the passenger seat was the late Lieutenant-Colonel Oryema and in the back seat were the late Oboth-Ofumbi and the late Archbishop Luwum.

"Before leaving the Nile Mansions, Major Okello told his passengers that he was taking them to Nakasero Officers' Mess for interrogation. He said that from Nile Mansions, he drove past the Kampala International Hotel and then branched off towards the Officers' Mess. But, before he arrived at the Mess, he was manhandled by the late Lt. Col. Oryema, who tried to seize the steering wheel. It was at this point that he lost control of the car, which later banged at a spot and place he did not know because, he said, he was then unconscious. He could not remember what had happened after the bang, he said, and he did not even know who removed him from the car. All he knew was that he had an escort car coming behind him.

"Asked at what speed he was driving, he said that he was driving between 30 mph and 40 mph. Asked what parts of his body had been injured, he said that although he had received no cuts on his body, he felt much pain in the chest and ribs. As to whether he remembered having seen any car in his way, Major Okello told the journalists that he could not recall anything of the sort, but reiterated that before the bang, he had been fighting with the attackers to keep control of the car.

"And as to whether the three passengers he was driving said anything before attacking him, Major Okello said that they did not say anything. Asked whether he was talking voluntarily, he replied that he was, and that, in fact, he was talking from the bottom of his heart. Asked whether at the time of the accident he had any gun, he said that he had only his pistol.

"Asked whether the late archbishop had made any attempt on him, Major Okello stated that he could remember what the late Lieutenant-Colonel Oryema did because he was seated by his side, but not the late archbishop. He said that it was impossible for him to tell who did what from the back seat. Asked how he had survived, Major Okello said that he did not know how he had survived, except God."

The document claimed that Captain Dr. Christopher Ntalo, of the Uganda Armed Forces Military Hospital, treated Major Okello soon after the accident. The doctor was reported to have said that when he received Major Okello in the Military Hospital VIP Ward, Okello had pieces of broken glass all over his body and his shirt was covered with blood, but he had no cuts.

"The doctor said that Major Okello was unconscious and was not responding to deep stimuli. He had bruises on his left knee and on the back side of the left shoulder and a closed head injury." Most significant was the next sentence: "He also had a concussion and was in mental instability up to the time of the interview."

Well, Amin's document said it, not us.

Naturally, few people outside Uganda (or inside), believed a word of the car accident story, and the murders shocked even those who had become blasé about Amin.

Based in Nairobi, the All Africa Conference of Churches, which had never been blasé about Amin, declared: "Member churches and churches throughout the world are urged to press their governments to censure and isolate the Uganda government for its flagrant violation of human rights and campaign of terror unleashed against Christians. Archbishop Luwum is one more victim of the wave of killing in Uganda against which the AACC has consistently protested."

The conference pointed to the cancellation of the archbishop's Namirembe funeral as proof—"If any proof were needed"—of the government's "cover-up."

"How much longer will the people of Uganda have to endure the tyranny of the Amin regime? Will Africa do nothing? Will the rest of the world do nothing?" asked the statement.

The conference also wrote to the then-Secretary General of the Arab League, Mahmoud Riad, and the Egyptian vice-president, appealing to Islamic states with any influence over Amin to help end all forms of persecution in Uganda.

"Moslems and Christians share a common veneration for sanctity of human life. Both religious traditions belong to Africa. It is therefore impossible to reconcile current events in Uganda with authentic Islamic or Christian teachings; just as it is not possible to see how such tragic happenings will contribute to the peace and solidarity between our two regions, which are so essential to the success of the struggles for liberation that our peoples are today waging."

There was some response from leading authorities across the world. Dr. Donald Coggan, the Archbishop of Canterbury, was so outraged with the killing of his friend Luwum, whom he described as "a big, strong, gentle man," that he called for an end to President Amin's rule.

"I want to see his regime broken, but how this happens remains to be seen. I'm astonished that he's gotten away with it for so long."

The archbishop also said that he was concerned for all Christians in Uganda and "anyone who stood for truth and justice."

And speaking only yards from where Thomas á Becket was martyred in Canterbury Cathedral, England, Canon Arthur Allchin said the truth was expressed by T. S. Eliot in *Murder in the Cathedral,* "A Christian martyrdom is never an accident."

In an understandably emotional statement, the National Christian Council of Kenya, based in Nairobi, said: "We wish to remind the government of Uganda that the cry of the blood of the martyrs has reached the ears of God."

The International Commission of Jurists, Geneva, also condemned the cover up. "The pretense that they were killed in a motor accident will deceive no one. This latest act of arbitrary violence gives added urgency to the case for an impartial investigation, by the United Nations Commission of Human Rights, of the consistent pattern of gross violation in Uganda."

In America, President Jimmy Carter deduced rightly that the murders in Uganda had disgusted the whole civilized world.

The *London Daily Telegraph* carried an eyewitness account by an African woman of how the accident had been faked by Amin's men. This report was carried in a letter from Uganda to a close friend. Part of the letter was reproduced. It said, "You know I was in Kampala the week when the incident took place near the Officers' Mess, formerly the Uganda Club, at Nakasero. These people were driven from the Mess in a red car toward the President's Lodge.

"Then there was a Range-Rover driven from the Lodge in a terrible speed towards the car. Then the car was knocked sideways. The bodies were thrown in a waiting Land-Rover, except one which was slowly put in a Benz [Mercedes-Benz].

"I saw it with my own eyes. It was planned but the archbishop was not there. The bodies were thrown in one Land-Rover. These people were killed first and put in a car to be smashed. It happened after five o'clock in the evening."

Journalists were quickly dispatched to find the truth about the death of the three men. One was John Penrose of the *London Daily Mirror*.

"I went to Nairobi with Eric Piper, a staff photographer, to see how we could get into Uganda," Penrose tells us.

"There were no scheduled flights into Kampala at the time and it was suicidal to go in unannounced. So from Nairobi we phoned 'Major' Bob Astles [the dictator's British-born special adviser] and spoke with him several times over a period of about three days.

"I told him that we wanted to come in and talk to Amin and find out what the truth was. It soon became clear that Astles was mounting a publicity exercise to get Amin off the hook.

"Anyway, he eventually agreed to let us in and we chartered a small plane and went to Entebbe. In fact, two planes went at the same time. In the other was a television camera crew.

"We were met at the airport by Astles, who told us immediately that Uganda was a lovely country and all these stories that we'd heard about it were untrue."

The media group was taken to a nearby hotel and given a breakfast of eggs and bacon, and then put in pickup trucks and automobiles and taken to hear Idi's speech at an African conference.

"When we arrived in Uganda, the African, Caribbean, and Pacific group of states were holding a conference in Kampala," says Penrose. "Idi's speech was delayed until we arrived at the hall.

"We were all shepherded into the hall. We could see that this was quite clearly a great publicity machine at work. As soon as we were in place, Idi rose to his feet and said he had heard rumors that he was the one who had killed the archbishop, but they were not true.

"After his speech, we were taken off to the Nile Mansions, a five-star hotel which was taken over by Amin and turned into apartments for visiting heads of state. He came and stood on the lawn and held a press conference for us all. We talked to him and he again denied having known anything about the archbishop's death.

"Then we were taken off to the scene of the so-called accident. There were some skid marks and some glass in the hedge-row. I remember thinking at the time that it all looked so terribly contrived. It looked more like a little bump-up on a Sunday morning and not the sort of crash where three people had been killed.

"We were then taken to an officers' mess, where Major Moses Okello was presented to us. He came out on crutches with a bandage round his head and limped very theatrically.

"It was quite remarkable. He leaned on a shooting stick and told us the story about how the minister had grabbed him and he went out of control and he couldn't remember what happened after that.

"Astles was there guiding us around, pointing out things and arranging Major Moses, and you could see he was clearly a very powerful man then and this was very much his show.

"Idi strutted around the lawns and then went on to say that he was coming to the British Commonwealth Conference in London. He said, 'I fear no one except God. I will be in London to meet the queen.'"

The British television crew then flew out to Nairobi with their film, and they were joined by photographer Eric Piper. Meanwhile John Penrose, BBC East Africa man; John Osman; and other journalists who were by now in the country all went back to their hotel, intending to leave the following morning.

"The next morning we thought we'd have a quick word with Idi and then leave. We were taken back up to the Nile Mansions where Astles said curtly, 'His Excellency has decided that you should remain in Uganda as his guests,' which was a very subtle way of saying that we weren't going to get out until Idi had dealt with us.

"Clearly, what he wanted was us to be his captive voice to the world. He obviously wanted to come over as the great leader, and we were kept waiting all day at the Nile Mansions.

"We were in a beautiful suite in his palatial place and everything was laid on for us. I slept in the bed that General Gowon, the former Nigerian head of state, had stayed in after being deposed.

"We stayed at Nile Mansions all day and there was still no sign of Idi. Astles kept saying that he had received reports from the front after a Tanzanian invasion and Idi was down there masterminding the troops."

As the day passed, "Major" Astles, who headed the anti-corruption unit with the honorary rank of major, kept them well supplied with reports of "this great action on the front and Idi's wonderful behavior."

It was during this enforced stay that Penrose discovered Amin's fanatical addiction to the BBC World Service, which he listened to day and night. "He had it piped through automatically to all the rooms in the hotel, so you had to have it on all the time," he says.

"And Bob Astles had in his car a special short wave radio ordered by Amin so he, too, could listen to world opinion."

Penrose filed a story to his paper from Kampala and hoped that he would now be free to leave, but he was not.

"We were then told that His Excellency would still like us to stay, and we'd have to stay that night," continues the journalist.

"We had a very late night with Astles and there were a couple of bodyguards with us all the time. They were sort of looking after us. We weren't allowed to leave the hotel room at all. On one occasion, Eric, who by now had returned, wanted to go downstairs to buy something, and they wouldn't let him go. Instead one of the 'boys' went off to get it for him.

"They kept our pilot with us as well, so there were six of us in the room that night.

"The next morning, Astles arranged that we should go 'and see how wonderful Uganda was,' and at about six in the morning, we came down to meet our transport. He had organized a police escort for us to be taken to a marketplace where we saw all the natives coming in to supposedly illustrate that, in fact, there was plentiful food for the Ugandans."

The group was then "encouraged" to photograph and interview local people.

"Then we were taken to a factory that made shirts, where we were taken around and shown 'how wonderful Ugandan industry was,' and we were 'encouraged' by Astles to interview the general manager of a store. We were presented with shirts to take away with us.

"Then we were taken back to have lunch at Nile Mansions."

The group was finally told they could leave, and Penrose, Osman, and Piper were put in a car heading for Entebbe. Suddenly they saw the ''Life President'' coming the other way at the wheel of his Range-Rover. He flashed his headlights, indicating that they should stop and jump in his vehicle.

''He promptly threw out his bodyguards and put us in his car. He said he'd drive us to Entebbe,'' says Penrose.

''On the way, he drove us into Entebbe Botanical Gardens and insisted on showing us 'how wonderful the place was.'

''Lots of little kids waved, and then we went to the Lake Victoria Hotel Entebbe, and he got out and strutted around and people stood up and shook his hand. He went over to the swimming pool and shook hands with a pilot who was staying at the hotel.

''After that, it was a tour of the local golf course for us.''

Penrose says that their unusual chauffeur drove along at quite a leisurely pace. ''He was very gorilla-like. He has an enormous bulk and sort of rolls around.

''The whole time he had the BBC World Service on his Range-Rover radio. He listened to it all the time. He was very concerned about what the world had to say about him.

''At the time he had threatened the two hundred Americans in the country with incarceration—although he backed down quickly when Carter threatened military action in return.

''Well, as we were driving along, a news item came over the air about this and he laughed his head off and said, 'Carter takes everything too seriously, doesn't he? I was only joking.'

''He was obviously a very cunning man. He had this strange habit of saying something and waiting to judge your reaction before reacting himself.

''If, for instance, he said something which he thought might be funny, then normal persons would react themselves. But he would say something which might be a joke and then wait to see how you reacted. There would be a rather pregnant pause while you worked out if he was being funny or serious and wonder if you should laugh at him or not. Then, if you'd laugh, he'd join in with you.

''When he did laugh he laughed uncontrollably and his whole body would shake.''

How did John Penrose assess this strange tyrant? ''He was an enormous man. One felt a great deal of respect for him, knowing that he had probably been responsible for the deaths of hundreds of thousands of people.

"What did come across to me were his spontaneous reactions. He was obviously a man who acted on impulse; for instance, stopping his car and kicking out his bodyguards and saying to us, 'Come on, I'll give you a ride.' This was not something that most world leaders would do. It's the sort of thing Amin would do. I think, quite clearly, if something upset him badly enough he would be capable of pulling out a gun and shooting someone there and then.

"He was a very dangerous man and obviously carried a great deal of power and control. People did click their heels and call him 'Your Excellency' when they saw him. They were remarkably servile, but I suppose with Amin's reputation, it would be silly not to be.

"Even Astles called him 'Your Excellency.' The 'major' was very humble in his presence, although it was quite clear to me that he, himself, was an ogre."

Then came another surprise for the tense trio. Amin took them to the old Entebbe terminal buildings, where the Israelis had freed the hostages in their historic raid.

Penrose summoned up the courage to ask Amin if he had seen the film, *Raid on Entebbe*. "Oh yes," he replied. "I've seen it twelve times, and I have my own private copy of it." Penrose swallowed hard, not knowing whether to laugh. Then Amin added: "I thought it was divine justice that the actor [Godfrey Cambridge] who played me had a heart attack."

We asked Penrose for his conclusions about the death of the archbishop. "Well, I feel clearly that the car accident didn't take place, and all the evidence points to the fact that Amin did carry out the killing. On the basis of the evidence I finally unearthed, I certainly couldn't grant him any benefit of the doubt. Amin must be guilty of the archbishop's murder."

Idi's cover had been blown.

The greatest problem facing the worldwide Anglican community in 1977 was the election of a new archbishop. Who would be willing to follow in the footsteps of Janani Luwum? Who would be prepared to put his life on the line with such a dangerous and difficult job?

No one was more surprised than Silvanus Wani to be elected to this high position by his fellow-bishops. "I had been praying that a young man be appointed as Janani's successor," he says. There was much agonizing on his part before he made his final decision. He knew that he, too, could be murdered by Amin. The fact that he came from the same Kakwa tribe as the president would be no deterrent.

At his Namirembe home, which still contains the two stuffed lions that Luwum loved so well, he spoke frankly about what it was like to be asked to step into the shoes of a martyr.

"This was a very trying time for me, filled with tremendous strain. In the beginning I was unhappy with their decision, but it was something, by the grace of God, I finally accepted. I realized I had come to a place of brokenness and humility.

"I had prayed, 'Lord, if it is Your will, please help me and give me Your strength so that I can accept Your call.'

"Eventually I felt that this was a call from God. So with the help of the Christians, including my brother bishops, I accepted the position."

The new archbishop said it was especially hard to move into Luwum's home. "My wife, in particular, was not happy to occupy this home. A period of six months elapsed before we finally made the move. According to our custom, when someone dies you shouldn't immediately occupy his house or property."

The self-effacing archbishop, who apologized for his "pidgin English," says it was difficult enough to take over Luwum's mantle at such a tense time. What made matters worse were attacks from several quarters which suggested that because of their tribal links, Idi Amin had personally appointed him to this office.

"President Amin had nothing to do with my appointment," he says firmly.

The new archbishop could not remain silent about the continued killings that were reaching alarming proportions. He says, "I went to President Amin and informed him that the massacring of people must be stopped and that on humanitarian grounds the church could not condone these activities.

"Amin would listen to some of my objections, and I think he did feel a bit guilty, but generally he did not pay much attention. Whenever I talked to him about putting a stop to these killings, he would remain quiet."

Archbishop Wani approached Amin about specific cases. "It was not easy for me to work with the former president. I felt a lot of pressure in his presence, but I knew that the Lord was with me. Often

I was accompanied by my brother bishops and at those times we were uplifted by the power of the Holy Spirit."

Archbishop Wani revealed that ironically the president strongly insisted that their meetings either be opened or closed with a word of prayer.

"I talked to the president about Christianity, but was constantly aware that the Islamic faith came first with him," he says.

"We in the church felt that he intended to get rid of a lot of Christians, thinking that eventually the people would turn to the Islamic faith."

With the double-faced Amin on the warpath against the Church of Uganda, the archbishop explained that there was much heart-searching as to whether they should cancel the Centenary Celebrations scheduled for June 30—the day on which the first Anglican missionaries arrived in the country.

"We almost canceled the centennial celebrations, but after prayer the Lord gave us renewed strength and courage. We had to begin again by writing a letter to all the bishops and Christians advising them that we would celebrate our Centenary as usual.

"By the grace of God these were truly jubilant days in the history of our church in Uganda."

9

Aftermath

AFTER THE KILLING of the archbishop, Amin turned his attention to the Anglican bishops who had signed the protest letter which sealed Luwum's fate. Many were told by their flocks to leave the country immediately, or they, too, could be murdered. "Be our voice in the outside world," the people implored them.

Bishop Festo Kivengere is probably the most famous of the exiled bishops. Now back in Uganda in his lovely Kigezi diocese, he recalls the heartbreaking day he was forced to leave his beloved land for an uncertain future.

Standing on the hill near his home, which overlooks Kabale, he says: "It was on the fateful evening of February 19, 1977, that my wife Mera and I had to leave this beautiful country because of the pressure of Amin.

"His men had been to our house three times that day, and when we arrived back from a trip to Kampala, the Christians were very upset. Most of them were in tears. They warned us that if we spent the night in our home, we would be placed under house arrest. They also said that if I tried to preach as usual in my cathedral on the following Sunday, I would be arrested during the service, and that would be the end for me."

The worried friends and colleagues told them: "You have something to accomplish in the wider world. Remember Peter. With the help of God's angel he escaped Herod's captivity and moved on to serve God elsewhere. Please go now!"

They packed in two hours and had to limit themselves to a suitcase apiece, leaving behind the possessions of a lifetime, including hundreds of books, sermon notes, furniture, and clothing.

"So, helped by friends, we drove off in a Land-Rover from our house on the hill. Our hearts were heavy and our eyes filled with tears. We had no idea whether or not we would encounter Amin's soldiers, which, of course, would have been fatal for us.

"Under the cover of night, surrounded with danger, and with fear and apprehension in our hearts because we were leaving our beloved friends, we started on the long journey. We proceeded towards Zaire along the road to the west, through the hills and around the lake, driving anxiously, yet filled with great hope.

"For a time we were lost behind a big hill so we circled back, trusting that we were on the right road. Looming behind that big hill we saw the lights of Kabale again. Our hearts sank, because we knew we had lost two hours on our escape. So we drove back over the same muddy path, nearly toppling twice into the lake, and then onto the main road to Zaire.

"When we reached nine thousand feet in the hills about forty-six miles from Kabale, we looked back, and I shall never forget the sight. The sun was rising, the mist covered the valleys, and it was very beautiful indeed. Yet my wife and I felt that we were fugitives in our own country. Africa is beautiful, but it had no place for us. We were running away because of a useless man called Idi Amin, who was only interested in killing Ugandans in order that he might take what he wanted.

"As we approached the border, we thought for sure this was it, and that Amin's men would be waiting for us on the road. But they were not. God had swept all our enemies out of the way. He helped us escape from the dangers of Uganda towards Zaire, and then on to Rwanda through those great mountains."

Bishop Kivengere and his wife eventually could go no farther in the Land-Rover. They continued all night on foot through the mountains and across muddy streams.

Very early that morning the young guide who was with them suddenly turned to Festo and Mera and said, "Just take three steps forward." He and his wife willingly complied in that misty dawn on the mountainside. It was 6:30 A.M. on Sunday, February 20, and they were finally in Rwanda and safety.

Once safely out of Uganda, as they walked through wheatfields into a village, they providentially came across a young Roman Catholic businessman. He took them in his Toyota truck seventy-five miles to Kigali, the country's capital, and let them off at the home of a pastor friend of theirs, who, they were confident, would know what to do next.

Kivengere recalls: "This dear brother had just finished his morning prayers. He had been praying for us after hearing the disturbing reports on the radio. Going to the door to see who had driven up, he saw me get out of the car and wave, and couldn't believe his eyes."

The Kivengeres rested for the next two days, then a flight was arranged for them to Nairobi. The Rwanda pastor escorted Festo and Mera to Kigali airport, but at the immigration control another crisis developed.

"This passport is not valid," said a grim-faced officer.

"What's the trouble?"

"You say you've come to Rwanda from Uganda. Why is there no stamp on your passport? You are an illegal immigrant." The Rwanda pastor thought rapidly as he stepped forward.

"Yes, but you see—he came out on a Sunday."

Obviously confused, the officer gave up. "Clergy," he muttered to himself as he reached for the stamp and regularized the passport. A scribble of chalk on the suitcases, and the refugees were cleared for Nairobi, and then a world-wide ministry for Kivengere that was to bring the appalling plight of Uganda's Christians to a then apathetic world.

As Kivengere was making his escape, a dear friend protected him at great cost to himself. Archdeacon Yosiya Banyenzaki was picked up at his home in the diocese of North Kigezi, the place where Kivengere was born and lived as a boy. As Kivengere was driving home that fateful day from Kampala, the army swooped on the arch deacon's home. A soldier told him: "We've come to find the guns that Bishop Festo Kivengere has brought for you and the people in your parish." The unwarranted accusation was as ridiculous as that made against Archbishop Luwum and Bishop Okoth, but the consequences could be just as perilous.

He told them: "I have no guns here and neither has anybody else in the parish. Festo has never given me a gun and he's never had a gun himself."

But the soldiers did not believe him and began to search his home from top to bottom. They even emptied all the sacks of food and looked through them, but found nothing.

"We don't believe what you're saying," said one of the soldiers. "You must come with us for questioning. Don't be afraid; we won't hurt you." The archdeacon knew better than that.

He was driven toward Mbarara to a large army barracks. It was there that many had lost their lives in savage tortures and executions.

Miss Joan Hall, home secretary of the Ruanda Mission CMS, says, "The army men, who were Moslems, didn't know the difference between a bishop, an archbishop, and an archdeacon, so they called him 'bishop.'

"As they rode along, they said, 'Bishop, why don't we get Bishop Kivengere as well?' The archdeacon immediately said, 'Well, you say I am a "bishop" so why do you bother about getting a second bishop?' He pleaded with them not to go to Kabale to find Festo. The marvelous thing about it was that if they had gone then to Kabale it would have been about the same time Festo was returning, and he would have certainly lost his life.

"Eventually the soldiers decided against going after Festo, and to the archdeacon's astonishment and delight he found himself being driven past the killer barracks, to Kampala. They took him to another barracks in Kampala and when they got him inside they beat him unmercifully. The ruthless beating continued into the early hours of the next morning.

"Finally they dragged him to his son's home in Kampala and, as the son opened the door they pushed him through, half-dead and said, 'Stay here and we'll come and collect you later.'

"He had been slashed with knives, beaten, and so badly bruised that his son immediately sent for a doctor to bind him up. To ease his pain the doctor administered morphine.

"They returned for him that morning and by then he was almost unconscious. Back at the barracks they again beat him and slashed him with knives.

"This terrible torture went on for about five days. The beatings continued each day, and at night they returned him to his son. One day his torturers said to him, 'Why don't you die like everybody else? You are the only one who has ever survived such a beating.'

"As he lay on the floor, near to death, he gasped, 'I'm alive because of Jesus. Jesus is in me and that's why I'm alive.'"

One day they took Archdeacon Banyenzaki into a room, propped him up and shot another man before his eyes. Blood was everywhere. As he watched this horrible spectacle, he said desperately to them, 'Why don't you shoot me now? I want to be with Jesus. Please don't wait any longer.'' The interrogators told him to be quiet. But he wouldn't. "If you want to shoot me, I am ready to go to be with Jesus. You can shoot me now.'' But for some reason they didn't.

"All the time this cruelty was taking place, they repeatedly said that they were going to kill all the Christians in Uganda,'' says Miss Hall. "Now that Archbishop Luwum was dead, they thought the Christian church would soon die. They felt all they needed to do was wipe out the believers that were left.

"Reluctantly they decided they could not break this man's spirit. So they sent him back to his son. When he was finally reunited with his wife, she could scarcely believe what she saw and wept uncontrollably.

"I saw him a few weeks later and my own eyes were brimming with tears as I listened to his personal account. He was a very courageous man.''

NICHOLAS ODONGPINY was in a car at the roadblock, which was set up like a steel trap beside the taxi park in the busy town of Masaka. His heart beat twice as fast as normal.

"I'm in your hands, Lord Jesus,'' Odongpiny, a clergyman in the Church of Uganda, silently prayed. The soldiers began examining identity cards and other documents belonging to occupants of the crowded taxi.

Odongpiny knew only too well what the soldiers were seeking. They were looking for members of the Acholi and Langi tribes, whom they were slaughtering indiscriminately.

Already more than two hundred corpses had been discovered in Mabira Forest between Kampala and Jinja. Most of the dead were from these two tribes, and it was reported that President Amin's execution squad was working its way through a death list of seven thousand.

But why such savagery against members of these northern peoples? One reason was that the late Archbishop Luwum was an Acholi, as were a large proportion of the armed forces during Milton Obote's period. Obote, too, belonged to the Langi tribe—sufficient reason for Amin's sick mind to suspect the entire tribe.

Wholesale slaughter was unleashed on thousands of members of both tribes, who Amin believed were potentially hostile to his regime in 1977 after the brutal killing of Luwum. But this was only one of many purges during Amin's bloody reign.

Odongpiny, the man in the taxi, had taken time out from his church work in a village near Gulu to attend a refresher course for rural service training at the Kabale District Farm Institute. When he heard of the slaying of the archbishop, he knew he would have to try to reach his home district before all the Acholis and Langis in the area were murdered.

"The people at the institute said that there was no chance of arriving in Kampala alive, let alone getting all the way to Gulu," says Odongpiny, who is now pastor of a parish church.

"But I knew God could keep me safe, and so I prayed, removed my dog collar, and set off in a taxi toward the capital. I had two friends with me. One was also Acholi, the other Langi.

"There were roadblocks every five miles along the way, but God had His own plan. At every roadblock the soldiers examined the papers of those at the front of the packed taxi and left us alone at the back.

"The people in the taxi with us were marvelous and didn't give us away.

"But then at Masaka, we were caught. A soldier told me to get out of the taxi and asked to see my papers.

"Then he said, 'Are you a pastor?' I said that I was, and he immediately pushed me to the ground and screamed, 'Why do you talk to me while you are standing? You have no right to do that. You are an Acholi and one of Luwum's people.'

"Then my friend, a Christian layman who came from the Langi tribe, was also shoved to the ground, as was my other friend. We all knew that we were in big trouble and could be killed at any moment."

These fanatical Moslem Nubians at the roadblock had devised a particularly horrible death for all the Acholis and Langis they could ensnare. They would take them to a nearby place, slash the bridge of their noses with a panga knife, and then force another captive to open the mouth of the victim, so that the blood ran down through the nostrils from the two cuts. He would have to do that until the wounded man choked to death by swallowing his own blood.

"As the soldiers examined our documents, they kept kicking us," says Odongpiny.

"They told us they were taking us a short distance away, to where the killing was taking place. I told them if they were going to kill me I preferred to be shot. I couldn't bear to be cut in such a way.

"Strangely, the Lord came to all of us in our hour of need and we had a deep confidence in Him. There was a complete absence of fear.

"I turned to one of the men and said, 'I have one thing to ask you.' 'What is that?' he said roughly, obviously relishing the thought of killing me. 'I want you to know that you will never kill my spirit. You will be just taking me from one home to another, and this new home will last forever.' I then asked him to let me pray before he did the evil deed.

"The soldiers watched for a moment and then became very angry and one said, 'Who is this Jesus you are talking about and praying to? Do you think we are playing games? Don't you see you are going to be cut open?'

"Then he blasphemed the name of Jesus. 'Do you think Jesus will help you now?' he sneered, then told me to put on my dog collar so that I would die with it on. 'When we show your body with the collar on, everyone will know you are one of Luwum's people,' he said.

"They dragged my luggage from the taxi. I pushed my hands into my luggage and found my dog collar and put it on. I then had prayer with my friends, who were lying on the ground near me.

"Each one of us had an askari [soldier] standing over us ready to kill us as we were praying. When I had finished my prayer, I turned to the one standing over me and said, 'You can now do whatever you like, because I have recommitted my life into the hands of God.'

"We were all waiting for death, when suddenly a Moslem taxi driver came over to the men and said, 'Excuse my interfering, but you should not kill these people. They are innocent.' One of the soldiers retorted, 'What do you mean, they are innocent? Don't you know that they are Acholis? They are Luwum's people who are trying to undermine our government.'

"He then pointed to me and said, 'This man is a pastor of the Church of Uganda. How can you say he is innocent?'

"With that they began beating him, and then dragged him away for further punishment.

"Then they came back to us, and suddenly another courageous

Moslem taxi driver came over. He also began to plead for our lives. At the time only Moslems were actually allowed to speak to the soldiers.

"The taxi man said, 'Look, these people are praying to their God, which we all know is useless. But why don't you just see if all their prayers will help them? There are roadblocks every five miles into Kampala, and if their prayers are worthless, as we both know they are, then they will not survive. But just in case this Jesus can help them, why don't you just let them try and get to Kampala?'

"The soldier wasn't convinced at all. 'You must be as big a fool as them,' he thundered. Then he and some of his colleagues began to quarrel about what should happen to us.

"They went nearly out of earshot and continued to argue among themselves. I just caught one or two things they said, and I heard one say to the main soldier, 'If you are going to free the people of Luwum, it's going to be you instead of them.'

"By that comment, it seemed as if we were really in danger, but then they came back and surprisingly said they had decided to leave us. They called the taxi driver who had brought us from Kabale and ordered him to take us on to Kampala.

"A Nubian then said, 'When you come to the next roadblock, make sure you've got your _____ _____ Jesus with you. Because you'll need Him.'"

The believers could hardly comprehend; they were still alive while hundreds were being slaughtered at the roadside. And, somehow, they got safely through the rest of the checkpoints to Kampala. As before, those up front handed over their papers. The soldiers, not bothering to check the "condemned three" at the back, waved the taxi through.

"When we got to Kampala, we decided to try to get to the Church of Uganda Guest House on Namirembe," says Odongpiny. "The problem was finding a taxi to take us there."

"In those days, the taxi drivers would outrageously overcharge everyone but the Moslems. They would demand six hundred shillings (eighty US dollars), for a three- or four-mile journey.

"But to our delight the first taxi man we spoke to said, 'You give me fifty shillings, and I'll take you.' We didn't tell him that we were going to the guest house, because he would have reported us, and we would have been picked out that night and arrested."

So they were dropped off quite a way from the guest house, which nestles below the Church of Uganda Cathedral, and is run by a brave young Ugandan, Naomi Gonahasa, and her husband, Stephen, a bishop's son.

As was their practice, this charming couple assisted the fugitives by not requiring them to sign the guest book—in case it was checked by State Research—and by regularly switching their rooms.

But the trio realized the sanctuary offered at the guest house couldn't last forever, so after a short stay, they were spirited away by a brave civil servant.

"This man was really courageous. He picked us up in his car," says Odingpiny. "He knew that no one was allowed to help an Acholi or Langi, yet he did, and he kept us hidden for a few days."

Then they caught a train heading towards Soroti. Despite numerous checks, the believers arrived there safely. It was a truly miraculous escape.

"I believe we escaped because God had not yet planned for our death," says the pastor. "Otherwise, we could not have passed through so many checks."

THE OPERATOR COULD HARDLY BELIEVE his ears when he heard the gruff voice on the line. "Kill Bishop Herd, and do it immediately," it said. The telephone operator at the Moroto exchange had put through the incoming call from the State Research man at Mbale to the local army commander, and stayed on the line to listen. It was the middle of the night. All else was quiet. The conversation became heated as the Moslem army man refused to have anything to do with the death order. "No, I won't kill him. He is a good man, and certainly not an enemy of Uganda," he yelled.

The news of this phone call was given the pastor just ten minutes after Ulster-born Brian Herd was seized by the police, who were taking him to Kampala—and possible execution.

The bishop and his future wife, Norma, had gone from Northern Ireland to Uganda in 1961. They were married there in 1963. After language study, Herd worked as a pastor at Namalu and Moroto before becoming Rural Dean in 1964. In 1965 this work was turned over to an African, and Herd became his adviser. He was made the first Archdeacon of Karamoja in 1970. When that vast tract of ten thousand square miles, with the lowest population density of any part of Uganda, became a missionary diocese in 1976, Herd was asked by Archbishop Janani Luwum to be its first bishop. Since all the other bishops were Ugandan, he became the only white bishop in Uganda.

Now, apparently because his name appeared on the bishops' letter to Amin—even though he wasn't at that Namirembe meeting—Brian Herd was to lose his diocese and possibly his life.

The bishop and his family now reside in Belfast, but he was too ill to be interviewed for this book. He had been hurt in a serious accident when a truck crossed the road and hit his car near Drogheda in Southern Ireland. So his wife described for us what happened on that traumatic day in 1977 when, two weeks after Janani's death, he was arrested.

"Brian was the only expatriate bishop in Uganda," she says. "He didn't sign the bishops' statement, but his name was on it and he has said that if he had been there he would have signed it anyway. Brian had attended the unofficial memorial service for Janani at Namirembe Cathedral. He was the only white bishop on the steps of the cathedral afterwards. He actually preached there that day in the afternoon and had two minutes of silence for Janani during the service.

"We also feel that somebody had been trying to frame him. Certainly the State Research people were out to get him. It truly was God's intervention, and the good will of other people, that helped us through that time. We learned that State Research meant to kill Brian, but the ordinary soldiers and police really did want to help us in that situation.

"We heard that a car full of State Research people had been driving around town during the night looking for our house, but were unable to find it. A fellow-minister encouraged us and said, 'Our God is a real God.' He felt that God had closed the eyes of the State Research people, making it impossible for them to find our home. Naturally in such a small town it would have been a simple matter. He reminded us that Elisha had a similar experience in Old Testament days when God shut the eyes of his enemies and he was able to pass by them unnoticed.

"There were a number of little things that contributed to the fact that they could not find him—for instance, the notice board outside the house. We had asked somebody to paint 'Bishop Herd' on it, but he hadn't done the job because of problems getting paint. I couldn't understand why these men hadn't asked someone where we lived, but the pastor explained they wouldn't do that because it would have indicated to local people that they were looking for him.

"Then the district commissioner, head of the police and the officer in charge of special branch, came to us and said that Brian should go to Kampala. They said there was a query about his passport and they told me, 'Madam, don't worry.' In fact, we were to discover the ordinary police were protecting my husband.

"My husband was taken to Kampala by car. A State Research chap wanted to take him personally, but our regular police refused. 'No, we will accompany him,' they said. So our head of police and also the chief of special branch accompanied him on the 350-mile journey to Kampala."

The policemen, who were making that long journey to ensure that the State Research men did not kill the bishop, told Mrs. Herd to follow and meet them at the Parliament Buildings in Kampala. In the capital, Mrs. Herd and an English friend, Deaconness Ann Wright, went to the British High Commission. The British representative there was very active and experienced in visiting the prisons and detention centers. He spent hours trying to find Bishop Herd and came back late at night feeling discouraged.

Mrs. Herd stayed overnight at the British High Commission where she heard the good news that her husband was to be immediately deported. So, along with Ann Wright, she dashed out to Entebbe Airport.

"It was then 8:30 A.M. and we were told he was to leave at 9:30 P.M.," Norma Herd recalls. "When we arrived, Brian was still waiting. There had been a serious delay in the flight out, and as we waited and waited all day one of the police officers was getting very jittery.

"He said to me, 'Madam, I just pray that this plane leaves tonight. Because we will not make it through another night.'"

Finally at 8:30 P.M. the plane was set to leave for Stansted, England, and the bishop was taken on board. "My husband was asked to pray with the two policemen before he departed, and he did so on the tarmac [runway]. As they closed their eyes he prayed for Uganda, for them, and for himself.

"The plane went directly to Britain and, as you can imagine, he was completely shattered. He arrived without any British money—I forgot to give him any—and was terribly apologetic that he didn't have a smallpox vaccination."

The bishop, who is sponsored by the Bible Churchmen's Missionary Society, was immediately surrounded by pressmen at the airport. He told them he still didn't know the real reason for his deportation. "I am told that some newspapers have connected it with a letter of protest to the Uganda authorities from church leaders there over events in Uganda. The truth is that I was not a signatory to that letter, as I was away at the time. Secondly, it has been reported in the national press that following my departure, the church in Uganda is in a state of collapse. With respect, I must stress that this is nonsense."

After collecting his thoughts, the bishop then told the Press, "The strength of the Uganda church lies in the whole body of believing Christians, even if some of the leaders are missing. The life is within the whole membership. We were saddened and perplexed by the death of the archbishop, but far from collapsing, the church in Uganda is vigorous, vibrant, and of steadfast faith.

"In Uganda, the churches are packed to the doors. People are finding Christ, and God's work is going forward."

Idi Amin, after seizing power in Uganda on January 25, 1971, is attending a thanksgiving service at Lubaga Cathedral in February.
On Amin's right is Lt. Col. Vincent Ocima, his chief of Protocol, who was killed by Amin early in 1972.

Amin with Archbishop (now Cardinal) Nsubuga at Entebbe Airport. They are awaiting the arrival of King Faisal of Saudi Arabia (September, 1972).

Idi Amin, King Faisal, and Chief Kadhi Sheik Matovu praying to Allah at Amin's Command Post in Kampala, Uganda (September, 1972).

Man accused
of being a guerilla
has been blindfolded
in preparation
for his execution
by firing squad
(February 10, 1973,
at Jinja, Uganda).

Residents
assembled by force
to watch the execution
of an alleged guerilla
at Mbale,
February 10, 1973.

Camerapix-Keystone

Lt. Col. Orinayo Oryema, Ugandan Minister for Lands and Water Reserves under Amin. He was arrested and then killed, supposedly in a car accident, with Archbishop Luwum.

Bottom left. Idi Amin congratulates Janani Luwum on his enthronement as Archbishop of Uganda, Rwanda, Burundi, and Boga-Zaire (Namirembe Cathedral, Kampala, Uganda, June, 1974).

The Archbishop of Uganda, the most Rev. Janani Luwum. He was arrested in Kampala on February 16, 1977, and killed by Amin the next day.

General Amin chats with Mr. Jong Jun Gi, North Korean Vice-Premier, while Russian Air Force Lt. Gen. Alexander Medvedev awaits his turn (Amin's fourth anniversary, Uganda).

Amin, with his Southern Sudanese henchmen in the background, holding an international press conference to explain the "car accident" in which Archbishop Luwum and two government ministers were killed. Looking on is his British advisor, Mr. Bob Astles.

Geoffrey Latim, Ugandan Olympic athlete, points out the site of his grass hut in the bush where he hid from Amin's men.

Mr. James Kahigiriza *(bearded man in center)* with his family the day after his release from the State Research Bureau (March, 1977). He was one of the last Christians to see Archbishop Luwum alive.

Naomi and Stephen
Gonahassi helped hide
many Christians from
Amin's killers.

Joseph Nyakairu
showing the very
trumpet he blew
when the
Makerere Church
believers were
being arrested.
He says, "My
trumpet was
'executed' and
now it is damaged
beyond repair."

Left. Survivors
from the
Makerere Church
imprisonment in
Kampala rejoice
that God
preserved them
through their
ordeal.

Ben Oluka worked in President Amin's office while conducting an underground church in his own home.

Sister Mary Nives Kizito helped run an underground railroad out of Uganda.

The furniture factory which was used as a front for an underground church.

Bottom. After walking through the furniture factory, believers go through a banana grove to hold an underground church service.

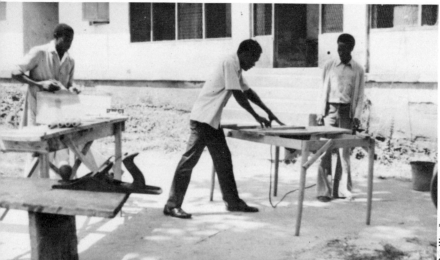

Dan Wooding

Dan Wooding

George Lukwiya revisits the dreaded death house run by the State Research Bureau. He holds the sort of club with which soldiers beat inmates to death.

Idi Amin, self-appointed President-for-Life.

Dan Wooding

The Nakasero Three who were arrested while witnessing about Christ. Benjamin Mwima, Imelda Lubega, and Paul Kinaatama.

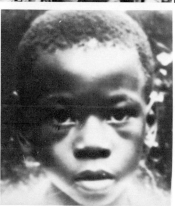

Geoffrey, Imelda's missing son, who was eight years old when they were arrested. When Imelda was released from prison, Geoffrey had disappeared.

Mary Hayward

Eight of Amin's sons at Kabale Preparatory School with Archbishop Silvanus Wani, Luwum's successor.

Outside Amin's headquarters, the State Research Bureau, just before the Tanzanian take-over. For three weeks Amin's soldiers held out against the Tanzanian invasion of Kampala. When they realized they would be forced to flee, they tortured and shot their remaining prisoners. Victims were killed, and their bodies left lying in the streets. This was the appalling last testimony of the works of Amin's secret police.

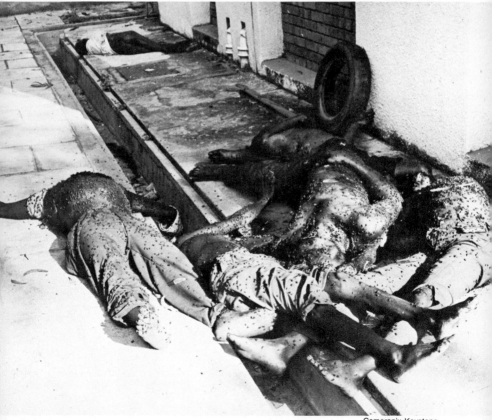

Camerapix-Keystone

Brigadier Stella Bywaters of
the Salvation Army frequently
greeted Amin's soldiers,
"From one Army to another!"
The surprised soldiers were
too flattered to arrest her.

Salvation Army uniforms were
supposedly confiscated, but
many were hidden away.
When liberation came, the
"soldiers" donned their
uniforms and marched in a
spontaneous parade.

After the fall of the Ugandan capital, some of the people, fearful that Amin would return, ransacked the State Research Bureau building.

Bottom. During Amin's reign bodies were often left where they had been shot.

Dan Brewster

World Vision International

Dan Brewster

Relatives check files for their missing family members who may have been killed at the State Research Bureau during Amin's eight-year rule.

The authors of *Uganda Holocaust* visit Uganda after the Tanzanian invasion to gain first-hand information. Dan Wooding, *left,* and Ray Barnett, *right,* outside Jinja.

Bishop Festo Kivengere
returns after exile.

10

The Work Goes On

IT SEEMS THAT SOME of the State Research officers found it hard to cope with the faith and courage of believers whom they arrested and planned to kill. They were afraid of the supernatural faith of the Christians. There were even times when they released them rather than face the witness of these disciples of Jesus Christ.

One such person was the Rev. Joshua Musoke, Pastor of the Makerere Gospel Mission to Uganda Church. His arrest came on a Monday, in February, 1977, when five soldiers barged into his home, close to his church, and accused him of being affiliated with the American CIA.

"We know that you have had ammunition sent to you from America," one of them barked.

The pastor retorted: "That is not true. The Bible is my only weapon. You men need salvation; you need to be born again."

That really upset Amin's men.

"Keep quiet, and don't tell us this nonsense," said their leader.

The soldiers grabbed the protesting pastor and hauled him to the Nakasero State Research building. After being checked in, the round-faced minister was taken down to a blood-and-urine-soaked basement.

"I knelt there and lifted my hands upward. I prayed at the top of my voice," recalls the bespectacled pastor. "Soon one of the guards came to me and said, 'What's wrong with you?' I told him that I was thanking God and also asking him to allow me to be shot rather than tortured. I knew then they were gouging out eyes and cutting ears off men and making them eat them."

The confused guard took him to see an interrogator, and as the man started to question the pastor, he again prayed loudly. "Lord Jesus, You are my God," he said.

"Are you crazy?" the man asked. "Have you lost your mind?"

But the minister just kept praying at the top of his voice. Unable to stand this constant stream of prayer, the State Research man finally, in exasperation, asked him to stop and said he could leave. So just four hours after he had been brought into this "house of death," the pastor was free again, leaving behind the guards nursing fantastic headaches from his noisy prayer sessions.

"It was miraculous," says Pastor Musoke. "When I arrived home people were praying for me. At first they could scarcely believe it was actually me. They thought maybe I was a ghost.

"When the unbelievers of the area saw that I was safe and free again, many of them accepted Christ. To them it was an absolute miracle."

ANOTHER MIRACLE saved the life of former Olympic athlete, Geoffrey Latim, from Gulu, who was forced into hiding and then exile after learning that his life was in danger.

Latim represented Uganda in the 110-meter hurdles at the 1968 Mexico Olympics. He was later team manager for the country's thirty-five-strong athletic squad at Montreal in 1976, when most of the black African countries withdrew in protest because of the controversy over New Zealand sportsmen competing against the country of South Africa.

As one of Uganda's top sporting ambassadors, Latim had met Idi Amin on many occasions. But after the killing of the archbishop, the Acholi athlete was considered an enemy. It was further complicated by the fact that he was also a committed Christian.

"Things began to deteriorate in 1976," says Latim, who was our guide at the beginning of our stay in Uganda. He relates his ordeal of hiding in the bush and tells us about his daring escape.

"I was by then headmaster of Gulu High School, and Amin suddenly announced that the Acholi and Langi headmasters had been collecting money for the liberation movement in Tanzania.

"There was certainly no truth in that as far as I was concerned, but there was still a move to remove all these headmasters, and several were arrested."

Then Latim received a phone call from the local governor's office. The man informed Latim that all the headmasters in the town were in great danger and that he ought to leave, "because they will be coming for you."

Latim had a brief but emotional time of prayer with his wife Asta at their bungalow in Gulu. He then left with Mr. Nyeko, head of Gulu Secondary School, and British missionary Mary Coleman, who is a member of the Church Missionary Society and was religious education adviser in the Diocese of Northern Uganda.

Mary Coleman was a likable person who seemed to specialize in working in danger zones. She had previously been based in Southern Sudan during a war and then in Jordan during the Six Day War. The former athlete asked her to drive him and Mr. Nyeko to Kampala. She did not then know that they were planning to go into hiding, but guessed something was up.

"We had problems all the way," recalls Latim. "After about fifty miles the car got a flat.

"We got out the jack, took off the wheel nuts, and had changed the tire, when Mary leaned on the roof of the car. Unfortunately, this caused the jack to break. So there we were with no way of putting on the other spare tire if it became necessary."

Latim had a big decision to make. Should he try to make it to Kampala in such a state, and put Mary at even more risk, or try to get back to the Gulu district and go into hiding in the bush?

He decided on the latter. Miraculously the car limped back to Gulu. As they were going back, they noted several State Research cars heading toward Kampala, and felt then that the jack accident had surely been providential. Had they continued toward the capital, they knew that any one of those cars could have overtaken their old vehicle and stopped them.

Latim, however, was still prepared for trouble. He warned his traveling companions, "If any one of them asks us to stop, we take off like lightning, and if we have a tire puncture, we take off into the bush." When they got back to Gulu, that's just what Latim did. He and hundreds of other endangered Ugandans just vanished into the bush and were forced to live off the land.

Latim built a grass hut in the long grass near his parents' home, six miles from the school. Mary Coleman says, "His Boy Scout training helped him to survive. Because in the scouts here each boy is required to go into the bush, build a grass hut, and live there for a few days.''

Often Latim's family would sneak into the bush, carrying a bucket as if going to a well. It was the only way they could take him food. Mary Coleman would sometimes, at great risk to herself, take his wife and their three daughters part of the way to the hide-out. They would make the rest of the journey on foot. Then she would visit some Catholic fathers at a local seminary for a cup of tea, so that if she was stopped she could truthfully say where she had been.

Why did she take such risks? ''The Bible says, 'Greater love has no one than this, that one lay down his life for his friends' [John 15:13]. That is what matters here,'' she says. ''People matter, and are willing to lay down their lives for a friend. It's not like the West at all.''

While Latim was in hiding, a group of Amin's soldiers arrived at Gulu High School, assembled all the pupils, and launched into a tirade of hate against the Acholi and Langis.

Among those in the hall at the time were Alex Latim, Geoffrey's brother, and his cousin Martin.

Alex says, ''They wanted to know where the headmaster was, and why he had disappeared. No one said a thing. Then they ordered all Acholis and Langis to stand up, but most of them refused.

''The pupils were very brave. None of them gave away the fact that Geoffrey was my brother, or that Martin was his cousin.''

Latim received the news that a reward was being offered for his capture. ''Apparently a lady teacher, who had been a friend of mine, was paid the equivalent of five thousand shillings to find me and the other Acholi who was in hiding,'' says Latim.

Erroneous reports of Latim's death reached his mother in Juba, southern Sudan, where she had gone for medical treatment. Heartbroken, she rushed back with his aunt. When she reached his grass hut, she was greatly relieved to find he was still safe.

But on March 22, 1977, it was decided that Latim must go on a ''make-or-break'' trek to the southern Sudan border. So his family prepared to help him in this highly dangerous escape plan.

Before leaving for the Sudan, there was a little farewell in his grass hut, with cakes provided by Mary Coleman. His wife was there and also a few members of his family. ''It was like the Last Supper,'' says Miss Coleman. ''He told us all that if his life was spared he would give it in the service of God.''

"My brother and aunt went by taxi on the red gravel road to Atiak, a town some forty-five miles away, and thirty miles from the border post," says Latim, "while my father and I left the same day on bicycles.

"It wasn't safe to ride during the day, so we decided to set off at night. The authorities had issued a directive that no one must ride after 7:00 P.M., so we figured we would take the risk after that time and keep our ears open for cars.

"Every time we heard a vehicle, we would dive off our bikes and either pretend to be mending a puncture or lie quietly in the bush at the side of the road until it passed."

By eight o'clock the next morning, despite several close calls, they arrived safely in Atiak. There they joined the "advance party" and formulated their plans for the border crossing.

"We tied all my belongings on the bikes, and I followed my brother into a nearby game park," says Latim.

"We walked deep into the bush, so Amin's men couldn't find us. The soldiers were all over the park trying to stop people escaping into Sudan. "But it wasn't just the soldiers that we had to avoid. The park was full of all kinds of wildlife, including elephants, lions, buffalo, jackals, and hyenas. It seemed we had escaped one danger only to face another."

The little group struggled along hour after hour, literally hauling the two bicycles through the deep undergrowth. They managed to cross two major rivers during this exhausting trek, but then realized to their dismay that they were completely lost.

"We decided to walk north," says Latim. "We felt we must eventually come to the Sudan, but it seemed we were crossing the same rivers time and again."

It then occurred to the little band of Christians that they had neglected to pray about the situation. So they stopped and urgently implored the Lord to help them in their desperate hour of need.

Then, amazingly, they came across a middle-aged tribesman dressed in rags and carrying a spear, who for a fee agreed to lead them safely through the park and into the Sudan—and freedom.

"Since this was the hottest time of year, we tried to avoid the rivers and trees, because that is where the wild animals gathered," says the former champion athlete.

"On the second night, as we approached Mount Gordon, I saw a 'hill' seemingly heading toward us. It took a few moments for me to realize the 'hill' was, in fact, a herd of about a hundred wild elephants moving in our direction.

"We all made a mad dash for a gorge to hide from them. I dived into the gorge with my bike, and broke one of the pedals. But I was thankful to be still alive."

Then, when the group was only about one and one-half miles from the Sudanese border, they came across a lion drinking at a river.

"My brother was completely exhausted and had terrible blisters on his feet, so we decided we should stop," says Latim. "We made a bonfire to scare the animals away and rested for a short time."

During their times of rest, the group prayed and thanked God for their safe deliverance thus far. "On one occasion, we were suddenly interrupted by a hoard of huge rats who raced by us, obviously escaping from other animals," he says.

"It was hard to sleep at night for fear of attack by an animal. We stayed awake often to the sound of a radio I carried. We would listen to the news from various parts of the world. On one Uganda radio broadcast, I heard the announcer say that all department heads of schools who hadn't reported should do so immediately. That was one order I certainly was not going to heed."

During the dead of night, after a brief rest, the group saw three lights ahead. They pressed on toward the middle one, which turned out to be a village where they were allowed to spend the rest of the night in a compound.

"We felt much safer there than in the game park," says Latim.

They finally found the Sudanese border post at Nimule. Latim immediately gave himself up and asked for asylum. He was well aware that he could possibly be sent back to Uganda—and certain death. But he found a kindhearted Sudanese commanding officer who, when he heard of Latim's case, ordered that he be granted political asylum.

His father, his brother, and the guide, with the two battered bikes, then boarded a truck going into Uganda, while Latim headed for Juba. He whispered a prayer for their safe return home, a plea that was answered.

Latim was then taken to a small refugee camp at Tarit for people who had escaped from Uganda, where he was given a medical check and vaccinated.

"At the camp I met the headmaster from Gulu, who had also been forced to flee," says Latim. "It was wonderful to see him again. He had escaped by a completely different route. When we first saw each other, we couldn't believe it. We just stood there, uttering, 'Praise the Lord. Praise the Lord.'" The pair shared a tent in the camp and had a lot of news to exchange.

Soon Latim arrived in Juba, the capital of southern Sudan, where he secured, through a British contact, a lecturing post at the university. His heart was heavy because he had left behind his wife and children, including an eight-month-old baby. He had sent a letter with his father to Asta, and in May she traveled by truck to Juba, posing as a single woman who was returning her sister's children. Her sister worked with the United Nations there, she claimed.

"It was May 11 when she arrived with the children," recalls Latim. "We had been separated since February 24, so you can imagine the reunion we had."

After awhile, it became obvious to Latim that even in Juba he was not safe from Amin's men, and in January, 1978, he decided to leave with his family by truck to Kenya. This, too, was a precarious journey. They traveled by bush truck route, which took them through a dangerous region full of primitive people who live by cattle rustling. Hundreds of tribesmen are killed in these raids.

Yet again the Lord protected them, and they arrived safely at the Kenya border, where, after a few formalities had been completed, they were allowed to go on to Nairobi. There, as an exile, Latim worked with the evangelical organization, African Evangelistic Enterprise, helping other refugees in the country.

"I ran with Jesus and he ran with me," says Latim. It was his finest victory.

SISTER MARY NIVES KIZITO, an attractive Ugandan, is head of the information service at the Catholic Secretariat in Kampala. She was involved in organizing daring escapes, such as that of Miss Helen Nabasuta, who was at Makerere University.

Trouble was no stranger to the university. It had erupted when a student, Paul Serwanga, was shot on the edge of the campus by Public Safety Unit personnel who were attempting to rape his girl friend. The incident, in March, 1976, was so well publicized that Amin was forced to appoint a "commission of inquiry." But as with all of his so-called inquiries, it never completed its task—one chairman after another was fired.

Then in June, Sister Kizito saw at firsthand how ruthless Amin's men could be. Her close friend, Mrs. Bukenya Nanziri, who was six-months pregnant, was dragged from her office and shot in the neck. Her body was dumped in the river, but later recovered and taken to Mulago Hospital mortuary where the fetus was removed from the body for separate burial, in conformity with Ugandan custom. The hospital staff was appalled at the barbaric killing of a pregnant woman.

So Sister Kizito was only too willing to help Helen Nabasuta when the State Research men turned their attentions to her.

"Helen was planning a trip to the United States for studies and we managed to get her a passport through normal channels," says the Sister. But Helen was visited by some of the president's men, who wanted her to give evidence against a Kenyan girl suspected of leaking stories to the Press in Nairobi.

"One afternoon she walked up to our house, disguised in ragged clothes, and said, 'You have to help me.' She explained her predicament and we appointed two Sisters to drive her to Tororo on the Kenyan border. They dressed her as a nun, and even the driver was not aware of the disguise. I went to her home to pick up a few things for her.

"They arrived in Tororo on Saturday afternoon. The next day they dressed her as an old woman, gave her a stick and a piece of old cloth to cover her head, and one of the Sisters, who was known to the border guards, went across with her to carry her suitcase. No one looked twice at the 'old lady,' and she went to a nearby convent.

"After arriving in Nairobi, she phoned me. I was very relieved to hear she was safe."

AMIN AND HIS ILLITERATE SOLDIERS seemed to reserve a special hatred for Makerere University, something we discovered from the Rev. Eustace Rutiba, a lecturer in religious studies and the university's Anglican chaplain for three years. This likable clergyman had become personally involved in the problems during March, 1977.

He tells us what happened on October 23, just one day before Amin was due to visit in his capacity as the Chancellor of the University. "My cousin, James Runyange, who was a cadet in the army, came to my house on the campus. That night he left with my son Ivan, and as he was walking home, James was shot and killed by a policeman.

"For some reason they thought he was an assassin. They forced him to sit and when he did they shot him in cold blood. My son ran off and they shot at him twice, but missed. Some of his friends hid him.

"When I went to see the body, the police arrested me and checked my house for a gun. I told them I didn't need a gun because I was protected by the blood of Christ. I was taken to Makerere police station, where I was given a special branch guard. I managed to phone the Church of Uganda provincial secretary's office and spoke to the secretary, Canon Wesonga. I told him, 'I want you to call the archbishop and tell him that I have been arrested.'

"They took me to the central police station and alleged that I had preached politics in the church. The commissioner of police interviewed me and read my file. Suddenly he told me that I could go home, but that I must remain on campus.

"Then they put me in a car and I thought they were taking me to an army post to be executed. They assigned four guards to watch me. These guards spent four weeks, either sitting idly by my office under the trees or wandering into the chapel to see what was happening. Some wore dark glasses. The majority of them were just young boys.

"I was quiet when they were there. However, after a month, I decided to preach straight again. I would elaborate on a pointed passage from the Bible which these men could not understand.

"I would welcome visitors to the services saying, 'You are welcome here whoever you are, whether you are here for reasons of your own or to listen to the message.'"

After the archbishop's death, Christians at the university were heartbroken. The chaplain found many students and staff weeping in the chapel. Every day at 6:00 P.M. for the entire month he held a service, and the building was full of people crying to the Lord to change Amin. Many of them were Acholis and Langis, whose lives were now in real danger.

So Rev. Rutiba felt duty bound to organize an escape route for these students. "We would receive an offering in the chapel and use the money to help them reach safety," he says. "Usually I would get other students who knew the border areas to help them. Some would go by bus to Kigezi and then cross the Rwanda border, and others would go to Busia and cross over the official route into Kenya. We instructed the students, that if they were checked, to use their student card rather than their government identity card, which would have given a clue as to their tribe.

"We had twenty Tanzanian students at the university who were in great danger, so we arranged for them to be smuggled out of the country."

Rev. Rutiba recalls the violence that erupted at the university in August, 1976, during his period as chaplain. "The students were threatened because they had complained about the food they were being served," he says. "The police and soldiers came twice that day and arrested many people. They forced some of them to walk on their bare knees on concrete for about half a mile, while others were made to hop. Then they were made to lie face down in rain water on the ground.

"The soldiers on this occasion were very inhuman. One medical student was badly beaten about the head and suffered brain damage. One girl was raped and a lecturer badly beaten.

"At two o'clock they returned, led by Amin's son, Taban. Scores of students leaped from windows to escape the police and soldiers. Some had broken limbs. We were told that three died during that time."

The chaplain showed real courage when Amin banned the free churches in 1977. "I gathered all the Protestant students under the Church of Uganda umbrella," says Rev. Rutiba. "For example, I gave the Seventh-Day Adventists the use of our chapel on Friday evenings and I arranged to have their own hymnbook printed. Naturally, I did not put a cover on it. I also arranged for them to be excused from exams on a Saturday, which is their Sabbath.

"I felt that our chapel was a neutral one for all Protestants. So I would let all the different groups meet and run their own service. I never preached for them.

"The Baptists and the Pentecostals also had their own service. I let them have free worship, and the Pentecostals could clap, dance, and speak in tongues in their meetings.

"We had a big problem when the news media reported that our chapel was hosting the banned churches. I immediately met with the chairman of the Christian Union and asked him to let me handle the situation. I then went to see the acting dean of the university and we drew up a charter in the Christian Union which said the Protestant students were all now part of the Church of Uganda. Then I announced in chapel that we were going to assist spiritually those who had 'joined us.' They understood that, although they were not allowed to call themselves by their old names, they were free to worship as they were accustomed.

"I wasn't really that courageous. It was my faith that brought me through. We knew that Amin was trying to Islamize this country. After I had been in prison, many people advised me to leave. But I wouldn't leave Makerere, as I decided it was not to be the will of God for me to die. I had a deep faith and conviction in the protection and power of the Holy Spirit.

"I was convinced that nothing could harm me if it were not the will of God. I saw the presence of the *whole church* as the future of this country. That is why I let the banned churches continue worshiping and did not leave my country."

Part IV

The Faithfulness
of the Church

11

A Chapter Out of the Book Acts

As I FASTENED MY SEAT BELT [writes Ray Barnett], the Belgian air hostess welcomed us all aboard Sabena flight 401 from Nairobi to Entebbe. For me the journey stirred memories of the daring raid by Israeli Defense Forces to rescue Jewish hostages held by Palestinian terrorists at the old Entebbe terminal building. This rescue had burned the name "Entebbe" into the minds of millions who followed the events of the hijacking of a routine Air France flight from Athens to Paris. The Israeli soldiers snatched their people from the jaws of certain death.

My mission to Uganda in September, 1978, was in accordance with Hebrews 13:3, "Remember them that are in bonds, as bound with them; and them which suffer adversity, as being yourselves also in the body" (KJV), an injunction from God not to forget those of the household of faith who were suffering and who were in prison. And where else in the world were believers suffering more than in Uganda?

As I sat in my seat on the Boeing 707, my thoughts moved to what lay ahead. I considered the conflicting reports I had heard about Idi Amin and his horrible persecution of believers. Was he deliberately intent on the systematic destruction of the church, or, as many claimed, arresting only Christians who happened to be involved in politics of violence? This was the question I was hoping to resolve in the days ahead. There were stories of mutilation and torture by the feared State Research Bureau. There was the killing of the late Archbishop Janani Luwum. What was the truth? The plane began its descent over beautiful Lake Victoria; the stewardess interrupted my thoughts with a request to return my seat back to an upright position and fasten my belt for the landing at Entebbe.

Descending, I dwelt on my other reasons to be concerned about my arrival in Uganda. My organization, Friends in the West, had just published in our journal "Between Friends," articles about the death of the archbishop and the mass arrest of the pastors and congregation at the Makerere church. The issue strongly condemned the regime of Idi Amin for its apparent violation of human rights. There was no way of knowing if copies of the magazine had found their way into Uganda, or indeed if they were in the possession of the State Research Bureau. That would have meant automatic arrest for me, and possibly death. In Uganda, at that time, anything could happen.

By this time the aircraft had taxied to its parking position outside the new terminal building. Despite the obvious dangers, I walked toward Passport Control, confident that my trip to Uganda was ordained of God, and completely dependent on the Holy Spirit for guidance. I was accompanied by an Englishman, who also felt called to undertake this hazardous journey.

Soldiers with automatic weapons were everywhere. I knew that my Canadian passport did not contain a visa for entry into Uganda, but I turned it over to the expressionless passport officer. To my relief he asked me how long I intended to stay. I replied, "Two weeks." My passport was duly stamped and handed back to me without comment. There only remained the usual check by the customs officer, and then I was waved into the airport, free to proceed!

Menacing State Security men thronged the area. They were easy to recognize; they all wore platform heels and, of course, dark glasses. Many had donned T-shirts which carried a smiling picture of their leader, and the inscription, "Idi Amin, Conqueror of the British Empire."

The next problem was how to go to Kampala and make contact with the believers there. A taxi, we decided, was out of the question since they were nearly all driven by State Research personnel, anxious to find out about visitors. I felt it vital that they have as little information about our whereabouts as possible.

We quickly approached a European priest, who was obviously waiting for someone to arrive on the flight. "Are you by any chance going into Kampala?" my colleague asked. "Yes," he replied, "I am waiting for several Sisters to join me. However, I am quite sure with two vehicles we will have enough room to accommodate you."

Soon the Catholic Sisters came through the customs hall and their baggage was quickly loaded on to the waiting Kombi. The priest signaled us into the car just behind and said, "Right, we're ready to go."

The trip from Entebbe to Kampala was filled with conversation and before we knew it, the Irish priest, whose name we discovered was Father McKee, asked, "Where would you like to be dropped off?" We suggested somewhere near the Bible Society headquarters. He appeared very reluctant just to leave us there. "Please take my telephone number," he said. "It might come in handy if you're in need of help." My colleague assured him that we would be fine, and with that we thanked him for his kindness and said good-by.

Quickly we darted across the street and into the Bible Society's book shop. There was a look of astonishment on the face of the manager. He could hardly believe his eyes at the sight of two Europeans appearing from nowhere.

After exchanging greetings, we asked to see the society's executive secretary, who turned out to be a man named Canon Akisoferi Wesonga. We were quickly ushered into his office. He was obviously curious about the purpose of our visit to the Bible Society, but my companion explained, "We are trying to make contact with a certain lawyer here in Kampala, who might be able to help us in our mission." He showed Canon Wesonga the name and telephone number scribbled on a piece of paper, and without further comment Mr. Wesonga dialed the number.

There was an animated exchange of words in a language completely foreign to us. Abruptly, the telephone was handed to my friend. From the end of the conversation I heard, I gathered we were to proceed to the International Hotel. The Bible Society secretary, obviously uneasy about what he was hearing, interrupted and took over the telephone. Again, a quick, emotional exchange took place.

Then Canon Wesonga turned to us and explained, "I told him how unwise I thought it was for you to wait at the International Hotel for him. I feel this is extremely dangerous. But the lawyer insisted this was the correct place to meet you. Before you leave, please sign my guest register, and my driver will take you there. You must be very careful."

Soon we were on our way in a vehicle I later discovered was

provided by Brother Andrew's organization, Open Doors. Canon Wesonga was one of the main Open Doors contacts in Uganda during the difficult years, and was understandably very uneasy.

The driver brought the vehicle to a screeching halt outside the main entrance of the famous Kampala International Hotel. As we walked in we could spot many of the secret police by the now-familiar dark glasses and platform heel shoes.

We sat on the veranda outside the coffee shop. Soon a waiter was towering over us, eyeing us suspiciously as he waited to see what we wanted. "A pot of tea," said my traveling companion. "It will be without milk or sugar," the waiter said abruptly, and off he went without waiting for a reply.

The tables around us were occupied by the secret police with their sneering grins. It appeared we were the center of their attention and conversation. Even without the milk and sugar the black liquid, laughingly called tea and costing about four dollars (US), was very welcome. Two hours passed and still no one came. We decided to have some lunch. The restaurant seemed to be filled with men wearing dark glasses and platform heels. They each had two bottles of beer, which my friend concluded must have been what their expense account allowed.

The lunch over, the tension inside both of us continued to build. The air seemed to be filled with electricity. Another hour passed, and we became acutely uncomfortable, both of us realizing that no one was going to come to our rescue. Somehow we should depart as quickly and unobtrusively as possible.

We picked out a taxi driver who, we thought, looked least like a State Research Bureau agent, and told him only that we were looking for a guest house near Namirembe Cathedral. Luckily we could get out swiftly, for everything we had brought into Uganda was packed in our briefcases. We sighed with relief as the taxi pulled away from the hotel and sped toward Namirembe.

The driver, who appeared to be a Moslem, pulled up at a filthy-looking guest house. My heart was in my mouth. The feeling about this place was not good. Fortunately, it turned out to be a Moslem guest house, and we explained that this was not the place we were seeking. He then indicated that he was lost. At this moment, we spotted a young lady coming down the hill, and so we suggested that he stop and we asked the girl for directions.

"We are looking for the Christian guest house. Can you help us?"

By this time a broad smile had spread across her face, and the girl, in her early twenties, indicated she knew where it was. In fact, the people in charge were friends of hers, she said. "I will come along with you. It will be easier that way."

As she got into the taxi, she smiled and said, "My name is Faith." It seemed the Lord was saying, "Relax, I am able to take care of you."

Soon Faith indicated to the driver that he must stop. We got out near the top of Namirembe Hill, paid him off, and then, with Faith leading the way, started walking. Later we discovered she didn't want the taxi driver to know exactly where we were going. We were soon at the guest house, nestling comfortably in the shadow of the cathedral, and were introduced to the lovely guest house manager, Naomi Gonahasa. She smiled beautifully, and said, "You are welcome." Faith then said good-by and quietly disappeared.

Naomi showed us to our whitewashed room, without the usual delay of having to sign the guest register. No sooner were we settled there than came a knock on the door. Standing before us was one of the workers with a tray, a pot of tea, milk and sugar, and a couple of bananas. Peace appeared to reign at this place overlooking the city of Kampala.

We paused and gave thanks to Almighty God for His care and direction. We were looking forward to the future with anticipation as we enjoyed the afternoon tea and bananas. What a contrast this haven was to the scary International Hotel.

After a refreshing wash, I cautiously moved outside. As I stood gazing down on the city, I was quietly joined by a young man who introduced himself as Stephen. "I'm Naomi's husband," he explained. I turned to him and said, "Stephen, I have come to Uganda under the direction of the Holy Spirit to encourage the believers and to find out what is really happening to the Christian church."

With tears in his eyes, Stephen said, "Only yesterday, we prayed specifically that the Lord would allow someone to come from America to visit us today. Surely the Lord has sent you." This seemed like an impossible prayer request, since they hadn't had any visitors from North America at the guest house for several years. This was another confirmation of being in the center of God's will.

With a tremble in his voice, and speaking softly, he continued, ''These are difficult days for the church in Uganda. Many brothers and sisters have been arrested. A vast majority of the churches have been banned, but praise God for His faithfulness. We are continuing to meet secretly. In spite of all the evil surrounding us, we are in the hands of God.''

I then asked Stephen if it would be possible to make contact with some of the Christian leaders. ''Word is already on the way,'' he replied. ''You must be patient because we do not have gasoline for cars, and messages must be taken by bicycle or on foot.''

It seemed like no time at all before a tall, distinguished-looking Ugandan was coming toward us. With genuine joy on his face, he introduced himself as Ben Oluka. He motioned us into the guest house lounge. As we sat down, he was quietly chuckling with amazement at our miraculous arrival. His heart was full of praise. He was continually thanking the Lord.

Very soon after his arrival, yet another leader appeared in the guest house lounge. He immediately began to praise God. The new arrival was Daniel Naaya. It turned out that he lived only a short distance from the guest house.

Again we stated the purpose of our trip to Uganda, carefully explaining that I was the president of a Christian Human Rights group based in Seattle, Washington, called Friends in the West, and why I was in Uganda.

I went on to explain that a leading American pastor had recently visited Uganda. After eighteen hours of discussion with President Idi Amin, he concluded that the dictator had changed, and that the only Christians in prison were those who had committed political crimes. Therefore, on this crucial visit we had to find out the real situation, so we could take the truth back to our Friends in the West.

Gradually, their story came, at first slowly and then pouring out. Although these brethren were justifiably cautious, they indicated that there was indeed persecution of believers who had no part in politics or any crime other than standing steadfastly for the Word of God.

They described to us the pressure of having their churches closed and how they had decided to worship underground until at one time there was a network of about eighty underground churches in the city of Kampala alone. I was very much impressed by their courage, faith, and victorious attitude in the face of what seemed to be relentless and unending persecution. They had an ability to trust God even for the simple necessities of everyday living as well as the protection of their lives.

"Is it true," I asked, "that an entire congregation was imprisoned last Easter?" "Yes," Oluka responded. "They were released after about three months."

"Would it be possible to meet the leader of that church?" I requested. Ben replied, "Yes, I think we can arrange this. His name is Pastor Mutebi, and we are in very close fellowship."

That evening Oluka and the other leaders present thought it would be good for us to worship next morning at one of the underground churches. This, they felt, would help us understand what was happening, and how they functioned in secret. I said, "This might be dangerous, and I am afraid if we are discovered it will have severe repercussions for you."

Oluka and Naaya brushed aside our objections and said, "We are in the hands of God. We have prayed about this matter and feel completely at peace." The following plan was decided upon.

They would come the next day in a taxi and take us to a furniture factory. This was a kind of cottage industry set up in a large house in Mengo, on the outskirts of Kampala. As agreed, the following day they came back, and when we arrived, the taxi driver was brought into the factory so that he might see where to collect us at the time designated. He looked at some of the furniture in its various stages, then left. He obviously thought we were importers coming to clinch a big deal.

After he had gone, Laban Jjumba, a leading elder in the underground church, showed us around the factory, which they had registered as a legitimate business. It served as a very convenient front, we concluded. We followed Laban out the back door, and through a banana grove, to the house of Daniel Naaya, where we entered the Sunday morning worship service. It was an experience I will never forget.

There were numerous testimonies of victory. The believers were amazed at our presence, which was a tremendous encouragement for them. To witness their love for the Lord Jesus was a moving experience. It seemed like a page out of the New Testament, because their love and concern for one another was so evident.

We were introduced by Laban Jjumba, who asked us to bring a

word of greeting. After both of us spoke there was prolonged applause. We felt a special bond of love.

We had been spiritually strengthened during the service, and left reluctantly. That afternoon and evening many of the brethren came for sharing and fellowship. Some of them walked many miles because they didn't have the luxury of even a bicycle.

Monday morning after breakfast, I sat on the patio of the guest house reflecting on all that we had learned since arriving in Uganda—the persecution, the miracles, the victorious faith, the joy, the love and concern. "Yes," I thought, "this is like a chapter out of the Book of Acts." Suddenly, the click of the latch on the iron gate leading into the garden broke into my thoughts. Coming in was a slightly built young man. There seemed to be something special about him.

As he came toward me, I rose to greet him. He said, "I am Jothum Mutebi." I asked him to repeat his name, since it sounded to me as if it was Joe and then thumb. I could scarcely conceal the smile on my face. In all seriousness he explained it was not Joe Thumb, but Jothum. That was my confusing introduction to one of the most gentle, loving Christians I have ever met. We felt an immediate bond of fellowship. I was amazed that after imprisonment and torture he had such gentleness of spirit and a compassion marking him as a man with a special anointing and a genuine Christ-like spirit.

Pastor Mutebi took up the story of the attack on the Makerere Church. He said, "We had decided to re-open the church that had been closed by the authorities, and as we were worshiping, suddenly the church was surrounded by soldiers in full battle dress with automatic weapons, including a heavy machine gun, which was mounted outside. We were shocked when the soldiers stormed into the church, firing their automatics as they came into the building." Mutebi went on to tell us that even though the church was packed, miraculously no one was shot. However, the musical instruments and the beautiful new church organ, as well as many pews, were completely destroyed under the continued pressure of automatic fire.

"We were herded outside and made to lie down on top of each other, the very old and very young were weeded out, but still about two hundred believers were forced into trucks and rushed off to prison. I knew this could be the end. When we arrived at the prison, I and the other leaders were separated and beaten without mercy."

He told of the plan to pour gasoline over the group, and of the vice-president's accident, which apparently saved them.

Pastor Mutebi promised me he would return to the guest house for prayer and more fellowship, then left as quickly as he had arrived.

I was astounded at the courage and faith of these believers. One testimony Mutebi shared with us on a subsequent visit was that of the sister who worked in the police headquarters. She used her position to take messages, even food, to the imprisoned believers. She also smuggled letters out to anxious relatives. If caught, she would undoubtedly have faced a horrible death at the hands of the secret police. Even now her name must remain secret.

Then there were the two brethren, Paul and Vincent, who insisted on driving us to Entebbe Airport on our departure. At great risk to themselves they insisted on accompanying us into the terminal building. We managed to get the last two seats on Sabena's flight to Nairobi.

When I asked these two men if they were worried, Paul replied, "The angels of the Lord are watching over us and we have nothing to fear." I knew as our plane took off that I must do everything possible to assist the church in Uganda, and that one day I would return.

Back in Nairobi, I was surprised when the telephone rang. The call was from Paul in Kampala. He said he was calling on behalf of the Christians, to make sure that, after they had left us to go through customs, we had gotten out of the country safely. They knew that many people had disappeared before actually boarding an aircraft.

As I later shared this story of courage and faith with Dan Wooding, my writer friend, we both vowed that when it was possible, we would go to Uganda and get the inside story of the *Uganda holocaust*—a chapter of church history that will never be forgotten.

12

The Ban Against Christian Groups

ARMED WITH A BIBLE, a series of Scripture studies, and sheets of postage stamps, an American Baptist missionary infiltrated the ranks of Amin's soldiers with the gospel.

The Rev. Webster Carroll, a missionary with the Southern Baptist Convention since July, 1963, had a tough decision to make when the president banned the 126 Baptist churches in Uganda. His dilemma was: Should he quit the country like many other expatriate missionaries, or remain and continue his ministry in low profile? He chose the latter.

In 1974, the same year that Janani Luwum was crowned archbishop, Amin announced his initial ban on some of the free church denominations. This meant that these independent Christian churches could no longer meet. In September, 1977, he announced the second ban, this time banning twenty-seven groups. He guaranteed freedom of worship through only four recognized religions—Islam, the Church of Uganda (Anglican), the Roman Catholic Church, and the Orthodox Church.

When the second ban went into effect, the Baptists were no longer permitted to conduct services. This decision led Webster Carroll into a new ministry. Amin's decision meant that many soldiers in his army were given an opportunity to learn about Jesus. They had been taught to hate, but now Carroll was able to show them how to love.

However, he was determined that his ministry should be law abiding. So Mr. Carroll made an appointment with Mr. Oguli, the Chief Education Officer in Kampala, and turned up at his office armed with the five textbooks for his "Bible Way Correspondence School."

"I wanted him to read them carefully and confirm that there was nothing sectarian in the lesson material," the dedicated missionary says in his smooth Southern drawl. "It was a very simple, general, Bible knowledge course which I believed was acceptable to all the churches of different denominations.

"Immediately, the Chief Education Officer turned to me and said, 'Mr. Carroll, I am a member of the Church of Uganda and I took my university work in America at the University of Kansas. I attended a Southern Baptist church near the campus and I know what you Baptists believe. I'm satisfied that you are not engaged in any subversive activities. I will therefore just consider this as a school and not missionary work as such.'"

It was a tremendous break for Webster Carroll who, so as to cause no offense, blocked out any reference to the word *Baptist* in the lesson books.

"We never used a word of advertising, and yet we continued to grow. The only promotion was by word of mouth, and we grew so much that we soon had about 650 students enrolled across the country. What was most interesting to us was that many of those students used one of the Uganda army military barracks as a return address. So even during the time of the ban, we felt we were able to have a Christian witness ministry by means of this Bible correspondence course."

Besides being a "third column" for the gospel into Amin's army bases, this missionary, who would not be cowed by the Ugandan leader, also opened up a low-key ministry of encouragement and comfort to the families of the victims of Amin and his murderers.

"This was a time when hundreds were being killed, and people would often say to me, 'Has God forgotten us? Why are we suffering as we are?' I visited the homes of many widows of those who had been murdered. All I could do was to give them hope. I prayed with them and emphasized that God is still in control. I stated that although they could not now understand why there was so much suffering and killing going on, God in His time would certainly bring the curtain down on this evil. God would bring peace again in our land.

"I was glad to reach out to the people in this situation. I never felt, after the ban, that God had prohibited me from having a ministry. God had called me to preach, but I felt so definitely that even though I was not permitted to speak publicly any more, God was giving me an opportunity to minister to individuals. I found just as much satisfaction out of that, during those Amin years, as in a public ministry.

"I'll always be grateful to the Lord for letting me stay in Uganda during those tragic years, and giving me the opportunity to serve Him in what little ways I could."

Being a Bible-believing Christian, Mr. Carroll felt he could do another important work in Uganda—helping to distribute Bibles throughout the land. In 1977, the year the Church of Uganda courageously celebrated its centenary despite the time of uncertainty, the Bible Society launched a worldwide appeal for $300,000 (US) to send 150,000 Good News Bibles into Uganda.

And as these volumes continued to pour into the Kampala headquarters of the Bible Society of Uganda, Mr. Carroll and his associate, James Rice (who was the mission treasurer/business manager and whose wife Linda helped conduct the correspondence school) offered their services in distributing the Scriptures throughout Uganda.

"We did so because they did not have any vehicles operating," said Mr. Carroll. "So we would load up our Land-Rover and take Bibles to every corner of the country.

"We were extremely concerned about the Bibles being distributed during those difficult years. This gave us a tremendous sense of service and ministry.

"It was particularly inspiring for me to realize that the one spot which seemingly had the greatest hunger for the Word of God was the West Nile. We made three trips from Kampala, loaded with Bibles and other Scriptures, to Arua, the administrative town in that district which is Amin's home.

"We couldn't keep enough Bibles up there. As soon as we could take another load they would be sold in the Church of Uganda bookshop within two or three days.

"So we always felt confident, even though our particular churches were banned, that as long as we could have a hand in distributing Bibles, we were actively engaged in missionary work. We were particularly grateful to God for giving us this wonderful opportunity."

Mr. Carroll says that in 1973 Amin's Ministry of Religious Affairs had urged the Southern Baptist Convention to merge with the Conservative Baptists, another American group working in the country. Both sides agreed.

"We feel that this was one very marked advantage that came to us during the Amin years," says Mr. Carroll. "We merged into the Baptist Union of Uganda. The two missions still exist in name only, so as to liaison with their mission boards and headquarters in the States, but that is all."

When the ban finally came, Webster Carroll paid an urgent visit to the Ministry of Religious Affairs. "The permanent secretary there, Mrs. Christine Tumubweine, assured me that the ban was against the churches only, not against individuals and expatriates, and that we were permitted to stay and engage in social services. So I felt very definitely guided of the Lord to stay and do what I could as a means of encouragement to our people

"She assured me that I could engage in social services of any kind, so I began to do more to enlarge an activity which I had started some two years previously. That was grafting citrus trees and trying to get as many orange trees planted in the village home compounds as possible, to be of some help to the nutritional needs of our people.

"I got a lot of personal satisfaction and also had a lot of fun doing it. It gave me the opportunity to visit our pastors and people and encourage them on a day-to-day basis."

As he traveled around the country, Carroll came to learn of the persecution of some of the Baptist pastors.

"Pastor Jackson from Bwamba, an area behind the Mountains of the Moon near the Zaire border, was beaten twice," says Carroll. "One Sunday morning his entire congregation was arrested by the local chief and taken to a public place in the village, where the pastor was beaten twice with a hippopotamus-skin whip. He came through it with a glowing testimony of his faith in the Lord."

DANGER WAS SOMETHING that Pastor Ponsiano Lwakatale also learned to live with. He was the supervisor of 165 Gospel Mission to Uganda churches in Ankole, Toro, and Kigezi, and was constantly living on a knife-edge.

After already being arrested twice, the Christian leader thanked God for his survival. He then continued his hazardous ministry to the underground believers of his large district.

On February 15, 1977, he was gathering with more than twenty people from the local church, when suddenly a sub-county chief arrived at the house with about forty howling followers. Each was armed with spears, pangas, and sticks. They began banging on the door and a pastor let them in.

"We have come to arrest you for holding an unlawful meeting," said the seething chief, armed with a spear and a panga knife.

"I told the angry chief that I had come to explain to these people about the ban and how they could obey the law," says Pastor Lwakatale. "I said they had no information on what has been happening, and so we leaders couldn't just leave them without telling them what they should do."

But the chief was not pacified. He screamed, "You Christians are giving us a hard time." Then without warning he lifted up his spear to kill the supervisor. "But somehow," says Pastor Lwakatale, "God held back his hand and he was powerless to spear me. No matter how hard he tried, he could not bring his arm down." As this was going on, the believers in the room were in silent prayer.

"I am convinced that God did a miracle," says Pastor Lwakatale.

Finally, after a strong warning, the chief told the pastor to leave the area and not return. And as the supervisor headed to his home in Masaka, he had a wry smile on his face.

He tells us: "What the chief didn't know was that I was also teaching them tricks they could use in their underground meetings, like having a cup of tea or coffee in their hands all the time so that if anyone discovered them they wouldn't look too suspicious.

"Of course, I was teaching them to obey the government, but I didn't tell the chief that I was also teaching them these other things."

ANOTHER GROUP of arrested believers were turned into slaves by local chiefs. Most of the eighteen who were taken into custody were pastors with the Gospel Mission to Uganda. The interruption of their house gathering was in the Bulemezi district some forty miles north of Kampala. "We were having supper when at about 8:30 P.M. we heard knocking on the door," says Pastor Wilson Sentongo, leader of the Senga church.

"When we opened the door, these men came rushing in, wielding panga knives and clubs. They tied us up and took us to a small house and began to threaten us.

"Next day they forced us to work as slaves picking coffee in the chief's garden. The chief told us that if we did a good job, he would let us go, but he deceived us and took us to the parish chief's office.

"After that we were taken to a prison which was just like a latrine, with urine all over the floor and no ventilators in the cells.

"Each day the rest of our group were sent out as slaves and made to dig holes and cultivate a garden. Police guarded them the whole time. But they wouldn't let me go because I was the leader of the church and they thought I might try to escape."

The group was constantly threatened with violent death. Then suddenly, after eighty days, they were summoned before the district commissioner, who told them they were free to leave.

"You are all confused, but go now and be good citizens," he said.

Did they call a halt to their underground services? "Certainly not," says Pastor Sentongo.

ONE ENCOURAGING SIDE EFFECT of the ban against Christian groups was the Church of Uganda's generosity in helping other churches in their time of need.

Webster Carroll says, "Immediately after the ban was pronounced and our Baptist churches were closed, Archbishop Wani and some of his bishops made a very definite point of opening their arms to us. They shared their sympathies and made sure that we understood that they would welcome people to worship with them in local churches around the country. And should they decide to become members of the Church of Uganda, they would be graciously received.

"Now this meant a great deal to us. First of all it was a clear indication of Christian charity and unity of the faith. We just cannot express to God enough gratitude for His Grace, Archbishop Wani, his bishops and pastors around the country, for their fellowship and love during this ban."

Carroll reveals that during early 1978, Baptist and Salvation Army leaders were called to the office of the archbishop who, along with a group of his bishops, said that an approach would be made to President Amin to lift the ban. The archbishop had gone on record as saying that the ban was "not in the interests of the Kingdom of God."

The approach was in vain. So then the archbishop said they were prepared to ask President Amin that Baptist churches be allowed to function as normal, but without the name Baptist being used. They would then come under the umbrella of the Church of Uganda.

Again, the dictator would not agree, but about fifteen Baptist churches continued to meet in their own buildings in small villages whose chiefs were Christians.

"The chiefs knew that they were not politically motivated and were not subversive in their activities. So they continued meeting for worship, but on a much smaller scale," says Carroll.

"However, the great majority of our people simply began worshiping with the Church of Uganda, and we felt that if individuals or congregations decided that the Lord was leading them into the Anglican community, we would accept this with joy, feeling that it was His will at that particular time."

Fellowship was so good between the two Christian denominations in Bugiri, a town fifty miles from Jinja, that two of the Baptist pastors there were invited to preach regularly in Church of Uganda pulpits.

But probably the most astonishing gesture by the Anglican archbishop was the assurance he gave to "his" Baptists that they could continue practicing baptism by immersion—something that has been a bone of contention between the two groups for years. (The Anglicans practice child baptism.)

"We felt that this was a tremendous gesture of love and unity as they sought to open their arms to us," says Carroll.

And on the subject of baptism by immersion, another of the banned groups, the Redeemed Church, not only continued this practice with its converts, but carried it out *at the bottom of Idi Amin's garden* in Entebbe. The new converts were baptized in water at the back of Cape Town View, a large house on the shores of Lake Victoria which Amin took over in 1975 from an English businessman.

In charge was Pastor Peter Sozi, who had been forced to leave his university science studies. He found himself being called to take charge of the Redeemed Church's fellowships after its leaders had left the country for various reasons.

"Because we had nowhere to baptize believers after going underground, we decided to go to Lake Victoria and there, behind Amin's house at Entebbe, we baptized eighty-two people in one session," says this Christian leader, who is in his early twenties.

"On another occasion thirty people were baptized in Lake Victoria. Through all of this we trusted God that the authorities would not find out what we had been doing. Local chiefs there knew what was going on, and they tried to stop us, but when they saw the power of the Holy Spirit in our lives, they decided to leave us alone."

THE REDEEMED CHURCH had five underground groups in Kampala, all meeting in homes. They had names like Jerusalem, Decapola, and Kabowa. And among the believers were a group of local policemen from Katwe police station.

"They would sometimes even bring people to our underground fellowships for prayer, and they would tip us off when there was the possibility of a raid," says Pastor Sozi.

However, the police believers couldn't be everywhere, and raids on Redeemed Church underground meetings did take place. During one raid, one of Amin's men rushed in and tripped. His gun went off and he shot himself. The police decided to leave quickly.

On another occasion, though, a Christian policeman did intervene. It happened when members of a Redeemed Church congregation in Makerere were found praying. They faced death for "conspiracy against the government." But a Christian policeman heard of their case and told his colleague, who had made the mass arrest, that there was no law against praying to God. They were released.

WEBSTER CARROLL speaks of an incident in early 1978 at the end of the regime. "Pastor Nicodemus of Mbale was arrested and taken to the local police station. Amin's men had found a cassette tape player in his home and, of course, these illiterate men claimed that this was definite proof he was having contact with the 'American Imperialists' whose purpose was to overthrow the government. So they arrested him.

"A military man ordered the commanding officer of the Mbale police to take him to Makindye Barracks in Kampala, one of Amin's horrible execution barracks from which very few people returned.

"But when the CO called the prisoner in to be taken to Kampala, he discovered that it was Nicodemas, his own brother-in-law. He knew him to be a man of God who was without political motivation and intention, and so he released him."

Carroll adds: "As far as I know, not one of our Baptist people was killed during that time."

The cassette player that Pastor Nicodemus had been caught with was part of another ministry in which Webster Carroll was involved. It had started in 1977, when the Uganda Baptist Church purchased about one hundred tape players.

"Our purpose was to distribute them among our pastors so that we could keep a lending library of cassette Bible studies and sermons for our people to listen to.

"We had stocked our library with a lot of Swahili language tapes, which we had purchased from a radio ministry in Tanzania. These were produced by the Anglican church, and were wonderful Bible tapes as well as sermons. We had lots of English language Bible studies and tapes.

"We had altogether about five hundred tapes in our library and most of them were from America. We used messages from American pastors who had a very simple English delivery and whose vocabulary would not be too difficult for our people in Uganda to understand.

"When the ban came, we felt no hesitation in placing these tape players and tapes as we had originally planned. They went mainly to Baptists, but we had a close fellowship with many Anglican pastors, who also received them free of charge.

"We were thrilled with the demand. I suppose we had about fifty tape players throughout the country, and some of these tapes literally wore out through constant use.

"We also placed many of these recorders in secondary schools. We found a faculty member who was a keen Christian, and he would keep the tapes available for students and staff.

"We had several tapes from British Bible teacher Major Ian Thomas, which were an extreme blessing to our people."

IN THOSE TRAUMATIC DAYS for the church in Uganda, age was no bar to being a leader. Seventeen-year-old "Brother Grace" became pastor of the "Holiness to God" underground church, which was linked to the Gospel Mission to Uganda.

While many of his brothers and sisters from the Makerere church were in custody, this teen-ager, who had been a Christian for only a year, had to assume a role of leadership in that house fellowship.

Wearing a shirt with the slogan, "Jesus is the Way," he tells us: "It was a big responsibility, because I had to know the special needs of the believers. I also had to practice not only the theology of Christianity, but also the social and practical side as well.

"We used to meet on Sunday for worship, on Wednesday evening for fasting and prayer, and on Thursday night we would have a Bible study and testimony meeting. It was a time when we all had to encourage each other.

"God gave me His wisdom, and I learned to fast and pray as I studied the Word, so that God would anoint my ministry."

FOR THOSE COURAGEOUS BELIEVERS who refused to bow to Amin's threats, the fear of arrest and violent death was very real. Pastor John Byamungu, who led the Gospel Mission to Uganda Church in a village in Masaka district, tells what happened to his group on January 27, 1978.

"We were meeting and worshiping God when local chiefs burst into the service and arrested us. They told us we were being charged with worshiping in a banned church," he says. "All the children in the church with us were left behind. They were aged between five and fourteen. They had to feed themselves in the bush for six days."

"There were twenty-nine Christians in the church when they came. They bound our hands behind our backs and then took us all off to the nearby administrative headquarters. There we were made to crawl on our knees as they beat us with sticks on the body and head. The believers were also forced to kneel down and hold heavy bricks in their hands for hours on end.

"Then the group was taken by military police, armed with rifles, to the nearby police station. While I was under arrest, men from the village raided and looted my home."

After being held for six days—during which time they prayed and preached to other prisoners—a judge heard the case against them and sent them home, saying they must return in a month's time.

Then Pastor Byamungu urgently felt he should visit the Makerere church to share with them the difficulties they were facing. He did so, but chose a bad time. He spoke to the packed church and had just taught the six-hundred-strong congregation a new song that fateful day when the soldiers began shooting. With many others, this longsuffering churchman was taken to Nakasero. While there, the Christian leader and his fellow prisoners were nearly burned alive in the sickening gasoline incident described in the first chapter of this book. Later Byamungu was taken to the Central Police Station and then to Luzira Prison, where each Christian prisoner was bludgeoned five times with a heavy stick.

After about three months, along with some of the others from Makerere, he was freed. The guard said: "Go back and do your work, but don't be confused by this religion brought in by the CIA."

When he finally arrived back in Masaka, the three chiefs who had arrested him and his congregation called him to see them. The chiefs told him that he had to leave his house within six days. He went to live in Masaka and was called with two other pastors to see the police commissioner. As the police chief hadn't yet arrived from the capital, they were detained, and spent one day in a police cell and then another in prison.

On the third day, when the commissioner had finally made it, they were taken to the Masaka Town Hall to meet the three local heads of religion—Church of Uganda, Roman Catholic, and Moslem—and told them that they must choose one of these religions. The prisoners stood quietly and made no comment. Suddenly they were released and no further action was taken against them or the others who were previously arrested.

Amin's persecution not only failed to destroy the churches, but actually strengthened them and drew them together in true unity in the body of Christ.

13

An Army for God

"I FOUND THE UGANDANS so friendly and willing to help," says Australian-born Brigadier Stella Bywaters, referring to her arrival in Uganda in 1962—thirty-one years after the Salvation Army had first started there. She had left her missionary work in Tanzania to run the Wandegeya Hostel for Handicapped Persons in Kampala, and became head of Social Services there.

"I think difficulties had drawn them together," she continues, "and they were more willing to help than any other group I had met. For instance, during my whole time in Uganda I was never stuck on the road without somebody coming to my aid."

She said that Amin's seizure of power from Obote did not at first affect the Salvation Army.

"Actually Amin called all the leaders of the church together and promised them complete freedom of preaching."

Trouble began for the "Army" in 1974 when Amin announced his initial ban on some free church denominations. However, despite the fact that the Army was not banned, some people had mistakenly assumed they were and began persecuting them.

"Our Entebbe Salvationists were the first to suffer," says Brigadier Bywaters. "They were marching to a memorial service in Kampala one Sunday morning, just after the first ban, when they were attacked and beaten up by a mob."

There was so much confusion about who was or who was not banned that, in the end, Brigadier Bywaters went to the Ministry of Religious Affairs to obtain the full list of "illegal" churches, and show people that the Salvation Army was still allowed to function freely.

After the second ban in 1977, Stella Bywaters began holding unofficial services at the hostel.

"When we had that first meeting, one of my colleagues got terrified and said, 'No music.' I said, 'Come on, we're not going to hide.'

"Then I invited the Salvationists who used to attend our Kampala Corps to visit us for Christmas. I had asked them to come and worship with us on Sundays, but they were a bit afraid. However, they did come over for Christmas celebrations. After that they came regularly, Sunday after Sunday."

Was Stella Bywaters frightened that first time? "My heart didn't know any fear then, but I was afraid for our people in case they suffered," she says. "So I used to watch the road through a window to see who was coming."

On that opening Sunday she even spotted a traffic policeman standing at the back of the house where the meeting was held, but despite the noise, he did not intervene.

As the numbers began to increase for the revived services, finding room to squeeze in all those who arrived became a real problem. "I used to wake up and say, 'Now Lord, if you don't want us to meet today, then let it rain.' There was only one wet Sunday during the whole time and that turned out to be a blessing in disguise as it prevented too many from coming in the morning. There were some up from Nairobi and I don't think we would have all fit into that little dining room. For those who couldn't attend in the morning, we had another big meeting in the afternoon."

Those meetings, says Brigadier Bywaters, were attended by an incredible range of people, from the handicapped to students, refugees, and even murderers.

Stella Bywaters, like some other Salvationists in Uganda, continued wearing her uniform, but with all the badges taken off. However, she kept the Salvation Army insignia on her car.

"We had no flag, but yet we still sang out of the banned Salvation Army songbook and we enrolled people under the Bible. I remember one occasion when we had a big group from Nairobi, including the Salvation Army commissioner and the chief secretary. We held an enrollment service and a dedication service christening."

That chief secretary was Lieutenant Colonel Stanley Walter, a Canadian who heads up the Salvation Army's Nairobi office. He told us how he always wore his uniform on visits to Uganda. "I wouldn't go without it," he says.

"I was going to see our Salvation Army social centers, and if the opportunity came to encourage the Salvationists while we were there, we did just that. We had a normal service—we had our songbooks and I preached the Scripture just as I would at any church."

During one trip, Lieutenant Walter visited Mrs. Christine Tumubweine, permanent secretary at the Ministry of Religious Affairs. The church itself had been banned for eight months, but now the Army was told it must abandon its social work.

"We told her we were disappointed at having to leave," he says. Did he register a strong protest with the Permanent Secretary? "You don't make protests about someone like President Amin . . . well, only to a point," he reports. "If he says, 'You're banned, you're *banned!*'"

Brigadier Bywaters knew that one day the Salvation Army could be discovered, because the ruthless Amin used to plant spies in church services across the land.

"The trouble was that I could never spot them," she says. "However, I know I never preached politics, but just gave them a good gospel message.

"State Research people surrounded us. They would often stand outside and shine their lights into our dining room on Sunday nights as we were having our time of singing. We really made beautiful noise unto the Lord and didn't care whether it was out of tune or not.

She adds: "I never felt any personal fear. If they had wanted to kill me, I was ready to live or to die."

Sometimes Stella Bywaters, like many other ex-patriate missionaries in the country, was harassed, "One time in 1976 my house was searched for gold," she recalls. "Some men came in without any authority to search the house and I told them, 'I have nothing to hide. The only gold I have is in my tooth.'"

The men, who claimed they were from the government, came back again, and this time she expressed her indignation. "Do you think that if I had gold in this house I'd be begging and pleading for money to help these people here?" she shouted.

"They then wanted to know what was in some of the baskets in the house. 'You don't believe a word I say,' I said. 'I told you that I have nothing but the gold in my tooth. Now, if you want to know what's in

166 / Uganda Holocaust

there, get up and get it yourself because I'm not going to.' All the
men found was a heap of dust.''

Brigadier Bywaters made an official protest to the Ministry of
Internal Affairs via the Ministry of Religious Affairs, and an ambush
was laid for these unofficial gold diggers, but they never turned up
again.

Stella Bywaters didn't usually "pull rank" on people, but she once
did so to good effect after being flagged down by some policemen.
They told her she had committed a traffic offense by towing another
vehicle. She knew that the officers wanted a bribe. They threatened to
take her to a notorious police station, where people were regularly
killed.

"After this man had finished snapping and snarling, he told me to
write down my full name and address," says Brigadier Bywaters. "I
didn't then use my rank in Uganda, but I did on that occasion.
Obviously he was impressed, and I then said calmly, 'It is a shame to
drag the Salvation Army through the mud, isn't it? Especially since I
was acting in complete ignorance. We are law-abiding citizens who
teach our people to do the same.' Finally he said, 'Oh, I think I'll let
you off this time, but next time it will be a six hundred shilling
fine.' ''

On another occasion, Stella Bywaters' rank saved a Salvation
Army old people's home from the Moslem Supreme Council. After
the Asians had been expelled from the country, the council had gone
around Uganda seizing properties which they had owned. Unfortunately, the council took over an old people's cottage on the edge of
the capital and painted their name on the outside of it.

On the advice of the Ministry of Religious Affairs, Miss Bywaters
decided personally to tackle the Council. "I took somebody with me
and my one prayer was, 'Lord, please don't let me get a military man
to talk to.' But to my consternation, when I was shown into this
lovely big room at their headquarters, there was an officer in full
military uniform.

"So I said quietly to the Lord, 'Now help me.' I walked up to the
soldier and said, 'Brigadier Bywaters.' He immediately rose to his
feet and saluted! I nearly laughed, but I was able to restrain myself
and I said, 'You have taken over our old people's cottage.' Then I
showed him our papers proving ownership. He apologized and then
pressed a bell. He told the man who came that the home was still ours.

"I said to him, 'From one soldier to another, from one Army to another, thank you.' I was so amused when he again stood up and saluted! And when I got outside and was safely in the car and out of earshot, I laughed and laughed. It was so funny.''

A surprising supporter of the Salvation Army's work was Amin's British-born aide, Major Bob Astles. He always spoke up for the "Army." On the night of the banning, when Stella Bywaters and her colleagues were feeling sick and didn't know which way to turn next, Astles phoned her and said, "I've just learned that your work is banned. His Excellency doesn't want this. I've just left him and I'm confident he doesn't know anything about it. Now I'm going straight back to see him, and I want you to continue with your social work. I can't do anything for your church work, but I can do something for the social work.''

So through this strange man's intervention, Stella Bywaters was able to press on with her important work for a further nine months. "We carried on exactly in the same spirit. The only difference was that we had no insignias on our uniforms.''

Stella Bywaters believes that Amin had not properly thought through the ban. "I don't think he actually pulled names out of a hat, but he thought that there should be only four churches left and all the rest should go,'' she says. "I am sure he didn't consider who they were. It probably was dependent on the mood he was in at that moment. He could be in a good mood one moment, and a foul one five minutes later.

"When I discovered we were banned, I was completely bewildered. Our place became like a railway station. Everybody was coming in to sympathize, and phone calls came from all over the world. It got so bad that I took the phone off the hook for two nights so I could have some peace, because people would call up at the most unearthly hours. All we seemed to do was make cups of tea for visitors who had come to say how sorry they were.''

Brigadier Bywaters admits there were many tight spots and times when she was inwardly apprehensive. "Every time we were stopped at a roadblock, the Lord was with me and I always managed to get through. Perspiration would be on my upper lip, but because I showed no fear I was able to meet them on their own ground. It was necessary for me to ascertain what sort of mood they were in. When they were in a good mood, I would laugh with them, and when they were in a bad mood, then I would speak straight to them.''

When a soldier would come over at a roadblock, Miss Bywaters would always smile, salute, and say, ''From one Army to another.'' Naturally, that usually went down well with the illiterate military men.

One of the most hair-raising experiences she had was at a roadblock on the day Amin had decided to publicly execute a man in Kampala—one of twelve around the country—and troops were rounding up people to watch.

''I decided it was the day I should go and pick up a wrecked car that had been repaired,'' she says. ''We were driving along—I had some others with me—and to my horror we approached a roadblock where people were being beaten up, apparently for not paying tax.'' The situation looked serious for Brigadier Bywaters and her friends, but she thought quickly.

''I noticed the man in front of me handing his log [car registration] book to the man at the roadblock. So when a soldier with a machine gun over his shoulder came to me, I said, 'Good morning, my friend. I suppose this is what you want.' I had asked the people with me to let me do the talking. He handed the log book back to me and then turned to those in the back, and said to them, 'Where are your tax cards?' I explained to the man that one was a probation officer, another a patient at our hostel. He said, 'Well, go then.' I am sure that if they had been on their own, they would have had a terrible time.''

Naturally Stella Bywaters trusted the Lord at all times but she told us that as an added protection she also carried a cap gun, a pepper pot, and a screwdriver in her car. ''The idea was that if someone put his head through a window he faced either the screwdriver or the pepper pot in his face,'' she explains.

Often thieves used a ''phony-drunk'' routine to rob unsuspecting people. ''I remember one night, coming back from the British High Commission, I observed some people staggering in the middle of the road as if they were drunk. The police had warned us that if that happened we should never stop, and if we hit them we should report it. I was going uphill when I saw these men and my heart thumped. So I changed gear and speeded up, and I've never seen so-called drunk people sober up so quickly and move out of the way.''

Brigadier Bywaters met Idi Amin on several occasions. ''The first time was when he was out of favor with Obote, before he seized power for himself. He was then Colonel Amin and he came to our sale of goods and stayed an hour. When I saw him I wasn't sure how to speak to him. I said, 'Good afternoon. We're very happy to see you here.' And he went into the dining room with his wife and a couple of children and had tea.''

After he became president, Amin invited Brigadier Bywaters to a special lunch at Cape Town Villas, one of his residences. "I was the only one at our table that he spoke to. After a short chat, when I explained briefly what we did, he said he was pleased with our work, and thanked me very much for it. Then he moved on. I was amazed he should stop to speak to me. I think he had a special feeling for the Salvation Army."

She adds: "However, after shaking hands with him I felt like washing my hands because they were so blood stained."

In 1976, Idi Amin gave Stella Bywaters one of his top awards—the Independence Medal, for meritorious service to Uganda. Why does she think Amin rewarded her with this medal? "He had a respect for the Army in some way or another," she says. "I think he also had a feeling for handicapped people. He wasn't worrying about the church or the spiritual work we did. He forgot we didn't do it just with our hands . . . we did it also with our hearts."

The Salvation Army work in Uganda consisted of seventeen churches and fourteen outposts [smaller churches]. There was also the Kampala hostel for the handicapped and a children's home in Tororo, 130 miles from Kampala, near the Kenya border.

Before she was finally forced to flee the country she loved so much, Brigadier Bywaters stayed with a brave Kenyan couple—the Ireris in Tororo. They told her, "We are not going to walk out, run out, or even crawl out . . . we're going with our heads up."

Brigadier Bywaters felt that despite the terrible slaughter around them, God had put the blood on their door post, as in Old Testament times. "Amin's men were searching from house to house looting and beating people up, but the house where we were staying was passed over.

"I do feel that this happened in many Christian homes throughout Uganda. I know, however, that after the archbishop died, many believers were cruelly persecuted. Though a tragedy, his death consolidated the Christian work in Uganda . . . so his dying was not in vain."

Sometimes the Salvation Army received help in unexpected ways. Amin's regime became so hated that even the most ardent non-Christians went as far as killing to protect the persecuted believers' right to worship freely.

In Wambingwa, Eastern Uganda, a group of Salvationists carried on worshiping in secret, probably in the forest, and some of Amin's soldiers were sent to deal with them. They stopped in a nearby village before going in for the believers, and got drunk in a bar there. They had obviously boasted about what they planned to do to the Salvationists. They were killed by villagers as they stumbled out of the primitive bar.

ANOTHER SALVATIONIST who witnessed the problems of his colleagues first hand was Major Paul Latham. During the Tanzanian invasion in 1979, he tells us, Salvationist John Mwalishi of Kigumba was determined that Amin's soldiers would not be allowed to use his farm tractor to grow food for themselves. So he took the vehicle apart piece by piece and hid it away in different parts of the forest. Major Latham says, "When Amin's army had finally fled the area, John went back around the forest to collect the hidden pieces, and it is now reassembled and working again."

Latham, an agriculturist who works in the planning and development department at the Army's international headquarters in London, England, went to the country to encourage the Young Farmers of Uganda program, which he helped set up in 1976. It is organized along with World Vision International, and assists hundreds involved in animal husbandry and agriculture.

"The idea is to uplift the young people of Uganda with help in food growing, bee keeping, and sunflower production," says Major Latham. "Most of them already have their own plots of land.

"I was trying to encourage these people, who, during those years, had been so resourceful. I think they can already teach other countries to be resourceful."

When the ban of the Army came, many of Uganda's Salvationists who belonged to the country's corps [churches] went underground —literally. They buried their uniforms, flags, and hymnals in metal boxes, anticipating the day when Amin would be overthrown and they could worship publicly again.

"They had to get rid of all evidence that they belonged to the

Army, and they either buried the things or sent them across the border by one of the unofficial routes," says Major Latham.

The British Salvationist who made a two-thousand-kilometer tour of Uganda after Amin's fall also told us of one particularly inventive "soldier."

"This chap buried his uniform outside his home and then built up a mound of earth to make it appear that it was a grave. To complete the illusion, he put a cross on the top."

The ruse worked, and he was later able to "exhume" his uniform and is now wearing it again.

Major Latham saw living proof of the success of the great "cover-up" when over eight hundred Salvationists marched through the town of Bombo.

Captain Joseph Waswa of the Salvation Army's Nairobi office also witnessed the march. He says, "They had dug up their uniforms, flags, books, and Bibles, and proudly marched along shouting praises to God for their deliverance and new-found freedom.

"The huge crowd also sang in Swahili a song about how the war against Amin had been won and how he had left the country."

Captain Nathan Nsango, another Kenyan from the Nairobi office, says, "It was a very emotional meeting, full of joy, clapping and singing and praising God."

Major Latham addressed an open air meeting in Bombo's market square, a service made even more poignant because it was held on the spot of the death of one of the Army's first martyrs—Joseph Mukhana, the Bombo Corps treasurer who had been killed three days before. He was gunned down by one of Amin's troops. Latham says, "I felt particularly privileged to be preaching on the very spot where a man gave his life, and I thought of how Jesus gave His life for us."

During his sermon, Major Latham spoke of Gamaliel's words to the council when he said, "For if this plan or action should be of men, it will be overthrown; but if it is of God, you will not be able to overthrow them; or else you may even be found fighting against God" (Acts 5:38–39). The Salvation Army in Uganda, he affirms, is of God.

14

The Underground Church

"WHERE ARE YOU EMPLOYED?" I asked Ben Oluka, the young Christian I met during my 1978 visit [writes Ray Barnett].

"The President's Office," he replied. The impact of what he said seemed to explode in my brain. Doubtfully, I asked, "You mean Idi Amin's office?" "Yes," said Oluka, matter-of-factly, "The President's Office for Religious Affairs."

As Oluka continued, I was even more amazed. "The orders for the banning of the churches and so forth are, in fact, enforced out of my office." I learned that Oluka was immediately under the permanent secretary, and as such was a senior civil servant. Little did the people in that office, or the State Research Bureau officers, realize that Oluka was one of the outstanding leaders of the underground church.

We visited Ben Oluka again. We went to see him at his new office at the Ministry of Information, Kampala. Because of the lack of transportation following the invasion, Obed Rubaiza, one of the leaders of the Makerere Church who had been imprisoned, took us there in two bumpy journeys on the back of his little Honda motorcycle. During each trip he had to stop for inspection at roadblocks, but we got through. We must have looked a strange sight to those soldiers as we jolted along on the back of the tiny machine.

The ministry building was guarded by Tanzanian militiamen and we noticed with a smile that the army youth who eventually waved us through had a hand grenade attached to his belt. Fortunately, the pin was still in it. Beside the entrance to the building lay a crumpled pile of hundreds of military camouflage uniforms abandoned by Amin's troops when Kampala fell.

In his office, Ben Oluka speaks of his undercover work on behalf of the Ugandan church. Ben was senior assistant secretary in the Department of Religious Affairs in Amin's office. "The department was set up so the government could control the religious sects and coordinate the activities of the religious organizations in the country," says Oluka, leaning back in his chair.

"It was really established for a bad reason, because the government felt these groups were collaborating with Imperialists and Zionists."

The department, says Oluka, also dealt with permits for resident missionaries in the country.

"After the ban in September, 1977, it became very difficult for me. I found I had to deal with some delicate cases which concerned members of banned religious sects who were found praying, reading the Bible, or meeting together. In some districts, the believers were forbidden to read the Bible.

"It was up to the local District Commissioner to decide how strictly he would enforce the ban. If the local commissioner was strict and a person was found reading the Bible and praying, that Christian could be arrested. Many were prosecuted for Bible study and prayer. Christians were most severely persecuted in Gulu, Soroti, Mbale, and Lugazi. Some believers from Lugazi were taken to court when they were found walking home from a meeting carrying their Bibles. One of the sisters who was arrested at that time was cruelly raped and became pregnant."

During these difficult years, Ben Oluka had used his influence in the president's office to bring about judgments on cases that probably resulted in many Christian lives being saved throughout Uganda.

But what Idi Amin did not realize was that Ben Oluka was not only doing what he could to assist suffering believers, but was also pastoring an underground church in his own home. It was a small group from the Deliverance Church, an indigenous Ugandan evangelical fellowship.

Oluka says, "At that time, I was working in the office that had to enforce the president's ban, and secretly I was running an underground church myself.

"When the ban was announced, much of the church went immediately underground, and house meetings sprang up throughout the country. There is a higher power, and when government restricts the freedom of worship, God's supremacy has to take over.

"The free churches decided to follow the example of Acts 20:20, where the believers went from house to house breaking bread and worshiping God.

"This was a very trying time because anyone caught in one of these gatherings could easily be taken to the State Research Bureau. Many of the underground churches were given names. Ours was called 'The Hill,' because that's where my home was—on top of a hill.''

What made this even more hazardous for Oluka was the fact that two of his neighbors were State Research personnel.

"So I needed much wisdom," he said. "We even had to avoid clapping our hands in time with the hymns and choruses because of the noise. Occasionally our worship service had to be held in a corridor of my house so we would not be heard outside.

"On Sunday mornings I would telephone my State Research neighbors to find out if they were home. Usually they were away at about 9:00 A.M. and I knew they would not return until between 5:00 and 6:00 in the afternoon. So we had plenty of time for our service.''

Often when a meeting was scheduled and his neighbors were at home, Oluka would invite them to go with him for a long walk in the cool of the evening. Often these strolls would last several hours. By the time they returned, the believers had come and gone.

Another serious problem Oluka had to deal with was a spy sent from State Research to discover what Oluka was up to at his home.

"When I saw him approaching, I would tell the group to hide and not to worship until I said so," says Oluka. "I would then meet him and take him out somewhere. As I left I would signal to my wife to continue the meeting.''

After this particular spy finally admitted defeat, others would attempt to detect any sign of illegal worshiping outside the Oluka house.

"I would watch them through the window, and stop and wait until they drove off. This happened two or three times a week. It was extremely dangerous for all of us. What I was doing was almost like committing suicide, but we were never discovered.''

And all this time, Oluka was on the president's staff supposedly helping to enforce the ban. He served in the Religious Affairs Department under Mrs. Christine Tumubweine, and would often have to plead the case of an arrested group or individual with her.

The most difficult problem he had to deal with, he says, was the mass arrest of the Makerere Gospel Mission to Uganda.

When they were first taken to Nakasero, Oluka immediately called his boss on the phone, but discovered that there was little he could do to intervene. "The following day, a Friday and a public holiday, I asked one of my State Research neighbors to take me to Nakasero to see these people.

"He offered the use of his office and suggested we could call them in one by one. My neighbor told me he had already pleaded for them the previous evening when they had been arrested, but his boss paid no attention."

Before the visit could be arranged, the majority of the group, with the exception of the "ringleaders," were transferred to Luzira Prison. Ben was informed he could not interview the "ringleaders."

He arranged for a Christian sister, who worked in the police headquarters to be a channel for messages, food, and clothing. In so doing, he helped set up an effective line of communication with the imprisoned congregation. He continued to do everything in his power to secure their release.

"I worked hard to negotiate with my boss, who was very cooperative at that time," he says. "But this was difficult, as the detention order had been personally directed by the president and signed by the vice-president, Mustafa Adrisi, who was also the Minister of Internal Affairs.

"I visited the believers later at the prison at Luzira. I could see the joy on their faces as they counted themselves worthy to suffer for the gospel's sake."

Oluka says he had been personally criticized over the imprisonment. "Some people thought I had betrayed them when actually I had been advising them that they should not go in the name of a document (which registered them as a company), but in the name of the Lord Jesus Christ." Oluka felt the congregation should not have met publicly in the church but should have stayed underground.

Oluka describes those tense days as "a very trying time for the church in Uganda." He adds: "It became almost impossible to proclaim the gospel, and people didn't want to accept Christian tracts anymore.

"I would personally give out tracts and people would ignore them or throw them away. Yet it was wonderful to witness for Christ at that time, despite the anti-Christ spirit that was around.

"I was personally ready for martyrdom."

And that was the feeling of tens of thousands of Ugandan believers, regardless of Amin's persecution. They were willing to die for Christ.

ANOTHER UNDERGROUND LEADER at that time was Pastor Nicholas Wafula, the overseer of the Deliverance Church, which started as the Young Christian Ambassador Fellowship. We met this courageous man on that same balcony at the Kampala International Hotel where Ray Barnett and his traveling companion had sat, surrounded by menacing State Research men, the previous September.

Pastor Wafula, a pencil-slim man with a friendly self-assured manner, explains, "In December, 1976, we had already started house fellowships, and so when the ban came we had some of these groups already set up. We would move from house to house, just like the early church. It was very perilous, because the banning order said none of the sects could have more than five of their group together at one time.

"We gave names to the underground house meetings. For instance, we had a branch, on Kira Road, and as the word Kira means Nile, we called it that. We could say to each other, 'Are you going to Nile tonight?' Another brother had a city-center fellowship which we nicknamed 'The Center.'"

Each secret worshiper knew only too well the dangers of their gatherings. One day several members of the Entebbe Fellowship of the Deliverance Church were arrested and taken to the local police station.

Apparently a major heard them praying, walked into the room where they were meeting, and arrested them. Pastor Wafula says, "When one of the group who was not arrested, a converted Moslem, heard of this, he went to the police station and gave his testimony to an officer. He told the man that Christ had died for him and added, 'Islam didn't help me.' He was promptly arrested, too. A tribunal was set up and they were interrogated by the military men. Before they were questioned, they were beaten with whips. Eventually they were released after three nights in custody."

Referring to the Mengo furniture factory "church," Pastor Wafula says, "The factory belongs to some of the brethren and they felt it was a perfect cover for them. At first the worshipers went through the factory, through the banana grove, and into a nearby house. Finally the church became so large they also held meetings in the factory itself.

"The first church there was called 'The Valley' and the factory was named 'The Annex.'"

Noise was a problem for them, too, and Pastor Wafula had to remind his flock that "the Lord can still move without a lot of noise."

Stephen Gonahasa, who attended "The Valley" church, says: "We made friends with people in the neighborhood. Realizing our predicament, they did not betray us. At 'The Valley,' we would hold all-night prayer meetings where we prayed for the nation."

Pastor Wafula tells of the clever ruses the believers would use to get around the ban. "When there was a wedding of one of our number, we would hold it in a Church of Uganda church. We would all come together for the service and then the reception, which would be used as a time to worship and minister. People would give testimonies, and the choir would sing. We also used birthday parties for the same purpose."

Disregarding the ban, the Deliverance group would still venture out into the streets and hand out Christian literature. "I was also continually invited to preach. Sometimes I would take our choir, The Revivals, along. Many of these meetings were Scripture Union groups who met in schools. Not one let on that we were part of an illegal church."

Each of the banned underground churches had ingenious ways of meeting for worship. Obed Rubiaza of the Gospel Mission to Uganda told us that one of their groups was called "The Upper Room."

He explains: "One of the brothers had a mud hut in the Mulago district and had built an upper room in it. The believers would climb a ladder and then pull it up and hold their worship service there. About thirty people would attend the meeting. They used to have a prayer meeting on Wednesday evenings and an all-night time of prayer on Thursday night, as Amin had by then decreed that Friday was to be a Moslem holiday."

Each of the "Gospel Mission" churches had Biblical names. One was called "The Goshen Church," named after the place where the children of Israel stayed during the plague. "Like those believers, we didn't lose one member, in spite of the fact that there were many killings in the area," says Rubiaza.

The "Gospel Mission" appointed John Nelson, the Makerere Church caretaker, as a full-time messenger to the different underground fellowships. "He would cycle around to each group with messages and duplicated sermons," recalls Rubaiza. "It was a very dangerous mission indeed."

One day "The Hebrew Church," which met in an old people's home in the compound of the Makerere Church, was raided by police and fifteen worshipers were arrested. "However, they just took away their Bibles and warned them to stop meeting, but of course they didn't," says Rubaiza.

One underground group had to swim for their lives, literally, when soldiers approached their baptismal service. An underground pastor felt it right to come out into the open to baptize his converts, and so they went with him to a river.

The service was going well when a lookout spotted soldiers approaching. The quick-thinking pastor instructed everyone to swim. Those not already in the water dived in, and the group splashed around with great vigor so that when the Amin men arrived on the scene, all they saw was a group of people enjoying a refreshing swim. After they had gone, the whole group burst into uncontrollable laughter, and then the baptismal service continued.

One lesson Pastor Wafula feels the church learned from that period was not to neglect the example of the early church. "Before the ban we were becoming more and more interested in big meetings, but the ban forced a return to the church of the Acts of the Apostles. Then as well as worshiping in the temple, they went from house to house.

"A great unity of Christians grew up, such as we had never experienced before in Uganda. The suffering brought us together. We had the same goals and we shared a genuine unity of suffering."

The ban had another unifying effect. It brought a group of key free church leaders together for weekly prayer sessions. One was Daniel Naaya, an owner of the furniture factory. The leaders met at different venues around Kampala, which were constantly being changed at short notice for security reasons.

"We had been troubled for some time about how we should pray for the nation and our leaders," says Naaya. "Then the Lord showed us that there was a 'horn of wickedness' in the land. We felt we had to pray against this evil. We knew the problem wasn't Amin, but it was a spiritual power that controlled him.

"So we gave the Lord two alternatives—either save Amin, or remove him completely . . ."

And God answered that prayer in His own way.

Part V

Final Days

15

Life in Uganda

WE WERE EN ROUTE to Uganda. Doris, a pretty Ugandan Airlines stewardess with a striking silver hair-band inscribed with the word "Love," smiled broadly as our small Fokker Friendship plane touched down at battle-scarred Entebbe Airport [writes Dan Wooding].

"Welcome home," she said softly over the plane's intercom-PA system, "welcome back to Uganda."

Tears began to well up in the eyes of refugees who had flown with us from Nairobi, Kenya, as they congratulated each other for actually making it back to *their* country. At times they must have given up hope. Many had been forced to flee for their lives; others had left their homeland for reasons of conscience, for they could no longer remain in a land so polluted by the presence of Idi Amin. But now that was over. They were home.

For several days Ray and I had been concerned about the unrest in Uganda. We had received disturbing reports of the continued violence in the country. Professor Yosef Lule had been deposed. Each day brought more news of murders, and we knew if we entered the country we, too, could possibly be targets.

We met to make our final decision in Nairobi with an old friend of mine, Arnie Newman, a missionary pilot from Zeeland, Michigan. He offered to fly into Entebbe at a moment's notice should we get into trouble while in Uganda. Newman, one of Africa's most experienced missionary pilots, had, three years previously flown me to Busia on the Uganda border where I interviewed refugees fleeing from Amin. Now he and his wife, Marilyn, who was also a pilot, were transferred from AIM Air, the flying wing of the Africa Inland Mission, which

183

they had set up for relief and medical assistance work in East and Central Africa.

As we talked with Newman and his hard-working wife, we discovered that he had probably flown in the first plane carrying medical relief supplies to Entebbe after the Tanzanians had taken the airport. Among those with him on that historic flight was Ken Knighton, director of MAP International, a medical assistance program based in Wheaton, Illinois, and the Southern Baptist Missionary, Webster Carroll.

"We didn't know what to expect," says Newman. "We did not get clearance to land. We just went in. There were soldiers everywhere at the airport and anti-aircraft guns were still in position.

"The Tanzanians had just pushed off the runway a huge Libyan Hercules that they had shot down, and there were big shell holes on the taxi-way.

"There was no immigration and customs then, so we just walked through the terminal building."

Newman and his party managed to get an army escort through to Kampala, which helped them through several potentially difficult roadblocks. The American flyer had had the foresight to take along something that was absolutely vital in those days—gasoline, and lots of it.

"It was necessary to take jerry cans of gas to fill the tank of whoever picked you up," he says. "Otherwise we would never have made it to Kampala. Gas was almost impossible to obtain inside Uganda."

Newman and the group visited various medical centers in, and around, the capital. "Some hospitals were cleared of nearly all medical supplies by looters," says Newman, who has an easy-going, James-Stewart-style accent. "Some of the looters even went into wards, lifted the patients off their beds, put them on the floor, and then left with the beds."

After talking with Arnie and Marilyn Newman, we decided we should go, and we committed the whole trip to the Lord.

We were seriously delayed by customs at Nairobi, and finally had to dash hurriedly to the departure gate. To our dismay the airplane was taxiing down the runway.

"Oh no, we've missed it," I groaned.

But we hadn't. We soon discovered that Ugandan time did not

coincide with our time. The flight was just arriving. It was forty-five minutes late from Entebbe. As we waited to board the aircraft, we had a brief time of prayer asking God to be in complete control of the unpredictable journey that lay ahead.

Flight UG357 from the Kenyan capital served as a gentle introduction to devastated post-war Uganda. Each passenger was served a stale bread roll—mine had a tiny piece of beef in it—and a plastic cup half-filled with orange concentrate and water.

As we flew over glittering Lake Victoria, which is dotted with hundreds of tiny islands, Doris apologized to the passengers for the lack of food. "Next time will be better. We are still trying to organize ourselves," she said.

I don't think any of the happy group of returning exiles were concerned one little bit about the stale rolls, the Aeroflot baggage labels, or even the Air Tanzania head-rest covers. And even if they knew that radio contact between the Entebbe control tower and approaching aircraft often faded out at a vital moment, I am sure they were too delirious to care.

My traveling companions on the one-hour flight were Dan Brewster, an American who was Relief and Development Associate at the Africa office of World Vision International, and of course, my co-author, Ray Barnett. Dr. Ken Tracey, director of the Africa Region of World Vision had kindly agreed to allow Ray and me to join one of their relief reconnoiters, and we were picking up a Volkswagen Kombi at Entebbe to take us on the long, but fascinating, journey into the heart of the Uganda holocaust.

The landing at Uganda's International Airport was smooth, but as we left the airplane, I noticed a huge presence of Tanzanian troops. About three hundred yards from where our plane had stopped, the notorious "Whisky Run" jet stood motionless and riddled with bullets. This Boeing 707 bearing the black, red, and yellow insignia of Uganda Airlines, used to make a weekly fourteen-hour flight to Stansted Airport in England, where Amin's men would load it up with "goodies for the killer squads." They paid for these with cash from the sale of coffee; often there was as much as forty tons in the airplane's hold. Booze—although they were Moslems—was always a priority. It was Amin's way of buying their loyalty.

As we went through the paper work, the immigration official asked, "Do you have any Kenyan newspapers? It gets so boring here with only two flights a day." (One flight was from Kenya and the other from Zaire).

Geoffrey Latim, the former Olympic athlete who fled the country for his life, was to be our guide. He led us to a Christian customs officer who, while being watched by a poker-faced Tanzanian soldier armed with a rifle, made a token check of our bags and then welcomed us to his country.

During our wait for transport, the Acholi officer joined us for a chat. He shared with us how God had saved his life. "I was going to be killed on April 7, 1979," he says. "But on the sixth, Entebbe was freed by the Tanzanians and my life was spared." He revealed that his name was on the death list found when the State Research Bureau headquarters, at Nakasero were liberated by the Tanzanians. He told of the heartbreak of his job during Amin's rule. "I saw many people passing through customs and I knew there was no way they would reach the aircraft. They would be intercepted by the State Research men and never be heard of again," he says.

"The State Research men were all over the airport. Most of them were illiterate."

The customs officer revealed that almost daily, Amin would arrive at Entebbe Airport on a bicycle, which was rather unusual for a head of state. "He would cycle here, leave his bike at the side of the airport, strut around the place for a time, talking to different people, and then leave on his bike.

"Along with the other customs officers, I would pray that he wouldn't talk to me."

An Ethiopian Catholic priest walked over to us. He, too, was waiting for a lift to the theological seminary, where he lectured. His transport finally arrived in the form of two Italian missionaries— Father Aroangelo Petri and Father Lubich Mariono—who told us how some of their friends had been killed during the retreat of Amin's troops.

One was Father Guiseppe Santi, who was cut down in Lira on April 14, 1979, on his way to a nearby police station to ask for protection for some school children.

Another was Father Oryant Annanias, who was also shot in April. His body was left to decompose at the side of the road for fifteen days. "Anyone who approached the body was killed," says Father Petri.

They tell of two Italians, Fathers Anthony Fiorantie and Silvio Dalmajo, based at the Pakwach Mission, who were awakened in their rooms and tied to a bed, one by his back, the other by the leg. Father Mariono says, "One was strangled and the other was killed when a bayonet pierced his ear.

"These are just a few of the horrors that have taken place here. But we must go now. May God be with you on your trip."

There was still no vehicle for us, so Ray and I decided to get a cup of coffee at the airport's restaurant. A white-coated waiter brought us some pretty awful liquid, but in Uganda's tropical heat it was still better than nothing.

As we paid, I was amazed to see that all the bank-notes still bore Idi Amin's face, a grim reminder for the whole population of those terrible days.

Eventually the Kombi arrived and we began the thirty-mile journey to Kampala. We were regularly stopped at roadblocks set up by Tanzanian soldiers, and on each occasion, Latim patiently explained to the soldiers—many of them carrying a rifle in one hand and a huge, noisy radio in the other—who we were and why we were in Uganda. Burned-out military hardware, including tanks, littered the side of the main highway into the capital.

Soon we were at the twenty-four bed Namirembe Guest House, run by the Church of Uganda, but originally set up by the Church Missionary Society of London.

We were greeted by the ever-smiling manager, Naomi Gonahasa. We soon realized the incredible difficulties under which Naomi and her staff were laboring. For a start, there was no running water, and so it had to be bought in jerry cans from people who dragged it up from the city on the back of a bicycle. They sold it for two dollars (US) per can. The lack of water also caused great problems with flushing the toilets. Each resident was rationed with one bottle of off-color liquid a day for everything. They had no gas for cooking, so they had to cook on a charcoal fire. What made it even more difficult was that the telephone was out of order, so we could not alert our contacts that we had arrived.

After dusk fell, we heard the sound of machine gun fire, then heavy explosions. The unnerving sounds of firing, screaming, and wailing went on all night. It was quite an introduction to post-Amin Uganda.

But despite the tension that was still in the air, a talk with Naomi and her husband, Stephen, an interior decorator, made me realize the caliber of this couple, who had risked all for Christ and were still doing so in their work.

I learned from them the secret codeword that they responded to when a person came to them for help. "This was a good hiding place from State Research," says Stephen. "People would turn up here and as long as they knew the codeword 'Goodyear,' we would hide them out. Their food was served in their rooms. Naturally we would not let them sign the guest register."

Adds Naomi: "We were not really frightened, because we believed that God was protecting us."

This sincere young couple—obvious targets for State Research —in addition to being in charge of the Church of Uganda Guest House were active members of an underground church.

Often believers from the Deliverance Church, one of the twenty-seven banned groups, would have meetings in the lounge of the guest house, the very place where Archbishop Luwum signed his own death warrant with his letter to the president.

Stephen referred to the time when Ray Barnett and his friend came to stay with him. "We had set a day apart for prayer and fasting and had particularly prayed that some brethren would come from abroad to encourage us.

"Of course Ray and his colleague did come, and they really lifted our faith here. They were at great risk, for had they been caught, they could have been killed.

"After they left, a friend of mine phoned me and said that the State Research Bureau was looking for 'the two white men.' Fortunately, by then, they had both safely left."

A highlight of the trip for Ray was seeing and talking with Faith Ojambo again, the young believer who had directed him on his previous visit to the Namirembe Guest House.

She told Ray: "When I first saw your taxi, I was afraid you might be spies. I thought you were stopping to arrest me. But it was wonderful to find you were believers."

Faith revealed that at that time she was a secret worker of the "Bethel" underground church.

We also met two friendly Dutch Christians, Gilbert Scherff and Kees Crezée, the advance party for 150 Dutch young people who had volunteered to give six weeks to help build a youth center in bomb-blasted Mbarara. Scherff, from the Worldwide Evangelization Crusade, and Crezée, from Operation Mobilization, were returning from Mbarara to Nairobi for a crisis meeting with the project leader, Leo Slingerland. He was a director with Evangelische Omroep (Dutch Evangelical Radio and Television) and also headed up the relief arm of this Christian broadcasting group, based in Hilversum.

The project came about after Slingerland made a film, televised in Holland, about the return to Uganda of Bishop Festo Kivengere, and the courage of the Christians who stayed. The Dutch people responded magnificently with aid and offers of manpower. Plans were immediately drawn up for a youth center to be constructed by these young volunteers. Raw materials and building aids were immediately purchased and shipped to Mombassa.

Deeply concerned about the daily killings, and for the safety of those volunteers who were about to fly from Amsterdam, Slingerland was forced to cancel their flight. Instead he decided to let Uganda labor build the center, with only supervisory help from a few courageous Dutch young people who insisted on going into Mbarara. Slingerland said, "Human lives are more important than a building."

Following a night's stay in Kampala, we left on a trip north, planning to visit Jinja, Mbale, Soroti, Kotido, and Gulu.

Again, there were roadblocks manned by Tanzanian soldiers, many armed only with spears. It was a big help to have a bishop traveling with us for part of the way. He was the Rt. Rev. Melkisedek Otim, Bishop of Lango. The purple-vested bishop would smile at the soldiers at each barrier and we would be waved through. However, occasionally a drunken soldier or policeman would flag us down and demand a ride. It was quite disconcerting to have these hitch-hikers sitting behind us with their rifles, because we knew that in their condition they could accidentally fire the weapon.

Upon our return to Kampala, we had the marvelous experience of worshiping with members of the previously imprisoned Makarere Gospel Mission to Uganda Church, and even speaking at their joyful morning service.

That evening, on a makeshift stage with curtains made from blankets, many of those who had been imprisoned and nearly burned alive for their faith, presented a play. We will never forget this play performed to a packed church, which still bore the scars of the shoot-out on its walls and ceilings.

The play began with one of the ex-prisoners reading out Idi Amin's fateful speech banning the twenty-seven sects, in September, 1977. Without mocking the ex-president, he read Amin's allegations that the group were part of the CIA, and added his instruction to soldiers to "beat and kill anybody found worshiping."

The play, written by a talented church member, was about Nehemiah going to Jerusalem to rebuild the temple after it had been destroyed. It had obvious significance for the churches of Uganda. It leaped from those Old Testament days to a clever scene in Amin's Uganda. For instance, Nehemiah's party of workers had to go through a border post manned by Idi's guards. The congregation applauded wildly as they saw that the border officer was dressed, and acted very much, like a State Research officer. He had on dark glasses, platform heels, and bell-bottom trousers.

Until Nehemiah arrived the officer had been confiscating all valuables from those who passed through his hands, and then many were sent for further treatment and possible death.

But when it came to the prophet, the man had to admit he was helpless, a lesson that Idi Amin took a long time to learn.

During our return stay at Namirembe, we met many great Christians who had survived the holocaust and each had a story to tell. One was Christian businessman Elijah Nkundizana from Kisoro, seven miles from the Rwanda border. Bespectacled Nkundizana would turn up for breakfast each morning armed with an extremely noisy radio which blared out a news program.

The affable Nkundizana tells, in a booming voice, of the comfort that radio had been to him during the war. "I would tune into overseas news broadcasts from the United States, West Germany, South Africa, and England to find out the latest news. It was exciting to hear more each day about the downfall of Idi Amin."

The incredible expatriate missionaries who stayed on in Uganda throughout the reign of Idi Amin had our deep admiration. One such person was Cynthia Mackay, the Church Missionary Society (CMS) representative in the country and religious Education Adviser at the Provincial Secretariat.

This former teacher at the Ngora Girls' School was suffering from a painful back complaint when Ray and I called on her in her tidy Namirembe bungalow close to the Church of Uganda's Provincial Office, where she now worked.

As she lay on her back, this gritty Yorkshire woman told of how the British High Commission became concerned about the dangers to her and other missionaries in remaining in the country. She recalled an episode when a High Commission official asked her to meet him in downtown Kampala.

"He called from the High Commission and made arrangements for a clandestine meeting. The man said in a confidential fashion, 'Park your car opposite the bookshop and I'll pick you up there.' This was shortly after the killing of the archbishop, so naturally they were very concerned for our safety. He picked me up, and as we drove around he told me that he was extremely worried. I told him that I wasn't unduly concerned. I explained to him the CMS rule that we should stay in our own place unless the church or government ask us to leave."

Soon after this meeting, the British High Commission themselves left Uganda. Their concern for her safety was correct, and was borne out by the fact that she was later savagely attacked in her home. Three men armed with panga knives burst into her house and tried unsuccessfully to rape her. The men had already killed the compound watchman, Samson. It was a terrible ordeal for this diminutive lady, but still wasn't enough to cause her to flee the country she believed God had called her to. God has since healed her mind of that dreadful incident.

She says the State Research Bureau was constantly trying to infiltrate Christian work, but was usually so obvious that its attempts were immediately spotted.

Our trip into Karamoja opened up a new aspect of the Uganda story. The incidence of crime was skyrocketing because of the large supply of guns and ammunition, some of which was left in the region by fleeing Amin soldiers, and some looted from army barracks.

About three thousand automatic rifles were seized from the Moroto army barracks, says Jim Rowland, an agriculturist with the BCMS whose work is supported by Christian Aid and other European agencies. Troops of the Uganda National Liberation Front forces, freedom fighters who helped the Tanzanian invasion, seized these rifles when they moved into the area.

Violent cattle rustling seems to be a way of life in this part of the country. Jim tells of one recent raid when seventy thousand cattle were seized at gunpoint by the powerful Jie tribe. No less than three hundred adults from the Dodoth tribe were killed in the battle—not including the children, who were trampled to death. Later, when the Dodoth regrouped and counterattacked, they got their cattle back, but this time six hundred people died. So in three days, about one thousand tribespeople perished.

Warriors from the eleven tribes and sub-tribes of Karamoja have lived this way since time immemorial. But now guns have made their attacks even more savage.

Brave missionaries are among the few people who know these gun-toting fighters well. Missionaries have maintained a witness in this primitive and violent area of Uganda that even Idi Amin could not conquer.

Amin knew Karamoja well. Although he was familiar with the cattle raiding first-hand, he didn't manage to do much about it.

Like other Ugandans, he felt ashamed that the Karamajong didn't wear many clothes. In his usual fashion of government by radio, he announced that all Karamojong should wear clothing. The next day a group of protestors were shot and killed in Kangole. For a long time the Karamojong tried to appear more dressed. But as the economy got worse, and clothes became too expensive, even the neck rings and headdresses largely disappeared.

The city of Moroto has suffered like the rest of Uganda, but the main problem of the area is lack of rain, resulting in famine. Before Amin's time the people could have sold a goat and bought maize seed. Now they have no hope, as Amin has destroyed even the little that they had. The water pumps of previous governments have been allowed to become useless. People often walk miles to get a bit of water. It's a tough land made tougher by Amin's neglect of proper government.

Since Karamoja became a missionary area it has been a focus for the rest of the Church of Uganda. Ugandan missionaries have gone to work there, most of them from the West Nile region which had been greatly influenced by the Revival Movement. Gradually Christian groups were formed in schools. In 1964 the Karamojong had their own New Testament.

As we toured part of the region with Jim and Jean Rowland, we were disturbed to see emaciated women and children at the nearby Kanawat Catholic Mission. There were women with babies whose bodies were wasting to skeletons and who had large, ballooning stomachs. A famine gripping the region has forced many to wander the countryside in search of wild greens or field rats because they cannot pay the exorbitant prices of the limited food supplies. These dying children are among the eighty thousand persons Uganda government officials say are in desperate need of food assistance until the region can recover from two successive seasons of crop failure.

"Starvation is rampant because of the war and the fact that the people are getting no vitamins," says Sister Lorenzina Magon, who runs the Kanawat dispensary.

"We need medicines such as antibiotics. We need milk, sugar, and blankets. We have no doctor here. No one will come."

Our final memory of Karamoja was not the Karamojong village we visited where we had to crawl on our hands and knees through the tiny holes made in the thorn bushes that surround the encampment, or the many other tiny gaps we had to scramble through to visit other parts of the village, but an old lady who was too weak to move, sitting silently in Kotido. The woman, who appeared to be near death, squatted by her open hut to keep out of the sun's rays. She said through an interpreter that she had eaten only wild greens for two months. She displayed large folds of loose skin around her rib cage.

Famine, more than Idi Amin, had taken its toll in Karamoja.

ON NAMIREMBE HILL, Kampala, outside the Church of Uganda Provincial Office, we met another delightful Christian who turned out to be possibly Uganda's most unusual evangelist. He was Frederick Lindo, a businessman in his sixties who told us that the combined problems of the Amin years and the Tanzanian attack on Masaka, where he had a 320-acre farm on which he grew coffee and sugar cane, had caused his business interests to crash.

"I am no longer a rich man. I lost twenty million shillings" (nearly three million US dollars), he says.

"But I am not heartbroken. I brought nothing into the world. God gave me all these things and He will care for me now."

At one time Lindo's farm was covered with the rich Uganda coffee so favored by Americans, whose caffeine addiction for years supported the machinery of the Amin regime. "Amin's troops came with guns to my factories, and demanded the coffee," reports Lindo.

"Then they sold the coffee to buy guns to shoot us. So I uprooted the coffee to plant sugar crops."

The agri-businessman's sugar crops also thrived, sustaining the three factories on his farm which employed 150 to 200 people. With his profit he paid school fees for his ten children, purchased more farm equipment, and supported Christian ministries.

Ugandan troops, retreating from a Tanzanian counterattack for Amin's aggression, dealt the first blow to Lindo's "Kingo Estates." The soldiers hijacked the farmer's four trucks, two old tractors, and six motors, while managing to eat or confiscate his hundred cows. Lindo and his family fled for their lives.

Then a two-hundred-man force of Tanzanians and Ugandan exiles hit Lindo's farm, eating his eighty goats and "liberating" his commercial passenger bus. "I have no quarrel about that," says Lindo, grateful for Uganda's new freedom and for the preservation of his family.

When the invading troops evacuated, villagers—oppressed and terrorized for eight years—celebrated their happy turn of events by looting Lindo's farm. "They took all my furniture, and ruined my three factories," reports Lindo. His bank was also bombed, destroying his savings.

"God is wonderful" exudes the stocky farmer, with the incredible lack of bitterness evident among most Ugandan Christians. "There is no way we could have pushed Amin out internally."

Hoping for a repeat of Old Testament rancher Job's recovery, Lindo plans to plant a fresh sugar crop. "While that takes two years to mature," explains the lay-preacher, "I'm going to travel this country with Life Ministry [Africa's Campus Crusade], encouraging people to build their relationships with God."

After a time, we had reluctantly to leave the guest house. The House of Bishops was meeting there and so Canon Wilson Baganizi kindly booked us into the Catholic Guest House at Rubaga, where we stayed for one night. Unfortunately, this proved even more remote from the city, and so as I continued interviews around Rubaga Hill, Ray tramped the two miles to the International Hotel where despite rebuffs, he persisted in the lobby for five hours until they finally allocated us a room.

Naturally, the hotel was much more convenient for interviews, but in some ways the facilities were worse than at the humble guest houses. There was no running water at the hotel and the only way we could get water for a time was from a nearby fire hydrant. But even that discolored water dried up. And being on the thirteenth floor without an elevator didn't help either. For part of the time we had an unofficial guest sleeping on the floor of our room. He was a top British businessman who had found himself without accommodation in the Ugandan capital. Knowing how dangerous that could be for him, we asked him to share with us. Each night we sat around the room talking to the sound of heavy gunfire around the hotel. (Many Tanzanian soldiers were staying there, and others were camping in a park at the side of the hotel.) At times the mysterious gun battles came a little too close for comfort. Even now we haven't discovered who was fighting whom.

Finally, when our time came to leave, we found to our regret that we had to walk through darkened and possibly dangerous streets to be at the Uganda Airlines office at 6:45 A.M. As the gunfire was still going on, this was not an appealing prospect. But—with considerable help from marvelous bell-hops from the hotel who went ahead of us and carried our luggage; we gingerly walked some twenty yards behind them—we made it. Then, the airline bus needed to be push-started by the passengers before we could head off for Entebbe.

But everyone on the bus took the whole thing in good humor. After all, that's life in Uganda!

16

Suffer the Little Children

THE AMIN CHILDREN were all safely tucked in bed and asleep when, late one night in March, 1979, an urgent telephone message was received at their school in Kabale.

Missionary Mary Hayward, matron of the Christian-staffed preparatory school for twenty-five years, answered the phone and received the terse instruction from the local army captain.

"Awaken the president's children, dress them quickly, and pack all their things," she was told. Miss Hayward hated to disturb them, but she knew that now their lives depended on it.

That tense night was the last time Mary, who is with the Ruanda Missions (CMS) saw her "special" children, whose ages ranged from five to thirteen.

By now the reign of the black Hitler of Africa was in its death throes. Amin was gathering his three dozen children around him to dash from the land he had ruled so unmercifully for eight years.

"We got all the staff up and went around the bedrooms waking the president's children," says Miss Hayward, who was also housekeeper at Kabale.

"The little girls couldn't believe it at first, and as we left them to get ready, they just piled into bed and went back to sleep. So we had to wake them up again.

"The boys were thrilled to bits with the excitement. Luyimbazi, one of them, said: 'Well, daddy said we've got to do this, so we've got to.'

"I hurried to get all their cases from the roof of the school and brought them down.

"Then a huge army bus with bullet-proof windows arrived. It was parked just outside the school and we took the children over to it.

"There were about nine young bodyguards on board, all with ammunition belts around their waists and carrying pistols and machine guns. They looked as scared as the little girls.

"We shook their hands and thanked them for taking the children to safety. One of these young men said to us, 'Thank you very much for taking care of them.' They were obviously under a tremendous strain and their handshakes were quite limp. None of them really knew if they would ever make Kampala alive.

"The Amin boys, however, didn't seem to mind the experience. The little ones were fighting for the front seats so they could see the road ahead.

"We got food for the journey, and blankets, and packed them in the bus. They were all wide-eyed, wondering what was happening.

"The road to Kampala, which was 250 miles away, was by now closed and so they took another route. We understand they first drove towards the Rwanda border and then went around the country lanes.

"We know they arrived safely in Kampala, because one of the children, Asha, was seen playing in Amin's garden two days later."

Miss Hayward believes the Amin children are all now in Tripoli, Libya. She thinks their cunning father is slipping unnoticed around the back streets of an Arab capital. The clue to this astonishing theory came when one of the boys, eight-year-old Geriga, woke up screaming at 10:00 P.M. on three consecutive nights.

"Each time I would rush up the corridor to his room, and finally, on the third night, I said, 'What's the matter, Geriga? What are you dreaming about?'

"He said, 'Well, when we were at home, Miss Hayward, a man dressed all in white used to come into our room and sit near us with his face covered up. I never knew who it was, then he would lift up the cover and we saw it was daddy. We would all laugh. He was dressed like an Arab. We didn't like it, but he kept doing it.'"

Miss Hayward says, "He is probably walking around the streets of Tripoli with his face covered, and no one recognizes him."

Although Amin, a man of many contrasts, could play this charade with his children, he is known to have involved the mother of three of them from the school in one of the sickest episodes in his disgraceful reign of terror. For he had his second wife, Kay, the daughter of a clergyman, murdered, dismembered, decapitated, and shoved in the trunk of a car.

The jealous dictator got it into his mind that Kay, a beautiful woman, had a lover—despite the fact that she was eight months pregnant. Early in August, 1974, she was arrested by his order on a trumped-up charge of possessing a pistol and ammunition.

She was taken to a police station, where she had a flaming argument through the bars of the cell with Amin, who had come to gloat. Kay shouted at him, "You can't have me arrested for keeping a pistol and ammunition which you are responsible for leaving in my house." His eyes bulging with rage, Amin called her a whore and said she deserved her punishment.

He stormed out, and next morning Kay was questioned by a magistrate. She explained to him that the gun and ammunition belonged to her husband. After a word of caution he released her.

However, shortly afterwards, on Sunday, August 13, she died in a most hidious way. In his book, *State of Blood,* Henry Kyemba describes what he saw at Mulago Hospital, Kampala, where her dismembered body was taken. After one of the doctors committed suicide, her body had been found in the trunk of his car.

"I drove back to the hospital, had the mortuary unlocked, and went in with two attendants," wrote Kyemba. "They opened one of the refrigeration units in which the bodies were kept. The shelf slid open and a body emerged. The sight that confronted me was the most horrible I have ever seen; it is one that still haunts me. The body was indeed that of Kay Amin, but it had been dismembered. The legs and arms had been cut off. Lying on the shelf was the torso, face up, with the head intact. The torso was lying in a burlap sack, which had been slit open and folded back to expose its contents and to ease the task of identification. More sacking lay beside the torso. Underneath were the legs and arms. The dissection had been neatly done; no bones were broken; the ligaments in the joints were carefully cut; there had been no tearing. The job was done by an expert with the correct surgical instruments. Too appalled even to speak, I took a step back in shock and simply nodded to the attendants to slide the shelf shut."

Amin had asked the Health Minister to go and see the body, saying he wanted to know "exactly what it is like." When Kyemba told him, Amin said: "Oh, is that what has been done? You go home now."

Back home, Kyemba had a call from Amin with an instruction that shocked him even more. The president told him to arrange for the limbs to be sewn back onto the body. He said the job must be done the following morning because he wanted to bring Kay's children (Kide, Masters, Lumumba, Adam, and Mao Mozambi), Kay's parents, and a group of friends to see the body. So next day after a post-mortem, the gruesome sewing-up job was done.

She was laid out on a bed and covered with a sheet up to the chin. Amin was determined that not only the children, aged between four and eight, and Kay's father, should see the body, but also the rest of the world. So he arranged for television cameras and reporters to stand by. When they were all assembled in the hospital room, he began shouting as if on cue at the children, "Your mother was a bad woman. See what has happened to her!" He told the terrified children: "Pray to Allah for your mother, who has died in sin."

The bizarre scene became a recurring nightmare to Lumumba Amin, one of the three Kabale pupils at the bedside. He had been named by the president after Patrice Lumumba, first premier of Congo, who was killed in 1964.

"Lumumba, like the others including Adam and Mao, had to kneel at the bedside and look at his dead mother," says Miss Hayward. "One night at evening prayers we were talking about what we could do if we ever became afraid. Suddenly Lumumba said, 'I didn't like seeing my mummy like that, so I asked Jesus to take it away from my mind, and He really did.'"

Idi Amin would often arrive at a local hotel, the White Horse Inn, where he had a permanent suite of rooms. He would immediately phone the school and ask for his children to be brought to see him.

"Sometimes he would fly in by helicopter; on the other occasions he would come by road," says Miss Hayward, who comes from Woking, England. "In the later days he never let people know which way he was traveling because he knew they could easily take a pot-shot at him.

"His children were always pestering him, saying, 'Daddy, why don't you come to the school?' So one day he decided to turn up unannounced.

"It happened that as he approached, the children were practicing marching for an important day. Suddenly the District Commissioner's car came around the corner and he called out to our headmis-

tress, 'The president's coming!' Thinking he meant that afternoon or the next day, she said, 'Oh, when?' He replied breathlessly, 'He's coming round the corner now.'

"She quickly pushed the marching children to one side. They stood in rows and did the traditional clapping as he passed through the middle of them.'' The bear-like Amin then shook hands with the startled staff and all the children.

"He behaved very nicely,'' says Miss Hayward. ''I remember that day he would only drink water while he was with us. He had Mama Sarah (wife number 5, formerly a go-go dancer in the jazz band of the 'Suicide Mechanized Unit') with him. She seemed to be a very nice little person.

"Then he called all his children to him and asked them how they were getting on at school. He also asked a teacher how they were doing. He was always asking about their progress, and on one occasion when he found that one of the boys wasn't doing too well because he wouldn't work hard, he took him away and the boy never returned, poor little chap.''

Unfortunately, not all the children were intellectual, in fact Mayi and Mariam were at the bottom of their classes during their short stay at the school.

"It wasn't because they were dumb, but because in the past they hadn't been treated properly,'' says Miss Hayward. ''They had never been to school before.''

After the giant president had left, young Geriga Amin came to the matron with tears streaming down his ebony face.

"What's the matter?'' she asked.

Between sobs, he said, ''Romeo [one of the other school boys] has been saying rude things about my daddy.''

"Oh dear! What's he been saying?'' said Miss Hayward.

"He said my daddy looks like a big fat hippo.''

The English matron found that she needed every bit of self-control not to burst into laughter at the comment—because she thought the other boy's description was quite fitting.

She tried to comfort the distraught Amin child, and then went off to find young Romeo and warn him to be careful what he called the president in the future.

"I had to act quickly. If that story went around the school and got to the childrens' parents, they would have been worried. And if one

of the Amin children went home and told their father that so and so's boy had called him a big fat hippo, the father of the family would have probably disappeared.

"I told Romeo, 'You musn't say things like that. It's not very kind, anyway, to say that about Geriga's daddy.'"

After recounting the story, Mary Hayward turned to us and with an infectious giggle said: "Well, he did look a bit like a hippo, didn't he?"

Most weeks Amin would telephone the school and say to whoever picked up the receiver, "This is the president speaking. How are my children?" Miss Hayward said he would insist on mentioning them by name, going through details of each individual child. If one of them wasn't well, he would ask if a helicopter was needed to pick him up and take him for medical treatment."

Like other members of the staff, Miss Hayward would sometimes get the opportunity to speak personally with the president during one of his infrequent visits to the school. As the soft-spoken Amin chatted with her, it was hard to imagine, because of his winning charm, that he was actually one of the most wicked men in history.

"I had to bear in mind his tribal background," she says. "The Kakwas and Nubians are known to be very brave, but cruel, soldiers. It is part of their tribal training.

"They are all tied up with the tribal custom that if you kill a man, you're supposed to taste his blood. This obviously came into his thinking. That was Amin's trouble; he never really seemed to be able to get away from it."

It may seem strange that the dictator should send his children to a Christian-staffed school. But Kabale Preparatory, which began informally in the 1930s as a "family" school for missionaries' children, was recognized as the top preparatory school in Uganda. Over the years it developed into a primary boarding school, integrated into the country's educational system, but with Christian teachers. And to be fair to Amin, he wanted only the best schooling for his children.

Miss Hayward believes that some of the Amin youngsters were truly born-again. "I think both Moses and Lumumba were, and what they learned at the school will come back to them. Moses especially had a quick grasp of the gospel. It's inside him, maybe now just a little seed in his brain, but nevertheless it's there. I believe this is true of all the children."

The enthusiastic faith of Moses nearly got the whole school staff into serious trouble with the Moslem dictator one day. Moses and his father were searching for a lost item and the youngster said, "Well, if we've lost it, why don't we pray about it like we do at school?" So the young Amin put his hands together, and said, "Dear Lord Jesus, please help us to find this. Amen."

Moses' father was shocked, and he began to question his aides to find out if his children were in fact being brought up as Christians at Kabale. Well, they were, and it was his fault for sending them there! He telephoned his Minister of Education and demanded immediate action. Knowing his head would roll if he did nothing, the minister contacted the local District Commissioner, who came to the school and said he would have to take some of the members of the staff to Kampala.

"It was just after the killing of Mrs. Dora Bloch and I didn't want a similar incident to happen to any of our staff, so I consulted with Bishop William, Festo Kivengere's assistant, and we finally agreed two of the staff would go with the DC," says Miss Hayward.

"The two staff members were both British teachers.

"They were asked what they taught, and they tactfully said, 'Well we don't teach them anything about being baptized and we don't teach them the Creed.' Finally they came through the interview safely. But we did have to have a Moslem teacher for the Amin children. This man was absolutely disgusted, as he had just finished his training and thought he would begin an ordinary teaching job. Now he found himself stuck teaching religion to these children. It was very difficult for him.

"Whenever we had a Scripture lesson, since the Amin children were forbidden to attend, he had to teach them the Moslem religion. They hated him, not because of himself, but because he kept them from prayers. One of the older girls was in tears quite often. 'Can't we come; please let us come,' she would sob."

Before this, his children always attended morning prayers, which consisted of a hymn, prayer, and a talk by a member of the staff, often about the lives of John or Paul, or possibly the parables of Jesus.

"The Amin children would be present at the little service and they genuinely did come to love the Lord and talk about Him as a person. Jesus was their friend and they loved to sing Christian choruses heartily."

The president was quite startled one day while at the White Horse Inn. He had become the proud possessor of a new toy—a cassette tape recorder—so he summoned his children to his suite and ordered them to sing. After they had gone through several secular songs, he ordered them to "sing me a special song." So the little group lined up and began singing the action chorus, "We have Jesus in our heart. You take Him, too." And as they sang, they pointed their fingers at their stunned father.

"We first learned of this on his next visit. He brought his tape recorder and said to us, 'Would you like to hear the music my children sang for me?' Naturally, we said 'yes,' and so he proceeded to play this chorus."

Fortunately, this time Amin was not angry. The staff managed to keep straight faces as he tapped his feet in time with the pointed chorus.

An occasional visitor to the school was the Archbishop of Uganda, the Most Rev. Silvanus Wani, who came from the same tribe as the president, the Kakwa, from the West Nile.

"He really loved those children and used to talk to them about loving Jesus, too," says Miss Hayward. "He would come to the school to take prayers and then he'd ask to see the Amin children.

"Ethically, he couldn't actually pray with them because they were supposed to be Moslems, and he felt that would have been wrong."

Although the children were forbidden to have Christian instruction, it was almost impossible to keep them from it in such a school.

"At Christmas time I remember we had trouble with some of them, as we felt they should not be allowed to take part in the carol service.

"Well, Miya, one of the older girls, came and said, 'Aren't we Amins going to be in the carol service?' So the headmistress said, 'Well, you know that your daddy doesn't want you to learn these Christian songs because you are being brought up as a Moslem.'

"Determined not to be beaten on this one, Miya said, 'Well, can I ring daddy and ask him?' So she called her father on his hot line and rattled to him in Swahili. The head also spoke to him and finally he said, 'Yes, they can.'

"I suppose he thought they'd quickly forget Christianity, just as many people think. But of course it doesn't happen like that. Anyway, the children all joined in and sang the carols with us."

Christian love was an ingredient that the Amin children received in abundance during their stay at Kabale. "You couldn't help loving them," says Miss Hayward. "They were delightful children.

"I always did a lot of cooking and was also school housekeeper. They would come to watch me and help out when they could. One of the girls learned to make ice cream and took the recipe home to her daddy. She told me later that he loved it. They lived, as much as possible, very normally with us."

Being in charge of such important children, staff at the school realized that their lives could, at times, be in danger, with Amin's unpredictable whims.

"It was just like Alice in Wonderland," says Miss Hayward. "You didn't know what was going to happen next. One day the Americans would be out of favor, then the British. You were aware you could literally be expelled from the country the next day.

"Once or twice we got packed and were ready to go. At one point we even discussed what we would do if soldiers came for the Amin children.

"So we obtained some British Airways overnight bags, packed them with food and a bottle of water, and prepared to leave. Fortunately, we didn't need them, so we just unpacked the bags and gave them to the house girls for Christmas presents."

Miss Hayward believes that many of the president's children were aware of some of the atrocities going on at that time. "They didn't know much, but we were never quite sure what the day children—the Amins were boarders—were telling them. We couldn't forbid them to speak to the president's children about these things, because children are children.

"In fact I am sure that some of them said more than they should have.

"Then Luyimbazi, an older boy, arrived with a radio. They would listen to it and sometimes become afraid. At times Maco was especially fearful. When the Tanzanians had begun their attack, he came to me and said, 'Miss Hayward, are they really fighting close by? Will it be all right?' It was pathetic."

Little Maco arrived back at school one day wearing a beautiful fur-lined coat, perhaps not the most suitable clothing for tropical Africa, though the Kabale area was a lot cooler than other parts of Uganda.

"He told me when he got back to school, 'One day during the

holidays, a lady came and brought me this coat, some toys, and some sweets. It was nice having her there. Then she went away, and afterwards, I discovered she was my very own mummy.'''

Amin had a very strange relationship with his son Moses—the real or the imposter—because he believed that through him, his life would be spared. A witch doctor told him that he would never be killed while Moses was by his side. Amin often took the youngster on long trips. He obviously believed what he had been told. He even took him to Nairobi in 1978 to attend the funeral of President Jomo Kenyatta.

When the younger Amin boys first arrived at the school, they were dressed in miniature battle fatigues, but as soon as she could, Miss Hayward changed them into school clothes.

"They loved wearing the fatigues, but I would put them away. After all, we weren't an army school," she explains.

The chairman of the school's Board of Governors is the Bishop of Kigezi, Festo Kivengere. He believes that the Amin children could definitely be among the Christians of tomorrow. "Oh, absolutely," he says. "They sang Christian songs and prayed with our beloved missionaries and teachers. We put seeds of Jesus into their hearts and we know those seeds will germinate."

17

The Nakasero Three

THE UNDERGROUND CHURCH SERVICE was over, and the team of happy believers, Benjamin Mwima, Paul Kinaatama, and Imelda Lubega, walked in a carefree manner along the Namirembe Road on the edge of Kampala. Imelda strolled behind, grasping the hand of her charming eight-year-old son, Geoffrey.

After the clandestine gathering in a private house, they were unable to find a taxi to take them home. Consequently, it was decided to use the two-kilometer hike usefully by distributing Christian tracts and booklets to everyone they met.

It was Sunday, March 18, 1979. The little group was attached to one of the network of underground fellowships linked to the Makerere Church, the church Idi Amin's vicious vice-president had arrested and nearly burned alive. Imelda and Paul had been imprisoned on that occasion, and barely escaped with their lives. From that experience, they knew only too well the dangers of what they were doing now. So great was their faith that they put the possible consequences out of their minds.

People coming in the opposite direction accepted copies of their evangelical leaflets, and many began reading them at the roadside. Twenty-four-year-old Benjamin, at that time a physics student at Makerere University, gave Christian literature to a group of people and began witnessing to them. A left-hand drive Fiat sedan drew up on the other side of the road and the driver began blasting his horn. It was unusual to see such a car in Uganda. Ben noted that the man was extremely dark, and probably of the Nubian tribe.

"He called me over and hastily I approached, thinking he was someone I knew," says Benjamin. "But as I drew closer I realized I had never seen him before.

"Then I thought he was probably interested in the literature I was giving out. He asked to see the material, and still I did not suspect anything unusual in his request. In fact, I was rejoicing in my heart that I was about to 'bait and catch a big fish.'

"I explained to the man that they were gospel tracts and booklets, full of the news of salvation through our Lord Jesus Christ. He quizzed me about salvation. Briefly and enthusiastically I told him how it could take place, explaining how Jesus died for our sins, that He rose again from the dead to prove that He was Lord of the dead and the living. Further I stated that through His blood men could receive justification."

By then the man was carefully reading the literature Benjamin had given him. Soon he asked who he was and what he was actually doing. Benjamin, a full-time evangelist with his church, began to get a little skeptical. Pointedly the man asked about his religious affiliations. "I clearly explained that I did not belong to any of the four religions then recognized by the government of Uganda," says the young preacher. "He was shocked and inquired more along this line. Firmly I asserted that I was simply a saved man who wasn't denominational at all.

"I went on to say that I was simply doing what Jesus commanded. He inquired as to what I believed and where I worshiped. His questioning was persistent and direct. Many of the queries he fired at me were surprising." Their conversation lasted for two hours.

Still the fresh-faced young evangelist didn't realize who he was talking to. "What would you say if the authorities caught you with these papers?" the Nubian eventually asked Benjamin.

"I would simply explain that they are gospel tracts and booklets which tell about the salvation of men by faith in Jesus Christ," he replied.

Then, completely without fear, Benjamin told the inquisitive stranger that Christians in Uganda were not afraid of Amin's men, despite the never-ending beatings and torturing of believers.

A look of triumph crossed the driver's face as he spotted the address of an American publisher on the literature, and he immediately demanded to see Benjamin's identity card. (Every Ugandan citizen was required by law to carry this card at all times.)

After scrutinizing the pass, the officious man discovered that Benjamin was a university student. He said sternly, ''What you are doing is illegal. Get those other people to come over here.''

Paul, Imelda, and Geoffrey had been waiting across the road for two hours, thinking all the while their friend was having a tremendous opportunity to witness to this apparently important man.

''When Benjamin finally beckoned, we ran happily across the road, thinking the driver was going to give us a lift home,'' recalls Imelda, a beautiful woman who works for the Uganda Commercial Bank in Kampala.

''The man told us to identify ourselves, and asked us to which of the accepted four religions we belonged.'' (The only four groups allowed then were Catholics, Church of Uganda, the Orthodox Church, and the Moslems.)

''With the Spirit of God helping me, I boldly declared that Jesus Christ had saved our lives. Standing there I remembered the verse in Luke 21:14, 'So make up your minds not to prepare beforehand to defend yourselves.' I explained that only Jesus could redeem a life, not any of these religions.''

The man, who by now they all concluded was a State Research officer, told the group that he was arresting all of them—including the little boy—for an ''illegal activity.'' At that moment a green Fiat 124 with an army officer at the wheel passed by. The Nubian officer honked for him to stop. As the two conferred, the believers caught a glimpse of a gun lying beneath the State Research man's seat.

''Right, you're going in to make a statement,'' he said, pointing to the green Fiat. ''Get in.'' The group climbed into the Italian car, and, with the officer following, headed for Uganda's notorious Nakasero State Research headquarters.

''Nakasero was normally a place of no return,'' says Imelda.

Previously Imelda had been held overnight at Nakasero, along with other members of her congregation. On the following day she had been transferred to the women's section at Luzira prison, where she spent three months. Imelda knew all too well what to expect, as her ''statement'' was being taken.

A person could be instantly killed by a sword, a hammer, or even by having his head smashed against a wall. The guards explained they used these methods because they didn't want to waste bullets.

Sometimes the guards would cut chunks out of a person's body over a period of days, with the intent that the prisoner would die a slow and agonizing death.

Strangely enough, the little group felt no fear. They knew that Amin's henchmen could kill only the body, not the soul.

Recalls Benjamin: "Inside me was a good feeling. I knew the time had come for me to suffer for Christ. I had heard and read about people imprisoned for Jesus' sake, so I was inwardly thrilled that Jesus had counted me worthy to suffer for Him. However, I did not know then that the prison I was going to in actuality was the worst place on earth."

This brave band of believers enthusiastically witnessed to their driver during the journey, while he tried to concentrate on the road. "He didn't seem to care about us, but he listened to the message all the same," says Benjamin. "We even brought out our Bibles and held them in our hands. We spoke freely and encouraged the army man to make a decision in his life for Christ."

When they arrived at Nakasero, they were taken into custody by a cruel-looking man in an army uniform who sat behind the reception desk. A large gun lay menacingly on the counter.

"The gun struck terror in my heart," says Benjamin. "We were then thoroughly checked. Our pockets were emptied, belts taken, shoes removed, and everything else confiscated except the clothes we were wearing. They examined our armpits, limbs, and so on, and finding we were not concealing anything, led us upstairs."

Young Geoffrey and his mother were separated, with tragic results. "One of the State Research men offered to look after my son while I was in prison," says Imelda. Having no choice in the matter and knowing that the Bureau was no place for such a tot, she reluctantly agreed.

"I have not seen him since," she says sadly. "I am waiting for a miracle from God." When the Tanzanian liberation forces took over Kampala, Imelda discovered that Geoffrey's guardian was killed. She was given to understand that a State Research woman fled Kampala with Geoffrey and may now be caring for him in northern Uganda or in southern Sudan.

"Please pray that I will be reunited with my son one day," she asks. "And please ask your readers to pray for him, too."

For the three adults, the ordeal was beginning. "The officer in charge commissioned two young men to guard us," says Ben. "One was in army uniform, the other was dressed as a civilian. Again they questioned us and we told them that as Christians we loved all people: presidents, Moslems, and everyone else.

"We climbed the stairs, and I must confess that they felt very cold under my bare feet. Fear was beginning to build up in my heart. The men were not very friendly and I anticipated difficult times ahead."

Benjamin predicted correctly. Soon the little group was to suffer a terrible humiliation.

But before that happened they were made to sit down against a blood-stained wall with a guard watching over them.

"Tension mounted, as I helplessly sat there facing an angry-looking armed man," says Benjamin. "I imagined we would have our skulls banged and crushed against the wall. Many people must have been killed that way, otherwise how did the blood-stains get there?

"The young man came back and ordered us to follow him; we did as he asked, leaving our property behind. He led us into an empty cell. There were two wooden benches near the wall and two dirty-looking buckets in one corner. A tattered suitcase with old ragged clothes lay in the other corner. Empty bottles and garbage lay on a wooden board nearby."

Left alone, the group resorted to prayer and committed their lives to God.

"We were still praying when a man came for me," says Imelda. "He took me to an office, where seven State Research men were waiting. It turned out to be the office of the head of the prison, Farouk Minawa. He had been nicknamed, 'The International Killer.' The room had a red carpet and on the table were at least six telephones."

Major Minawa, the brutish Nubian who headed up the Bureau, was reputed to be the executioner of Entebbe hostage, Mrs. Dora Bloch. Ugandan sources have said he and Captain Nasur Ondaga, Chief of Protocol to the President, marched into her ward at Mulago Hospital dressed in civilian clothes and carrying pistols. They shouted to the staff to stand back, then they hauled Mrs. Bloch out of bed, grabbing her by both arms. The men frog-marched her down three flights of stairs, leaving behind her cane, purse, shoes, and dress. She screamed continuously, as they half-dragged, half-carried her. She was then taken to a forest, where, it is said, Minawa shot her.

Imelda takes up her story again. "One at a time the seven men began questioning me. They thoroughly checked everything in my bag. The Lord helped me to answer all their questions with Scripture. They could not grasp how a person could have Jesus without religion. I quoted John 14:6, in which Jesus said, 'I am the way, and the truth, and the life; no one comes to the Father, but through Me.'

"One of them spoke Latin, and because of that he claimed to know God more than us. I said that our Lord did not have a religion, and in the Bible God did not give a religion to the world as a way to heaven.

"Another of the men gave me a soda, but still we disagreed. Spiritually, they were too blind to see Jesus."

Imelda was accused of being an agent of the American Central Intelligence Agency, of creating political unrest, and of backing the Israelis in a plot against the Ugandan government.

"You preach your gospel and earn a salary from America," one of the accusers claimed.

They soon realized that Imelda was unmarried. (She had lived with her son's father until she committed her life to Christ, then felt it was wrong to continue living in such a way.)

"Why isn't one of these two men your husband?" one of them snapped.

"Because one of them is only eighteen, and the other twenty-four, and I am twenty-eight," she explained.

As Imelda was being interrogated in the early hours of that morning, her two friends were earnestly interceding for her. Another woman prisoner was brought into their cell, but was almost immediately taken out again. They supposed she was about to be raped and then savagely murdered, so they prayed fervently for her, too. Many of the State Research men would gang-rape a woman prisoner until she died.

"I pleaded the 'blood of Jesus' for her [a prayer for divine intervention]. If anything protected us, it was the 'blood of Jesus.' I lost count of the times I pleaded it," says Benjamin.

It wasn't long before Benjamin was roughly escorted from the cell. "The guards led me to a room with the title, 'Head of Technical Operations,' on the door. I was welcomed into the room and then ordered to sit on the carpeted floor.

"Imelda was sitting on a sofa at one end of the room, with a soda bottle in her hands. I sat facing the table with my legs in front of me. I rested my hands around my knees.

"The room had three sofa chairs along the walls, a large office table and chair with an odd assortment of items piled behind it. One of the men was lying on a sofa. He was on my right-hand side.

"Guns were lying underneath the sofas, and pictures covered part of the walls. The other men were sitting around drinking."

Benjamin exchanged glances with Imelda, who sat quietly on the sofa. He drew courage and braced himself for the questioning, as he considered Luke 21:13, "It will lead to an opportunity for your testimony." He decided that whatever they asked him, he would turn the confrontation into a personal testimony.

"They began to interrogate me randomly," says Benjamin. "When asked about my religion, I told them I did not belong to any of the four religious groups, but was a born-again child of God. They asked me why this was so, and I explained how I had been converted and what the salvation of Jesus meant to me.

"They did not like hearing my words and only seemed interested in incriminating me. I was asked where I went to church and what books we read there. 'The church where God's children meet and we read the Bible,' I responded."

Benjamin expressed the idea that religion would not save anyone, only the blood of Christ and faith in Him.

"These men really hated Jesus. They did not want to hear His name and tried their best to divert my conversation from Him.

"They tried to make me admit that I had been brainwashed and was a CIA agent. I denied it and told them again of Jesus. The Lord gave me a tremendous boldness."

As they conversed, a tall, bearded man, with a frightening air about him, came into the room. He was obviously a powerful man at the house of killing.

The newcomer leaned forward on his desk, littered with telephones and said accusingly: "You are an agent of the CIA." (At that time Amin's men had a paranoia about this American organization, and seemed to see an agent under every bed.)

He added: "You are trying to establish a fifth religion in Uganda." Benjamin denied this ludicrous suggestion and patiently asked to be allowed to explain the true situation. Almost as soon as he started talking again, the giant man harshly ordered him to shut up. Benjamin's constant use of the Lord's name irritated him. Benjamin goes on: "He didn't like the name of Jesus, and we know also that Satan doesn't like that name. It is a terror to him. The devil in that man was trembling and shouted at me to stop talking of Jesus.

"The man stood up and angrily pulled out his pistol at his waist. He threatened to shoot me on the spot if I wouldn't be silent. My life was spared due to the intervention of one of the other interrogators."

"Okay, now let's talk sensibly," said the man. "I've been to a theological seminary and I know the Bible better than you.

"Admit that you have been brainwashed and have been working as a secret agent, and all will be okay."

At gunpoint, he ordered Benjamin to stop preaching to him about Jesus, but that was like trying to dam the Nile with a toothpick. Benjamin pleaded for one last chance to defend himself, like Paul, who told the Romans in Acts 22:1, "Brethren and fathers, hear my defense which I now offer to you." His interrogators vainly tried to get him off the subject of Christ and the New Birth.

"Clearly it wasn't me speaking at this time, but the Holy Ghost," says Benjamin.

Then, Paul, a teen-ager, was brought into the room. They questioned him along the same lines. To the astonishment of the soldiers, his answers were the same as Benjamin's.

The massive man behind the desk came over to Benjamin, and squatted in front of him. "Look, stop talking about God and Jesus and start talking like a normal man," he said.

"I guess by 'a normal man' he meant someone who didn't speak about the things of God," says Benjamin. "Refusing to admit to any of the allegations, I told them they were all lies. He offered me a cigarette. I declined. At this time he was very patient with me. However, the other men began violently kicking me on the jaw and in my ribs.

"The leader snapped—he grabbed hold of my shirt by its collar, then transferred his grip to my neck. He spread his large fingers over my windpipe, trying to strangle me. It was obvious he could have easily done so, as he was a trained killer. I struggled fiercely to get loose. The man's grasp relaxed and he let me go. Surely God had come to my aid!

"He cursed aloud and ripped my shirt open, apparently thinking a recording device was concealed there."

The conversation then took a decidedly sick turn as the soldiers began a crude discussion about sex. They commanded the believers to undress. "I thought they were joking," recalls Benjamin. "But unfortunately, the soldiers were very serious. They said they wanted to see if it was possible for me to fornicate with sister Imelda. Can you imagine the ungodliness?

"Imelda was taken to another room and forced to undress while we remained in that room dressed only in our underwear [shorts]. When Imelda was brought back, she was completely naked and was sobbing with streams of tears running down her face. Paul and I were then compelled to undress completely."

During this whole unsavory episode, the three drew comfort from the knowledge that Jesus Himself was stripped, before He was led away to be crucified.

Benjamin was then ordered to rape Imelda. He refused and this so incensed one of the men that he lunged at Ben with an empty bottle. He struggled to force him to commit the sex act with distraught Imelda. He repeatedly crashed the bottle down on the young preacher's head and body, in an attempt to make him proceed with the evil deed. Ben's arms were terribly bruised as he tried to protect his head. Again he took solace from a Bible incident when Jesus was beaten with reeds before His death.

Imelda pleaded with the men, "What you are doing is not right." Taking no heed to her cries, they violently slapped her on the face. After they finished with Benjamin, they ordered Paul to take his place.

"Paul also refused to do as they asked and was beaten and kicked unmercifully," says Benjamin. "This was the most agonizing time of all. I can still remember him shouting at the top of his voice that this was something God would not allow. He said, 'Mungu anakata,' a Swahili expression which means, 'God has refused.'

"They hit us with bottles as we wriggled helplessly on the carpet, all the while taking photographs of the brutal acts.

"Then one man, with all his might, hit me over the head with a bottle. It shattered into many small pieces all over the floor. I began to lose consciousness, with a sharp noise echoing in my ears. Later, Paul told me he was ready to meet the Lord, 'there and then.'"

Suddenly, without explanation, the torturers stopped their beating, told the trio to get dressed, and took the shocked and injured believers back to their cell. There the three continued to pray and call on the Lord for His deliverance.

"During this time I was gripped by fear and panic and we became less talkative," admits Benjamin.

The brave Ugandans tried to snatch some sleep on the bare cement floor. They took turns lying uncomfortably on top of the wooden bench. Continually their sleep was interrupted by State Research men coming in and out, firing questions at them.

"They were bloodthirsty men. The sounds of their guns being cocked became a sort of nightmare for us," says Benjamin. "Despite the fear that gripped us, God gave us courage and strength when we found the demons of torture, anger, and drunkenness in them. We also pleaded the blood of Jesus for our protection."

The next day the trio was escorted to an office, and personal background information was obtained. That was the last time that Imelda caught a brief glimpse of her son, Geoffrey, a bright-eyed, friendly lad.

They noticed one of the officers standing with a sword in his hand and a man lying on the floor. He was badly mutilated. After a short interrogation the three were returned to their cell.

"We sang praises to God and witnessed to fellow prisoners," says Benjamin. "The imprisonment of Paul and Silas came to mind as we sat there. We remembered how the prison foundations were shaken and the doors opened, as they prayed and sang praises to God.

"Right after a meal we always found time to pray and sing. This was when we had the most strength. During the greater part of the day we were very weak. Like Paul and Silas, we were indeed in the 'inner prison' of Uganda. Only murderous armed men worked there. Nakasero had become infamous for its killings and rarely did anyone come out of it alive—that is unless he or she was a Christian whom God hadn't yet desired to call back to Himself.

"No one would easily enter its heavily guarded gates; except of course the Lord Jesus Christ. Even high ranking government officials were not allowed in. It was the top security military prison in Uganda. No communication of any sort was allowed between the prisoners and the outside world. I realized how completely cut off from the outside world I was. A keen desire rose in me to see again the beauty of God's creation. How I longed to look into the heavens, to hear the conversation of normal men, to walk and drink in the fresh Uganda air."

This testing time was not all horror for these dedicated and courageous believers. "One woman prisoner accepted Christ Jesus as her Savior in her cell," relates Benjamin. "Later she was released; after she witnessed to two men, they were also converted. Shortly afterwards, in the night, one of them was called out. I suppose he was killed. The other convert was removed from his cell but later brought back. He had been badly beaten. His face was disfigured and he was bleeding from his nose and mouth.

"Just then I was sharing Christ with an important-looking man. He panicked at the bloody sight and said he would wait to consider whether or not to accept Christ. As far as I know he didn't get saved and I gather he died there of starvation.

"Often at night, one of us would be taken to an office and we used the opportunity to preach to the soldiers on duty. Whoever was left in the cell would immediately start praying for the 'preacher.' I understand we became famous in that place as 'the three religious people who didn't belong to any religion.'" Others in the prison gained courage to speak of their faith because of our stand. They told us they were 'people of God,' too.

"On one occasion a State Research man angrily asked me questions with a knife in his hand. I knew if my answers were not satisfactory during this interrogation, he would drive this weapon into me. Fortunately, a superior ordered him to put the knife away."

Imelda said for a time she was confused about the reason for her imprisonment. "Every day we were undergoing afflictions and torture. For a whole week, both day and night, we faced the same cruel treatment.

"Then one evening while talking to God I reminded Him of His promise in Jeremiah 1:19, 'And they will fight against you, but they will not overcome you, for I am with you to deliver you.' I also thought of First Peter 5:7, 'Casting all your anxiety upon Him, because He cares for you.' Then I heard a voice asking me, 'What about My work?' Right then I realized God's purpose for our being in that place. When I told the brothers, they said they had also asked the same question.

"In our underground church we had often prayed all night, fasting and waiting on God for His work in Uganda. We came to understand there was a great work for us to do as witnesses in this very place, and that God would not bring someone else to do it.

"Many people joined us in our cell. On one particular occasion we started to preach the gospel to them. Several got saved and many others were convicted.''

Although the three had great courage, they experienced a very natural fear of a possible brutal death. Says Benjamin: ''I could not stand the thought of being killed, my body being thrown out somewhere in the bush, and no one knowing about it. This was the practice of this prison—many people were killed, driven away in the trunks of cars, and dumped in forests. Only a few people knew where we were. Many thought we had been immediately killed.''

They became so physically weak that they thought they were dying. They felt there was no more point in their friends outside praying for them, so they committed themselves to God. However, believers discovered their location and were prepared to offer twenty-thousand shillings (approximately $2,700 US) for their release.

After a week, twelve people were in the cell, and the men were suddenly removed. ''Being together with the men that whole week was surely God's protection,'' says Imelda, ''for it was very unusual. The men were taken to another room.

The three women already in our cell remained and two other women joined us. Being separated from my brothers caused me great grief. They had encouraged me many times, and I thought I would never see them again.''

It seems an illness saved Imelda from being gang-raped like some of the other women. ''The fever was God's way of saving me from these brutal men, who came for other women,'' she says. ''I had sleepless nights because of the hard floor. The meals were becoming less and less, until there was no food at all.

''I was not allowed to wash my clothes or take a bath; and I was really filthy. This was a time of surrendering my whole life to God. I had personally concluded that I would not live much longer as the fever had increased and there was no food.

''I thank God that two of the women sharing the cell with me got saved. One of them prayed and laid her hands on me. Miraculously, I was healed.''

Meanwhile the two men were taken out and an execution was set up for them and some of the other prisoners. ''Large, tall men in commando uniforms lined up about three meters in front of us, cocked their rifles, and ordered us to look down,'' says Benjamin. ''I was certain the hour had come at last when I was to join my Lord. I began to pray what I believed to be my last prayer.

"I asked God to forgive me all my sins and receive my spirit. The next moments were the worst of my life. I expected bullets to go right through my body. Paul sat beside me and was also praying. We both thought death was imminent.

"But the execution order proved to be only a cruel hoax to frighten us. At that moment, we were ordered to stand up and move ahead. We were taken to another cell, bursting with about thirty people.

"The conditions were more appalling than the other cell. There was very little fresh air. We had our shirts off most of the time and used them as fans. The waste buckets were overflowing, and maggots were crawling on the floor. I took my position right by the maggots and had the job of constantly pushing them back to provide some space for myself.

"There was hardly enough room to stretch out. Sleep was rare, so we sat up most of the time on the hard floor."

For a while they were given just one meal a day, and water became scarce. Only four plates were provided for all thirty prisoners. Food was slopped on banana leaves, a slimy sauce was poured on top, and it was slid onto the filthy floor.

"The situation always worsened at night," says Benjamin. "Seldom was it possible to find a comfortable position to sleep. Most of the times our legs were in the air.

"During the night there was a constant exchange of prisoners. The moment we heard the familiar clanking of the keys on the iron chain, we knew it was a guard coming to check on us.

"Many of those brought in were bleeding, and their clothes were covered with blood. One man had his ear lobe cut off and an arm badly fractured. Of those taken, few ever returned. Death was hanging over our heads all the time.

"We found strength to call upon God to deliver us. But the chances of ever leaving this particular cell alive looked very slim."

One miracle occurred when the pair prayed desperately for water. People throughout the prison were slowly dying for lack of it. "As a direct answer to prayer, water was brought into the cell," says Benjamin. "It was carefully rationed so that we would all get a share. Quickly we drank it. What a relief it was to us. Water became everything to us, because there was no food."

One day, a guard came to their cell and selected several people, including Benjamin, to clean up "some mess in a cell."

He reports: "Together with four other prisoners I scrubbed the floor of some corridors and the doors of some of the offices. Human blood lay thick on the walls and stairs. It was only by the grace of God that I endured the horrible sight. Pools of blood and water lay on the floor at the bottom of the stairs. We had to scoop it up into buckets and pour it into a small toilet nearby.

"This was the blood of men killed there. Hundreds had lost their lives in those underground cells, especially one, which was like a tunnel. It was very low and dark and void of fresh air. This was the place where our friends from the church were kept for twenty-four hours and is known as 'the grave.'

"As I worked, I imagined the awful deaths of those people. Such a death, I knew, could also soon be mine, but the Lord encouraged my heart and strengthened me."

The pair, by now like human skeletons for lack of food and water, were then moved to their third and final cell.

"That Friday night, I prayed again desperately for water," says Benjamin. "Almost immediately it rained. I took a small plastic plate and eased it underneath the glass window shutter. It was raining heavily, but I was able to collect a very small amount to quench my burning thirst.

"I had to be careful that the soldiers didn't see me, as that would have been dangerous. I drank down the little water I had collected. It was some relief."

Others were less fortunate. "A fellow prisoner at my side asked for water but was disappointed. There was only one bucket with filthy water in it, and some of the prisoners went ahead and drank from it. It was a crucial time for every one of us. Driven by excessive hunger, some of the men even resorted to trying to eat coffee beans. I, too, tried but gave up. The taste was too awful even for me, a starving man."

One day, as the seriously ill prisoners were locked in their cells, war planes were heard passing overhead. They realized that the liberation forces were approaching the city. But would the prisoners survive to be freed? That was the question that haunted all of them.

Abruptly, on Saturday, March 31, 1979, the impossible happened. Soldiers entered the cells of Imelda and the two men and said: "Where are God's children?"

After identifying themselves, they were escorted out and their names were called.

"You are all free!" the officer said solemnly. It was like a dream. Even though they looked like scarecrows, and could hardly walk, they embraced.

A guard took pity on them and drove them to Imelda's home. Sadly, her house no longer rang with the happy sounds of her little son Geoffrey.

On arriving home, Imelda received the tragic news that Geoffrey's father had been arrested, taken to the State Research, and accused of being a CIA spy. He was later shot.

18

The Final Chapter

FOR THE FIRST TIME since the dreaded reign of Idi Amin began, All
Saints Church in Kampala was packed to capacity. It was Sunday
morning, April 15, 1979, and many of the congregation were standing in line still waiting to enter the famous cathedral. No longer did
the church members glance nervously toward the pink-painted building standing behind barbed wire about four hundred yards away.

Over there, inside the headquarters and torture center of the infamous State Research Bureau, lay the appalling last testimony of the
works of Amin's secret police—hundreds of twisted, tortured bodies,
many of whom were Christians. In the stifling, mid-morning heat, the
stench of the corpses pervaded the air in the garden of Amin's lodge,
strategically placed on Nakasero Hill overlooking the SRB building.
There the black Hitler of Africa and his evil henchmen had perpe-
trated some of the most evil crimes known to man.

Inside the pink building was the bloody aftermath of a final massacre of anti-Amin prisoners by the State Research Bureau, who were
well trained for their brutality by Russians and Czechs. Grenades had
been thrown into the crowded cells, killing one hundred prisoners.
Another one hundred lay hacked to death in the unlit basement. Some
had been killed with a sledge hammer. There were more bodies
sprawled in the hall and on the stairs, tortured and then shot.

In the garden lay a grim reminder of the atrocities. George Lukwiya remembers the metal bars used by the soldiers as clubs to beat
the prisoners, often causing death. A full head of hair had fallen off a
tortured man's body, which had lain there a few days. In all, 650
bodies were found, including some of Amin's supporters, killed in
the fighting. A blood-soaked torture chamber was found in a barred

upstairs room. It was there that hundreds of Ugandans were tortured to death. Others had their eyes gouged out by the secret police.

The new and later deposed president, Professor Yusef Lule, a member of the Church of Uganda, had estimated that the butcher Amin and his followers were responsible for the deaths of 500,000 people.

IT WAS ON OCTOBER 30, 1978, that, shielded by tank columns and bombardment from the air, three thousand Ugandan soldiers streamed across the frontier into remote northwestern Tanzania. President Amin was making a bid for glory. His so-called Suicide Strike Force led the onslaught, which took by surprise Tanzania's scattered border defenses. The Ugandans pushed on toward the Kagera River, looting, killing, and pillaging as they went.

Hundreds of defenseless villagers were killed in the advance. Some were tortured or beheaded as soldiers swept through hamlets, shooting at anything, and hurling tear gas canisters into huts.

"What Amin's troops did on the northern side of the Kagera River during the days of occupation amounts to genocide," says Ferdinand Ruhinda, editor of the Tanzania government newspapers, the *Daily News* and *Sunday News,* and one of the first journalists to visit the area. "We saw the remains of people who must have been tortured, then beheaded, before their bodies were dumped along the roadside in a barbaric display of savage triumph."

After Amin's barbaric invasion, Nyerere, President of Tanzania, vowed that he would now allow the Ugandan leader's evil deeds to go unpunished.

"We are going to fight until this snake is out of our house," Nyerere declared angrily.

As the Tanzanians began to counterattack, Amin suggested a crazy solution to the dispute. He declared that the matter should be settled in the boxing ring. "I am keeping fit so that I can challenge President Nyerere in the boxing ring and fight it out there, rather than having the soldiers lose their lives on the field of battle," he said. Amin said that Muhammud Ali would be an ideal referee for the bout. Amin, as the former Uganda heavyweight champ, would give the small, white-haired Nyerere a sporting chance by fighting with one arm tied behind his back, and his legs shackled with weights. This proposal was rejected outright.

The Tanzanian government-controlled mass media reinforced their president's stand. A spokesman said: "To accept mediation is to turn the other cheek to a butcher."

Soon it was the Tanzanians' turn to take the offensive. First the towns of Masaka and Mbarara were reduced to smoldering rubble. They looked as if they had been hit by an earthquake. Then, as the Tanzanians, with the help of Ugandan exiles, discovered there was very little resistance from Amin's troops, they decided to go all the way to Kampala to rid the country once and for all of the vile dictator.

But as they marched, Amin, as always, was full of bluff words. He boomed out over the radio: "Like the prophet Mohammed, who sacrificed his life and his property for the good of Islam, I am ready to die for my country."

However, when the Tanzanians showed how determined they were, he and his troops quickly retreated. Amin's army would have continued to run had it not been for an eleventh hour decision by Libya's strongman, Colonel Gadhafi, to back his homicidal friend to the hilt.

Libyan troops stepped in to reinforce the demoralized Ugandan army at key defenses. They delayed the capture of Kampala for several weeks.

This action precipitated a black African resentment over the Libyan action: namely the arrogant push of Moslem influence deep into Christian Africa at any expense, even when it meant supporting a ruthless and discredited regime, such as Amin's. And most of Africa knew Uganda to be one of the continent's most Christianized countries. In fact, it is the only African country to have internationally recognized saints, and the only one to be visited by a pope.

After Entebbe Airport and town had fallen, the Tanzanian troops began their bombardment of Kampala. As they did so, some six hundred people flocked to the hilltop grounds of the Roman Catholic Rubaga Cathedral. There they were cared for by priests, nuns, and even the Catholic archbishop until the guns ceased firing.

Among the priests who helped in this massive relief operation for people from every faith seeking sanctuary, was Father Yves Tourigny, a French-Canadian who is the Catholic Church's Uganda archivist.

"As the shelling started, people of all ages appeared here," he says in his office next to the towering Roman-Norman style cathedral.

"There was a wonderful spirit among the men, women, children, and old people who stayed here. We had to organize a dispensary for those who were sick, and a place for the food to be prepared. It was marvelous to see the men actually help the women to prepare food, something previously unheard of in Uganda.

"The bombardment lasted about three weeks and during the last week we had sixteen bombs explode here. Yet no one was hurt and not one window in the cathedral was damaged. There was a direct hit on our hospital at the back of us, but fortunately the ward that was damaged had already been cleared of patients."

Cardinal Emmanuel Nsubuga, the Archbishop of Kampala, really involved himself in the situation. "The cardinal and his staff spent nearly all their time with the refugees," says Father Tourigny. "In fact, people were sleeping all over his residence.

"During a lull in the fighting, the cardinal would sneak out with a Red Cross sign on his vehicle to a nearby farm to bring food. This went into the common store, which was kept full with our provisions and food brought in by the refugees. We shared everything in common."

Much of Father Tourigny's time was spent walking around talking to people. "One day, as I was walking, the first stage of a missile burst above my head before shooting off toward its target," he says. "The bang was so loud that I jumped several feet in the air. The people were watching me and I felt that I should set an example, so I just stood there, calmly relit my pipe, and continued walking. Mind you, I didn't feel so calm inside."

The Catholics made no stipulation about the faiths of those who stayed there. Among the books handed out to comfort the fugitives were the Koran for the Moslems and the Bible for the Christians of all denominations.

"We told the Moslems and the Church of Uganda people that they could hold their own services if they wished, but they decided to join us for ours," says Tourigny.

During this period, a distraught man arrived with his one-month-old baby. He said that his wife had been killed and he had three other children to look after. A woman from a nearby village, who was staying at the cardinal's home, immediately "adopted" the helpless baby and he is now part of her happy family.

As the stubborn Moslem's world was crumbling, his audacity continued unabated. For instance, he appealed for papal intervention.

"Nyerere is a Catholic," said Amin. "We hope that he would heed an appeal by the pope. We appeal to Pope John Paul II to use his good offices to ensure Nyerere orders his forces to withdraw."

Christian centers seemed to draw refugees like bees to a honeypot. Another five hundred crowded into Gayaza High School, a school twelve miles outside of Kampala. This school has had a great influence on the Christian leadership of the country for more than fifty years.

"We were one of the few secondary schools which managed to complete that first term of the school year," says English-born Miss Janice Hobday, who has been at Gayaza School since 1965. "So many other schools had buildings destroyed and property looted or burned, and this made our deliverance seem all the more miraculous.

"Our school became a place of real refuge during the shelling in this part of the country. Three hundred of the girls stayed here with us all the way through. About 240 went home with their parents, but school life continued as normally as possible. Many families came out from Kampala as refugees for two days up to two weeks, and our buildings became homes."

Says Miss Ann Cutler, another British member of the staff: "For two days, when fighting in Kampala was at its worst, we must have had about five hundred refugees with us. Every available space was full, even the table tennis room and the two dormitories. Fortunately every group fed themselves, and even the dubious characters among them were kept busy in their search for food, water, and firewood for cooking."

The staff really believes that God protected them from the shelling during that critical time. "Gradually, I became convinced that we were going to be safe, and I rejected all suggestions that we would be bombed, taken over by the army, and raped. Any of those things could have happened," says headmistress, Miss Sheelagh Warren. "When the Tanzanian soldiers came to look around the school later, they said, 'We had no idea there was such a place here; we thought it was a forest and we might have shelled you." The teacher on duty said, 'But God knew we were here and He looked after us.'

"He surely did. The Tanzanians had a device which could detect the presence of four or more soldiers and score a direct hit. This was proved many times by the deadly accuracy of their bombs."

Cynthia Mackay, a missionary from Yorkshire, England, kept a gripping diary of those heady but frightening days. Here are a few excerpts:

"*April 5*. We heard that the 'enemy' were within a mile of the centre of Kampala, so did not move far from home today, as we thought there might be street fighting. Of course the 'enemy' were really our friends, the Liberation Army, whom we were longing to see. It is a topsy-turvy kind of war to be in when you are hoping your side will not win and can't wait for the 'enemy' to arrive. There was heavy shelling early on, but then a quiet night. They have been very careful in their shelling to do as little damage as possible and have kept their fire for places where they knew army were hiding or where Amin himself was hiding out. Some buildings at Makerere and Mulago were hit because of Amin's men taking refuge there at night.

"*April 8*. At our fellowship this evening we sang softly, and then as shooting seemed to be very near, we had a Bible Quiz instead of singing, and quietly read and prayed with only one more Palm Sunday hymn, 'Ride On, Ride On in Majesty,' sung very softly. From about midnight to 2:30 A.M. there was shooting and shelling, but then it quieted down and we slept.

"*April 9*. This was the night that in his sermon last Sunday Canon Shalita called 'that night,' and we all knew which one he meant! The shelling was very intensive and very near and we were shivering with fright. We thought every shell whining over must land on us. Tragically, a doctor friend of two from our fellowship, Godfrey and Elina, who lived very near them at Mulago, was killed that night with his brother. Three others were also killed near there. At Mengo Hospital the only shell which landed was on a store, so there were no casualties at the hospital.

"*April 10*. In spite of the fearful night, we rejoiced this morning because it poured with rain and we were able to catch enough from the roof to fill our baths and every container in the house. There has not been water in the taps for ages and this was a great blessing. Shelling continued all morning and we stayed in our houses. The telephone was still working then and Godfrey rang up to tell us about Dr. Wandera's death. Most of the people, including Godfrey, Elina, and Bernard, from the 'Doctors' Village' there at Mulago, decided to move away and walk to Gayaza about twelve miles away."

On April 10 Miss Mackay described what happened when the troops arrived. "At about 4:00 P.M. we suddenly heard cheering and shouts outside and rushed out to hear people shouting, 'They've come! They are here!'' The Liberation Army had arrived at last. People from the top of the hill came dashing down to tell us that there were hundreds of soldiers taking up position on the top. Wilson Baganizi, our provincial secretary, whose home commands a magnificent view of the city, told how he watched them coming in from three directions, marching in two's and filling the city in their thousands. The fact that they were walking took Amin's army by surprise, we think. They were probably looking out for tanks and lorries [trucks]. We too had been getting impatient and saying, 'Why don't they hurry up and arrive?' Most of them have been walking for six months all the way from Dar-es-Salaam. There were many Ugandan exiles in front and thousands of Tanzanians. It was a very thrilling moment, and we realized something of what it must have meant to Holland and other occupied countries in Europe when the American and British troops arrived.

"There was no news on Radio Uganda that night, but some unusually good music including Gilbert and Sullivan songs such as, 'They've Got Him on the List!'''

Miss Mackay then went on to describe what happened on April 13 (Good Friday). She said: "I love Africa for the lovely bits of informality that so often come into a formal occasion. After his speech, President Lule suggested the crowd sing the Tanzanian National Anthem. There was no band and no one knew the words and few the tune, but he said, 'Just sing it to "la" if you don't know the words,' and they did! Rather he did, with a few following the 'las.'''

Then she described that wonderful Easter Day. "We were up by 5:30 A.M. and out by 6:00 A.M. (fourteen of us) all singing 'Jesus Lives,' 'He Arose,' 'Jesus Is Risen Today,' 'He Is Risen,' and other Easter hymns at houses round the hill as we walked along. We finished at Mengo Hospital at Dr. John Davies' home, where we had a cup of tea before going on to church.

"Canon Shalita's sermon at an absolutely packed All Saints this morning was magnificent. With such experiences as we had just been through in our minds we were all prepared to be reminded that outward liberation and freedom can be lost and spoiled so easily. The terrible looting and destruction showed only too clearly the need for liberation by Christ from greed, revenge, hatred, selfishness, lack of thought for others, and similar evils.

"It was joyous to see people after the service meeting each other and so relieved to see their friends still alive."

Cynthia Mackay added that there were so many people at the church for all the services that day that enough bread could not be found in the city for all the communion services, so they had to use biscuits brought by the liberators.

"The fascist dictator is finished," broadcast the loudspeaker vans that drove through Kampala. For the first time in post-colonial history, one African country had invaded another. Amin was well and truly on the run.

As he was running for his life, the people at Kampala went on a terrible orgy of looting and destruction. Dr. Ken Tracey, director of the Africa Region of World Vision International, explains why he believes the government building received special attention from the wreckers.

"Many of the population of Kampala felt that Amin was so devil-inspired that there was no way they could get rid of him," says New-Zealand-born Dr. Tracey. "They were convinced that he would come back.

"What they were trying to do was to make it impossible for him to rule again. So they smashed everything. They burned every file they could lay their hands on. They smashed computers and all this sort of thing. Typewriters were taken out into the streets and absolutely mangled.

"This meant that there was no machinery of government, and that's what has made things so difficult for this government."

BUT AS THE PEOPLE OF KAMPALA rejoiced, the rest of the unliberated land still suffered. For instance, as Amin troops fled to the north to escape from the Tanzanians, there were some horrible reports of killing by the Nubians. A Catholic priest and nun brought dreadful stories to Kampala of child victims seen stuck on stakes by fleeing Nubians near Bombo on the road north to the Sudan and Zaire. The European nun said that the women fleeing in the Nubian convoys of cars and trucks were armed and killing, too.

Right up to the end of the war, Amin's men were still carrying out a plan of systematic killing of Christians and other key people.

Says American journalist Bev Hubble, who visited Uganda shortly after the fall: "Even as Amin's soldiers retreated through different towns, they would pause and take time to look up specific people on their death list, and kill them.

"It does seem amazing that in retreat they would do that, but it just shows how determined they were to murder specific targets."

Miss Hubble says she came across instances of miraculous escapes by Christians in the town of Jinja.

"Several of my Ugandan friends said that their fathers were on a death list in Jinja. They had been selected to appear before a firing squad on the exact day that the Tanzanian soldiers liberated Jinja," she says.

"Documents were found later which showed that the local Moslem Council had planned which of their neighbors were going to be murdered as Christian targets.

"Christians in Jinja interpreted their escape from being eliminated as a miracle of God's timing."

Another unusual escape in Jinja came from Dora Kantungamo, who works for an evangelical organization in Nairobi, Kenya. She says that when the dictator's henchmen swept through Jinja, her uncle, who had been warned that soldiers were tracking him, climbed a tree for refuge. Local children occasionally screamed to prevent him from slumbering during his three-day perch in those branches. When his little friends announced the arrival of liberation troops and begged him to climb down, he refused—unable to believe Jinja's terror was past.

Many Ugandans still bear the mental, emotional, and psychological scars. "The minds of people have been destroyed," says one Ph.D. in the new government, describing the emotional paralysis created by years of tyranny.

It was really tragic that one of the Church of Uganda bishops who survived Amin's reign of terror should die so tragically at the end. The Bishop of Mbale, the Rt. Rev. John Wasikye, was murdered by Idi Amin's fleeing soldiers at Jinja. Mr. Wanedeya, the lone survivor of the bishop's party, which was on a trip to Kampala, felt that two factors may have led to the bishop's death. One was that, while under arrest, he protested against the murderous acts of Amin's soldiers when they seized an army captain, who shared his cell, and strangled him to death. The other theory was that he was sent by some people in Mbale to deliver a message to the Uganda National Liberation Front administration in Kampala, asking for the immediate rescue of the people in the eastern part of the country where Amin's soldiers were killing indiscriminately. It is possible that this message fell into the hands of soldiers at a roadblock near Jinja.

Wanedeya, a staunch Christian businessman in Mbale, offered to take the bishop to Kampala. They embarked on their journey but were taken prisoner when they got to a roadblock just before Jinja. They were ordered to sit down and later were taken to Gadhafi Garrison, where they were put in a cell.

At the barracks, soldiers were massacring people arrested on a bus earlier that day. Soon after the rattling of the gun ceased, they heard a voice and their cell door was flung open. It remained so for some time.

Wanedeya and the others in the cell could see soldiers loading bodies into a truck. The soldiers, who spoke Swahili mixed with Kakwa and Nubian, came back in the morning and read out the names of those in the cell. They told the bishop that there was no respect due to people like him who thought they were "big." They closed the door and at 10:00 A.M. two of them returned and ordered some of the prisoners out to go and meet "the boss." The others were forced to board a truck, in the presence of Major Muhammed and the former provincial police officer E. K. Kwakanengyere. The soldiers who went with them had orders to shoot them, and later some of these prisoners' bodies were found floating in a river near Bujagali shooting range outside Jinja.

Bishop Wasikye is reported to have approached Kwakanengyere, who assured him that he was arranging for his release. They and the businessman were asked to go back to the cell while their arrest was closely investigated.

In the cell, one of the prisoners, an ex-army officer, said he doubted they would survive the night, for soldiers had by then started indiscriminately killing any civilian they came across. When they asked for food, Major Muhammed said, "You ask for food here? You think this is your home. Keep quiet now. You will get food to eat if it is available."

In the night, soldiers armed with torches, ropes, guns, and pangas, opened the cell door. One of them asked for the whereabouts of "captain" and the ex-army officer cried as they advanced toward him. They put a rope around his neck and pulled him toward the cell door. Bishop Wasikye protested against this, telling the soldiers that they were committing an evil act, but he was told to "shut up." A soldier added: "You can explain to us when your turn comes." The gangster then strangled the ex-officer.

Prisoners inside the cell could clearly see what was happening because the soldiers had flashlights. Wanedeya recalls they laughed excitedly as they performed their acts of murder. Some victims were strangled with ropes, others shot, and the rest bayonetted.

Then the killers came to the bishop's cell and one said proudly: "We are back to hear from that big man [the bishop] who thinks he can boss us around with orders here." One of the soldiers then threw a noosed rope around the bishop's neck while three others tried to pounce on him.

Another prisoner called upon his cellmates to resist these random killings. A group of prisoners, including a woman soldier, followed the soldiers who were pulling the bishop, in a futile attempt to rescue him. But a soldier who was guarding the door opened fire. A man and the woman soldier rushed past him, but the guard chased them and killed them with his bayonet.

The bishop was killed in the confusion, and the only survivor of that terrible day, Mr. Wanedeya, kept quiet in the cell until the soldiers had left and silence had enveloped the death yard. He sneaked out of the cell, clambering over the dead bodies, and managed to get to the inner gate of the barracks.

A guard spotted him and fired three times, but missed as the businessman rolled on the group. The soldier kept watching and raised the alarm to alert the other guards. Wanedeya quickly crawled to a nearby fence and spent an agonizing time trying to find a hole to crawl through. "My desperate attempts were rewarded. I eventually found an opening," he says.

The bishop's body still has not been found.

As the Tanzanians continued their relentless push forward, those in areas which had not yet been freed from Amin waited impatiently for their turn to come. One of those places was Fort Portal, which is in the extreme west of Uganda, bordering on Zaire. Kampala-born Miss Elizabeth Kerr, the daughter of CMS missionaries, who now teaches at Kyebambe Secondary School at Fort Portal, was one anxious "waiter."

She first speaks of the excitement on Thursday, April 5, 1979, when they heard that Kampala had at last been taken by the invaders. "At night some brave, or foolhardy, souls near us celebrated by flashing lights, hooting, beating drums, and blowing whistles. That naturally annoyed the army, and there was some frightening shooting and our first experience of the sound of a mortar shell, which made a sort of dull bang.

"As one of the girls said, 'I could feel my bed shaking with fright.' Somehow it was odd going on teaching as usual; there was little time for marking papers as we turned out lights around 8:00 P.M."

Miss Kerr says that on April 8 (Palm Sunday) many of the girls at the school began making a "frightening" noise in the dining room, saying they wanted to go home—even though three-quarters of them were boarders and would not be able to. So it was decided that the local girls could leave, plus those who would be collected by their parents.

"We feared bombing and I don't know what else, and also that we would run out of food and money. So in record time, all before lunch, the textbooks were handed in and at least half the girls were gone. I plowed on with a tiny group in my class and others on two succeeding mornings. We listened to Shakespeare's *Twelfth Night* on records, more to keep them occupied than anything else."

By April 12 only one hundred and fifty pupils were left in the school. "They were very depressed and fearful," says Miss Kerr. "We had our Holy Communion early because of the curfew. It was a service I shall never forget because of the feeling throughout the school at the time that this was our last evening on earth.

"The girls were convinced that the cathedral was going to be bombed, and, as we were just behind it, we were going to die."

The preacher that night spoke about the words in Luke, "When the hour came . . ." and then as he began to talk of the Last Supper, he asked a question that brought home to the girls exactly where they were at that moment. "Are you ready to eat the Last Supper with Jesus?" he asked, and suddenly they discovered a new-found courage and responded with a confident "Yes."

As Amin's soldiers were trying to escape from the Tanzanians, they were stealing buses, cars, and trucks, so they could travel quickly. Miss Kerr, like so many other missionaries, was held at gunpoint by four heavily armed and desperate soldiers, who ordered her out of the car. Along with some colleagues she was ordered into a little room in a ruined gas station, and they all wondered for a moment if they were to be murdered.

"But all they wanted was money, and they were so annoyed that we had so little, just our collection. One of them took the car and rolled it down the road, and we hoped they would not get it started. But they did; they got petrol at gunpoint and then drove madly down the road and up to Bunyoro. The car had 'Diocese of Rwenzori' on the doors, so it was somewhat conspicuous and lots of people saw it speeding north."

Miss Kerr and other staff members spent Easter night in the bush, hiding. "I remembered as we were standing or sitting on dried banana leaves in the bush, that at that time (we left the house at about 9:00 P.M. after we'd had our supper), it was the time perhaps when Jesus came to the disciples. They were also in hiding, in the room behind locked doors, that first Easter, and He said, 'Peace be to you.'"

Finally, on Wednesday, April 18, the town was liberated. Says Miss Kerr: "I've never seen the town go absolutely wild with joy before. It was so exciting, so warming to see men in battle dress smiling and relaxed. Everyone wanted to greet them and shake hands with them."

The Tanzanian troops went through town accompanied by crowds of people, shouting and blasting their car horns and riding decorated bicycles. They waved and yelled at the three giant tanks as they roared slowly into the town, covered with waving, tired soldiers.

Miss Kerr adds: "I learned a lot about fear during those few days, mostly that it's frequently illogical, an emotion that you can't reason with."

All over Uganda, desperate Amin soldiers seized transport at gunpoint. But many people hated the regime so much that they did their best to sabotage the vehicles.

One Italian priest, a Verona Father from Kaabong, which is fifty miles from the southern Sudan border and twenty-five miles from Kenya, was really crafty.

"Amin's men came and said they wanted my old car," says the priest. "I had to think quickly, so I invited them in for a cup of coffee before their long journey, and whispered to one of my men to close the gap on one of the spark plugs.

"When they set off, the engine was running very badly and after chugging along for about two kilometers, they gave up and brought the vehicle back.

"It was quite astonishing. After they'd gone and I'd fixed the plug, it was working as well as ever again."

THERE WAS A TIME when the Roman Catholics of Gulu did not get on very well with their Church of Uganda counterparts. As with Protestants and Catholics all over the world, there had been times of mutual suspicion.

But the war changed that, when three VIPs sought sanctuary with a group of Catholic brothers at the Alokolum National Seminary, which trains priests from all over Uganda.

The VIPs were three veteran British missionaries, Phebe Cave-Browne-Cave, Mildred Brown, and Mary Coleman, who lived in separate houses on a compound at the back of the Anglican Cathedral in Gulu.

"We were only about two kilometers from the local barracks and we had heard a lot of shooting," says Mary Coleman. "We were told that if Kampala fell to the Tanzanians, we ought to be at least five miles from the barracks, because the Amin soldiers were going to kill anyone in that radius.

"So on Thursday morning, April 5, I went to see the Ugandan father-rector at Alokolum, who had always been very helpful to us. I asked him if we could stay there for one night."

The father-rector and his international team of teacher/priests from the United States, Germany, Holland, and Ireland, welcomed the three women.

"But Kampala didn't fall the next day, and in fact we stayed for several weeks."

The next day, Miss Coleman, who comes from Acton, West London, tried to return to her bungalow, but found the entrance to the compound blocked by a tree trunk and guarded by a soldier who seemed to enjoy playing with a hand grenade.

"We were going to shoot at your car yesterday, thinking you were guerrillas," the soldier told a shaking Mary Coleman.

With that she decided to return to the seminary, and despite problems at a roadblock manned by Amin's troops, arrived safely.

A priest put them in guest rooms at the front of the buildings. But soon the local base commander decided to provide a 'guard' for the seminary in the form of a handful of teen-age soldiers. These young men were in fact far from helpful, and their disgraceful behavior was a constant nightmare for everyone at the training center.

One white Father, who asked not to be named, says, "We suffered constant intimidation and terror from our so-called proectors. They would go out at night and loot things like radios and bicycles from nearby homes. They also brought back girls they had stopped at gunpoint and would rape them here."

"We carried our passports at all times and we were ready to run into the bush at a moment's notice," says Miss Coleman. The "bush" was at the back of the seminary, but the problem they faced was elderly Phebe Cave-Browne-Cave, now in her eighties. This brave woman went to Uganda in 1927 and had taught many of the country's political and religious leaders, including the late archbishop, Janani Luwum. Miss Coleman was worried that Miss Cave-Browne-Cave might not be able to make a quick escape because of her advanced years, although all the women knew that if necessary, the priests would carry them on their backs.

The news that Kampala had fallen came through on Wednesday, April 11. As the three Protestant missionaries emerged from early morning prayers next day with the staff and students, there was shooting going on all over the seminary. Then some of the soldiers seized about fifteen vehicles and drove them away. Many of them were used for looting local houses in and around Gulu. Mary Coleman later discovered that her car had been impounded and used in thefts from the Catholic bishop's home.

Gulu was a base not only for the Chwi (Leopard) battalion of Amin's army, but also for the air force. After the fall of Kampala, the retreating forces found their way north through the town. What little military discipline there was rapidly broke down. The local commander, a Sudanese, who knew Father Jordan, the vice-rector, twice said that he was leaving because of the conditions. Each time, however, he returned and there was a slight semblance of order. The young guards assigned to the seminary would get drunk, and then loot and attack villagers.

Three times they got news that the soldiers were evacuating the barracks, but twice many of them came back. They would be out looting, go off to the West Nile, and then come back to Gulu for more.

While Mary Coleman was at the refuge, soldiers raided her house. Later, at the site of the mayhem, she says, "It seems that somebody led them here."

The soldiers got into the house by shooting through the locks and then through some of the windows. They seized, among other things, some of her letters; her Kenyan bank book which showed that she had been secretly helping exiles like Geoffrey Latim; and her diary containing Latim's address.

"When I heard the papers had been taken, I began to think that maybe State Research was behind it," she says. "All I can say is that I am glad I wasn't there when they came." Miss Coleman's home had previously been raided, in February, so Amin's men knew roughly what was there. Even if they had discovered anything of Mary's involvement with people who had fled the country, they never came to get her.

"Most of the students at the seminary had tried to get back to their homes, but for about a third of them it was out of the question to attempt it," says Miss Coleman.

"There were at least sixteen of us for meals and twenty-nine students. But we never went without food.

"We lived largely on rice. It provided not only lunch and supper but often breakfast as well, with sugarless jam. On Good Friday I made hot cross buns, and I made biscuits to celebrate birthdays. The seminary garden provided some vegetables and avocado pears to give a little variety, and occasionally we got some meat.

"But prices soared. At Easter someone wanted to sell us a goat for two thousand shillings (about $267 US), ten times the normal price. Later we were able to buy it for six hundred shillings ($80 US) to celebrate liberation.

The uncertainty of what was really happening in the country hindered everyone at the seminary. "Nobody was supposed to listen to their radios. The soldiers had been told that Kampala had not fallen and that all these stories about the Tanzanian advance were rumors," says Mary Coleman.

"The psalms in the morning and evening prayer spoke so much to our situation. I shall always remember saying the Lord's Prayer at Easter. As we came to 'deliver us from evil,' there was the sound of a truck outside. Looters, I thought, as the fathers on the alert at the back moved out to see.

"What saved us was that Alokolum had two drums of petrol. Whenever soldiers arrived, the fathers always had jerry cans of petrol ready. They took these out and poured the petrol into the vehicles. They always smiled as they did so. At least the soldiers could then go on somewhere else."

On Thursday, May 17, most of the soldiers left. Mary Coleman says, "We learned later that all the Roman Catholic institutions, including the seminary, had been marked out for shelling by the Tanzanians because Amin's troops were believed to be occupying them. An Italian brother from another college was able to get a message through which prevented this shelling.

"I know we were kept by the power of prayer. Had I been at my house when it was raided I would have been killed. And had that message not got through to the Tanzanians we could all have been killed by the shelling of the seminary."

Eventually Gulu fell to the Tanzanians and most of the soldiers from the town took off for the Sudan in their stolen vehicles. But on May 20 the priest persuaded the three soldiers left at the seminary to give themselves up as prisoners of war. They disarmed them and gave them civilian clothes, but one fifteen-year-old soldier sensed trouble ahead and sat sobbing on the floor. The priests led these three young men, who had caused them so much trouble, to a roadblock and asked the Tanzanians there if they would accept them as prisoners. The officer in charge said he would and that they would be safe.

Heaving a sigh of relief, the priests returned to the seminary. But just after they had left, a mob from the town came down the road, and when they spotted the three young prisoners, they went for them and literally tore them limb from limb. The soldiers could not, or would not, do anything to save them. Within seconds they died a terrible death, their dismembered bodies thrown at the side of the road.

For them, the three missionary women, for the priests—for all the Christians of Uganda—Amin's holocaust had ended. The reign of a man who has been the most unpredictable and complex ruler on earth was all but over.

What will happen in Uganda in the future remains to be seen. But the faith and courage of the Ugandan church during those eight years will live on.

Appendix

"MY INTEREST IN PERSECUTED BELIEVERS began in Stockholm, Sweden, in the fall of 1966," says Ray Barnett. "I was coordinating an international businessmen's convention in the Swedish capital, and before the meetings began, several witness teams had been sent to various parts of Europe. One went to Talinin, Estonia, in the Soviet Union. They were accompanied by Krista Maeots, a young Canadian newspaper reporter and a self-confessed atheist.

"When Krista returned to the convention headquarters in Stockholm, she presented me with indisputable facts proving that many Christians in the USSR were being beaten, harassed, and imprisoned for their faith. Krista, who was deeply moved by what she had discovered, said, 'Why don't you help them?' So began my efforts on behalf of Christian Human Rights.

"Friends in the West was born. It's aim was, and still is, to open up lines of communication with believers suffering for their faith in any country of the world."

AS A REPORTER, I worked on several projects with Ray Barnett and his Christian Human Rights group, Friends in the West. The first assignment was an undercover reporting job in the Soviet Union, specifically a demonstration by fifty-three young Christians from all over the world, who were protesting religious persecution. The believers held their protest meeting just outside Moscow on May Day, 1974. Shortly afterwards, we were all placed under house arrest in Kallinen, near the capital, with about one hundred Russian soldiers armed with rifles guarding the perimeter of our "prison" motel.

Finally we were freed, and I filed the story from a tiny Finnish border post cafeteria, to newspapers and news agencies around the world.

We also worked together on publicizing the strange case of the Moscow Seven, a group of Siberian believers who took refuge in the US Embassy in Moscow on June 27, 1978. They sought exit visas to the United States so they could worship God in freedom, and were representative of three thousand other Christian families who also wished to leave the Soviet Union. Originally the Soviets insisted they leave the embassy before their request would even be considered. But these believers refused to leave until their visas were granted.

UNREGISTERED SOVIET BAPTIST LEADER Georgi Vins looked pale and gaunt when, in May, 1979, I met with him briefly in a New York hotel, just days after his release from a Siberian labor camp.

But his suffering-pinched face lit up and he was deeply moved when I handed him a "Prisoners for Christ" bracelet inscribed with his name, similar to those which had been worn by thousands of Americans who had prayed daily for him and his family.

Vins was one of the five Soviet "dissidents" who was released to enforced exile in the United States in return for two Russian spies, and I had gone to meet him along with Pastor Gary Short, a leader of Friends in the West and a pastor of the Church of Blessed Hope located in Seattle, Washington. Ray Barnett wished us to explain to Pastor Vins that this was just one of scores of bracelets engraved with the names of different Christian captives, distributed by his organization on behalf of Christian prisoners around the world, and that God was answering prayers in a miraculous way in freeing many of them.

As I stood in the lobby of the UN Plaza Hotel, talking to the bearded Vins via the Rev. Michael Bordeaux of Keston College, England (the Center for the Study of Religion and Comunism), who was translating for the exiled Baptist leader, little did I realize that this meeting would indirectly lead me into the heart of the *Uganda holocaust,* a Christian human rights story almost beyond belief in its horror and courage—a trip, in a sense, from Siberia to Uganda.

When Gary Short and I returned to Seattle to report to Ray Barnett about the meeting, I discovered that after his trip to Uganda in 1978, he had gone to East Germany to see a lawyer, Dr. Wolfgang Vogel, to ask him to intervene in the case of Vins. Dr. Vogel was, at the time, acting as a go-between for the super powers in an exchange deal, and did not then have Vins on his list of Soviet dissidents to be exchanged for two Russian spies. When Ray arrived at his East Berlin office, Vogel expressed surprise at his mission and said he was the first person who had ever contacted him on behalf of a Christian believer, though Jewish groups regularly came to see him.

On Vins' release, the press reported that Dr. Vogel had played a leading part in securing freedom.

In Seattle, Ray told me the story of his Iron Curtain trip and then outlined the heroism he had found among the Ugandan believers. It was then the seeds were planted to write a book about their story, which we believed to be one of the most inspiring, yet shocking, in the history of the Christian church—a story that must be told. We felt we could not do justice to this from the safety of a newpaper clippings library. Information had to be gathered first hand.

So we set out to do just that. We visited Uganda shortly after the fall of Amin and traveled extensively throughout the country. We interviewed and photographed the people who survived Amin's terror machine, and the relatives of those who didn't survive.

—Dan Wooding

IF YOU WOULD LIKE to assist Ugandan Christians or find out more about Friends in the West, write to: Box 66515, Seattle, Washington 98166, United States of America.

Glossary

Vice-President Mustafa Adrisi (a-DREE-see)—Idi Amin's second in command
Idi Amin (a-MEEN)—President of Uganda
Kay Amin—Second wife of Idi Amin. Murdered, dismembered, decapitated. Daughter of a clergyman
Malyamu Amin—Amin's first wife. Sister of Wanume Kibedi (former Foreign Minister of Uganda, now practicing law in London, England)
Sarah Amin—Amin's fifth wife
Major Bob Astles—Amin's British-born special adviser

Emperor Bokassa I—Former emperor of Central African Empire
Pastor John Byamungu (bee-ah-MOON-goo)—Pastor of Gospel Mission to Uganda Church in village in Masaka District
Brigadier Stella Bywaters—Commanding officer of the Salvation Army in Uganda

Rev. Webster Carroll—Missionary with the Southern Baptist Convention
Lillian Clarke—Retired British missionary. Former associate of Bishop Festo Kivengere. Director of Christian Education in Uganda
Mary Coleman—British missionary

King Faisal—Former Saudi Arabia Head of State
Margaret Ford—Bishop Janani Luwum's secretary

Colonel Muammar Gadhafi—Chairman of Libya's Revolutionary Council

Naomi Gonahasa (gahn-a-HA-sah)—Manager of Uganda Guest House on Namerimbe Hill (a place of secret refuge for those hiding from secret police)

Stephen Gonahasa—Manager, with his wife, of Church of Uganda Guest House

Bishop Brian Herd—Bishop of Karamoja. Expelled from Uganda

Laban Jjumba (JOOM-bah)—Leading elder in furniture factory secret church in Mengo, outside Kampala

Michael Kaggwa (kah-GWA)—President of the Industrial Court in Uganda

James Kahigiriza (kah-HEE-ge-REE-za)—Former Prime Minister in the Acholi Kingdom government during time when Uganda was still a British Protectorate

Kampala (kam-PA-la)—Capital city of Uganda

Dr. George Kanyeihamba (kan-ye-HAM-bah)—Attorney-General during Lule's short term as President of Uganda. Presently leader of Uganda Human Rights Organization based in London, England

Karamoja (kah-rah-MO-jah)—An area in northeastern Uganda where the tribal people refused to accept Amin's control

Wanume Kibedi (ki-BEH-dee)—Former Foreign Minister of Uganda and brother-in-law to Idi Amin

Father Clement Kiggundu (KEE-goon-doo)—Editor of *Munno*

Paul Kinaatama (KEE-nah-tah-mah)—Teen-age prisoner from Makerere Uganda Mission Church

Bishop Festo Kivengere (ki-VEN-gair-ree)—exiled Bishop of Kigezi, Church of Uganda. Worldwide spokesman for Uganda refugees

Benedicto Kiwanuka (KEE-wan-oo-kah)—Chief Justice and former Prime Minister of Uganda

Mary Nives Kizito (kee-ZEE-toe)—Sister who worked at Information Service at Catholic Secretariat in Kampala

Henry Kyemba (kee-YEM-bah)—Amin's former Health Minister

Geoffrey Latim (la-TEEM)—Represented Uganda in 110-meter hur- dles at 1968 Mexican Olympics. Later team manager in Montreal in 1976. Headmaster of Gulu High School

Apollo Lawoko (la-WO-ko)—Senior Civil Servant. Cellmate of Archbishop Luwum. Witnessed Amin killing prisoners

Geoffrey Lubega (LOO-beh-gah)—Son of Imelda Lubega. Taken from mother at time of her imprisonment. Later kidnapped, possibly to Sudan

Imelda Lubega—One of the Nakasero Three

Yosef Lule (loo-LAY)—President of Uganda who succeeded Amin

Archbishop Janani Luwum (loo-WOOM)—African Archbishop of Uganda. Martyred by Amin

Pastor Ponsiano Lwakatale (loo-WAH-kah-tah-lay)—Supervisor of 165 Gospel Mission to Uganda Churches

Cynthia Mackay—CMS (Church Missionary Society) missionary. Religious Education Advisor in Province of Kampala.

Makerere (mak-KEH-reh-reh)—Church in Kampala

Makindye Prison (mah-KIN-dee)—Execution barracks in Kampala

Mbale (MM-bah-lee)—City in Eastern Uganda

Major Farouk Minawa (MEE-nah-wah)—Commanding Officer of State Research Bureau at Nakasero

Munno—Influential Roman Catholic daily newspaper in Kampala

Rev. Joshua Musoke (moo-SO-kay)—Senior pastor of Makerere Gospel Mission and leader of all Gospel Mission to Uganda churches

Jothum Mutebi (muh-TEH-bee)—Assistant pastor of Makerere Gos- pel Mission to Uganda

Sir Edward Mutesa (muh-TEH-sah)—Head of State and President of Uganda in 1961

George Muwanga-Kamya (muh-WAHN-gah-kam-yah)—Present editor of *Munno*

Benjamin Mwima (MOE-wi-mah)—One of the Nakasero Three

Daniel Naaya (NEE-yah)—Underground pastor of "Furniture Fac- tory" church

Nakasero (naa-kah-SEH-ro)—Headquarters of the State Research Bureau in Kampala (Amin's police force)

Namirembe (nam-a-RIM-bee)—Hill in Kampala

Joseph Nyakairu—Trumpeter at the Makerere Church
President Nyerere—Head of State of Tanzania

Milton Obote (oh-BO-tay)—Former president of Uganda. Deposed in a coup by Amin
Charles Oboth-Ofumbi (OH-both-oh-foom-bee)—Minister of Internal Affairs. In "car accident" with Luwum
Major Moses Okello (oh-KEL-lo)—Alleged driver of Land Rover that supposedly crashed with Archbishop Luwum and ministers
Ben Oluka (oh-LOO-kah)—Senior Assistant Secretary employed in the President's Office for Religious Affairs. Leading underground church leader
Lieutenant Colonel Erinayo Oryema (OR-i-em-ah)—Minister for Land and Water Resources. In "car accident" with Luwum

Obed Rubaiza (roo-bah-EE-zah)—Young elder in the Makerere Gospel Church
Rev. Eustace Rutiba—Anglican chaplain of Makerere University

Archbishop Erica Sabiti (sah-BEE-tee)—First African Archbishop
Canon Shalita (sha-LEE-tah)—Pastor of All Saints' Cathedral

Tanzania (tan-zah-NEE-ah)—Country to the south of Uganda
Dr. Ken Tracey—Director of African Region World Vision International
Mrs. Christine Tumubweine (toom-ah-BWAY-nay)—Minister of Religious Affairs under Amin

Uganda (you-GAN-duh)—Country in east central Africa

Pastor Nicholas Wafula (WAH-foo-lah)—Overseer of the Deliverance Church
Most Rev. Silvanus Wani (WAH-nee)—Successor to Janani Luwum
Canon Wesonga (weh-SON-gah)—Provincial Secretary of Church of Uganda. Manager of Bible Society Book Shop in Kampala
Dr. Ted Williams—Founder of Kuluva Hospital in West Nile (Amin's home region)

Index